Tourism, Globalisation and Cultural Change

TOURISM AND CULTURAL CHANGE
Series Editor: Professor Mike Robinson, *Centre for Tourism and Cultural Change,*
Sheffield Hallam University

Understanding tourism's relationships with culture(s) and vice versa, is of
ever-increasing significance in a globalising world. This series will critically examine
the dynamic inter-relationships between tourism and culture(s). Theoretical
explorations, research-informed analyses, and detailed historical reviews from a
variety of disciplinary perspectives are invited to consider such relationships.

Other Books in the Series
Irish Tourism: Image, Culture and Identity
    Michael Cronin and Barbara O'Connor (eds)
The Global Nomad: Backpacker Travel in Theory and Practice
    Greg Richards and Julie Wilson (eds)

Other Books of Interest
Classic Reviews in Tourism
    Chris Cooper (ed.)
Coastal Mass Tourism: Diversification and Sustainable Development in Southern
Europe
    Bill Bramwell (ed.)
Dynamic Tourism: Journeying with Change
    Priscilla Boniface
Managing Educational Tourism
    Brent W. Ritchie
Marine Ecotourism: Issues and Experiences
    Brian Garrod and Julie C. Wilson (eds)
Natural Area Tourism: Ecology, Impacts and Management
    D. Newsome, S.A. Moore and R. Dowling
Progressing Tourism Research
    Bill Faulkner, edited by Liz Fredline, Leo Jago and Chris Cooper
Recreational Tourism: Demand and Impacts
    Chris Ryan
Shopping Tourism: Retailing and Leisure
    Dallen Timothy
Sport Tourism Development
    Thomas Hinch and James Higham
Sport Tourism: Interrelationships, Impact and Issues
    Brent Ritchie and Daryl Adair (eds)
Tourism Collaboration and Partnerships
    Bill Bramwell and Bernard Lane (eds)
Tourism and Development: Concepts and Issues
    Richard Sharpley and David Telfer (eds)
Tourism Employment: Analysis and Planning
    Michael Riley, Adele Ladkin, and Edith Szivas
Tourism in Peripheral Areas: Case Studies
    Frances Brown and Derek Hall (eds)

Please contact us for the latest book information:
Channel View Publications, Frankfurt Lodge, Clevedon Hall,
Victoria Road, Clevedon, BS21 7HH, England
http://www.channelviewpublications.com

TOURISM AND CULTURAL CHANGE
Series Editor. Mike Robinson
Centre for Tourism and Cultural Change, Sheffield Hallam University, UK

Tourism, Globalisation and Cultural Change
An Island Community Perspective

Donald V.L. Macleod

CHANNEL VIEW PUBLICATIONS
Clevedon • Buffalo • Toronto

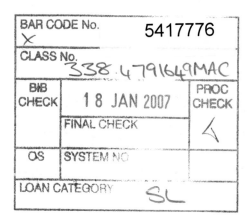

Library of Congress Cataloging in Publication Data
Macleod, Donald V.L.
Tourism, Globalization, and Cultural Change: An Island Community Perspective
Donald V.L. Macleod. 1st ed.
Tourism and Cultural Change
Includes bibliographical references.
1. Tourism–Canary Islands–Gomera. 2. Tourism–Social aspects–Canary
Islands–Gomera. 3. Tourism. 4. Tourism–Social aspects. I. Title. II. Series.
G155.C32M346 2004
338.4'791649–dc22   2003024108

British Library Cataloguing in Publication Data
A catalogue entry for this book is available from the British Library.

ISBN 1-873150- 72-5 (hbk)
ISBN 1-873150- 71-7 (pbk)

Channel View Publications
An imprint of Multilingual Matters Ltd

UK: Frankfurt Lodge, Clevedon Hall, Victoria Road, Clevedon BS21 7SJ.
USA: 2250 Military Road, Tonawanda, NY 14150, USA.
Canada: 5201 Dufferin Street, North York, Ontario, Canada M3H 5T8.

Typeset by Archetype-IT Ltd (http://www.archetype-it.com).
Printed and bound in Great Britain by the Cromwell Press.

Contents

Preface viii
Acknowledgements x

Part 1: The Issues, The Community and the Tourists
1. Tourism, Globalisation and Cultural Change 3
   Introduction 3
   Theoretical Concerns 4
      Globalisation, change and agency 4
      Identity, authenticity and the gaze. 11
      Islands and tourism 14
      Accounts of history 17
   The Fieldwork Site 18

2. Valle Gran Rey: A Changing Destination 23
   La Gomera in Context 23
   The Physical Setting 24
      Vueltas: the settlement. 33
   Perspectives on History 41
      Recorded history 41
      Local observations 47
      Fishing development and decline 52
      Individual voices. 54

3. The Tourists: Types and Motivation 66
   Examining Tourists. 66
   The Growth of Tourism 66
   The Variety of Visitors. 68
      Seasons and tourists 70
   Tourists: Motivations and Experiences 77
      Motivation 77
      German women and Gomeran men 81
      Cultural stereotypes 85

Foreign Settlers 90
Change and the Future 93

Part 2: The Influence of Tourism
4. Work and Property 99
Introduction. 99
The Transforming Economy 101
Overview 101
Employment and social stratification. 103
Tourist types and specific impacts 104
Business and Employment in Vueltas 105
The working environment. 105
The business of fishing 115
Changing Attitudes Towards Work and Property 124
Gender and the division of labour 124
Tourism and new work 125
Business attitudes and new opportunities 127
Property 130

5. Power and Conflict. 135
Introduction 135
Global Events: The European Union and its Impact on
Vueltas 136
Local Politics. 138
Formal structure 138
The elections. 139
Personalities in politics. 141
Political power and patronage 144
Local Conflicts and Global Issues: The Protest. 147

6. Social Identity. 155
Introduction 155
Local Identities 156
Pre-Hispanic influences on identity 156
The Gomero 161
The fisherman 163
Gender roles. 168
Global Influences 173
Strangers. 174
Mass media and education 180
Tourism and social boundaries 182

7. Family, Belief and Values 187
Introduction 187

The Family in Vueltas 187
    Specific family groups 192
    La casa 195
    Potential marriage partners 197
Belief and Values 198
    Religious behaviour 198
    Supernatural powers 200
    Envy, competition and criticism 203
    Respect and shame 205
Local Attitudes and Global Ideas 207

8. The Ability of Tourism to Change Culture 213
    The Environment and Identity 213
    Tourism and the Globalisation of an Island 217
    Tourism and Cultural Change. 219
        General overview 219
        The specific influences of tourism and tourists 223

References 229
Index 240

Preface

What influence do tourists have on a community? This was one of the motivating questions that drove me to live in a remote Canary Island fishing settlement for a year. Back in 1989, there were just a handful of books within the discipline of social anthropology that dealt head on with the impact of tourists and tourism. Following a reconnaissance trip to the Canary Islands with the original intention of studying pre-Hispanic traditions manifest in contemporary culture, I changed the emphasis of my study to what I perceived as a more important and interesting issue: change in a community and the influence of tourism.

Over the years there have been many changes and one of the tasks of this research is to highlight those changes that can be most directly associated with tourists and tourism. Related to this is the conviction that specific tourists will have specific influences. The majority of visitors to La Gomera are those whom I term 'alternative', and as a result of their characteristics, I argue that they communicate and interact with and consequently influence the local community to a greater extent than would package tourists. These influences and changes penetrate almost all areas of culture and most of the population's lives: personal as well as public. A longitudinal research project, in this case covering the years 1990–2002, which includes a full continuous year of intensive participant observation fieldwork, is a particularly good way of enabling the researcher to appreciate the breadth and depth of tourism's influence on a community.

Despite its intensive focus on one community, this study has ramifications worldwide and, in true anthropological tradition, comparisons are made with examples taken from a wide canvas, in space and in time. Furthermore, the relevance to other island communities is made clear throughout the book and all peripheral communities experiencing tourism will be able to draw parallels with their own experience. The bulk of academic literature and sources are taken from anthropological works, with much support from sociology and geography, and the area of Tourism Studies with its collection of academics from a wide variety of backgrounds has also supplied much material.

Nevertheless, it must be pointed out that the majority of material is primary research data, gleaned through talking with people in the community – fishermen, shopkeepers, foreign settlers, tourists and so on. This is the stuff of ethnographic fieldwork: the fieldworker tries to blend in with the community and pick up information without overly distorting or influencing opinions and conversation. The book, therefore, contains a diverse collection of opinions, ideas and perspectives, which further increases its richness: an intended goal that partly supports the contention that tourism, globalisation and cultural change are complex by nature. Nevertheless, I have developed arguments that run through the book relating to the subject of globalisation, the nature and causes of cultural change, the influence of specific types of tourist, the immense influence of tourism, the relevance of power, the social construction of identity and the importance of individual human agency in the entire process. Furthermore, in the tradition of the ethnographic monograph, I hope that the reader will gain a good picture of the people described and a general insight into the human condition.

Acknowledgements

Special thanks are due to numerous people, organisations and funds and I will attempt to acknowledge them in rough order of their appearance in the making of this text.

At the University of Oxford, where the adventure began, the Pirie–Reid Scholarship funded three years of postgraduate studies; Brasenose College provided a warm collegiate embrace, the award of the Hulme Continuation Grant and a Travel Scholarship; the Institute of Socal and Cultural Anthropology provided an excellent research environment and the Peter Lienhardt Travel Scholarship – Peter had been an enlightening first supervisor in social anthropology; Marcus Banks gave inspired and conscientious doctoral supervision; and Peter Riviere offered support and insightful comments.

In the Canary Islands, I acknowledge the help of Alberto Galván-Tudela and Juan Pascual-Jimenez for their initial encouragement and in particular, I thank the people of Vueltas who were a most welcoming community and have proved to be enduring friends.

More recently, the University of Glasgow Crichton Campus has provided a good base for reflection and a vigorous one for research in the Crichton Tourism Research Centre. During the latest development stages of the book, Mike Robinson has given excellent advice and been an invaluable reader of the material. Finally, I would like to thank my immediate family for their continuing and good-humoured support.

Part 1

The Issues, The Community and the Tourists

Chapter 1

Tourism, Globalisation and Cultural Change

Introduction

Tourism is a genuinely powerful and unique force for change in the community. This study outlines its impact on economic, social and cultural life: all these are embraced by the broad term 'culture' but, for the sake of the analysis, the different elements which make up a culture are broken into specific areas.[1] Anthropologists and others have sought to view different elements of society in a unified, holistic way, intending to highlight their interdependence. For example, in this work we see how families as kinship groups often form the workforce for business operations and influence political inclinations, social identity and values. By understanding the interconnections within a society, we are better able to appreciate the repercussions of external influences such as tourism and the major and deeply felt changes that such phenomena as the introduction of ex-tourists into the family through marriage can have. However, these types of changes are not as obvious as the more salient material developments relating to construction and the economy.

Here, it is argued that the community of Valle Gran Rey (VGR) on the Canary Island of La Gomera has experienced tremendous changes in a short period of time since the early 1980s when tourism began to develop seriously. Moreover, the type of tourists has had a particularly strong impact due to their propensity to communicate with and live in close association with the local population. It is suggested that the experience of La Gomera may be comparable with other isolated communities, especially islands, around the world. The advantage of long-term research is that various transformations can be traced over time and family groups can be observed in such a way that the agents of change – local people, tourists, foreign settlers and others – become real personalities. Throughout this book, quotations from those involved in this process are given. Field research has spanned more than a decade, from 1990 to 2002, with the bulk of the intensive fieldwork taking place during 1990–91 followed by intermittent return visits.

Research has shown that tourism is a very complex business, as are the responses from the destination community, itself composed of different groups with differing interests. Much of the conflict regarding the resources supplied by tourism and demanded by tourists seems to be between local factions. In some way tourism has accentuated and put pressure on fissures within the local social landscape. Political interests were particularly divided over a proposed development plan for the beach – and a massive protest, accompanied by wide media coverage, led to a historic climb down by the mayor and his supporters. Tourism has become a very important part of the political agenda.

The book is divided into two parts: the first 'The Issues, The Community and The Tourists' provides a grounding, giving an overview for the reader, embracing the theoretical concerns, a detailed description of the destination and its history and an examination of the tourists who visit the region. The second part 'The Influence of Tourism' focuses on the specific changes that tourism and tourists have initiated in the community: in particular it explores the areas of work and property, power and conflict, social identity and family and belief. These chapters give detailed descriptions of the people, their lifestyle and their relationship with tourists and tourism. Finally, the concluding chapter ' The Ability of Tourism to Change Culture' draws these issues together, reaching conclusions on the environment and identity, globalisation and tourism and tourism's specific influence on cultural change. It summarises the findings of the research as well as presenting final arguments and thoughts about the role of tourism in changing the culture of a community.

As the introductory chapter, this one outlines the central theoretical concerns of the research, draws attention to the experience of islands and tourism making comparative generalisations, describes the place of 'history' in the book and, finally, places the fieldwork site and research into context.

Theoretical Concerns

Globalisation, change and agency

Tourism is very much part of the globalisation process.[2] In essence, globalisation involves the exchange and flow of economic and intellectual items in terms of goods, knowledge, values and images, as well as people, on a global scale (cf. Featherstone, 1990a, b; Featherstone & Lash, 1995). We will regard it as a process that has its historical roots in the European trading expansion of the 16th century, the opening of the trans-Atlantic routes and the beginnings of the Eurocentric worldwide network. Scholars such as Wallerstein (1974) and Wolf (1982) have examined this phenomenon, perceiving the origins of the modern world system as lying in the development of the processes that we describe today as global. Other interpretations of globalisation see it as beginning at the dawn of recorded history or with the post-industrialisation of society (Waters, 1995). We can theorise that globalisation as a concept and experience does not necessarily have to be confined to a specific time or place but should be seen as (a) implying a group's efforts to homogenise their 'global' environment as they see it and (b) the development through communication and trade of a vast network. Both notions are grounded in the cultural worldviews of the participating actors.[3] However, for the purposes of this book, we will focus on the European-based expansion and, in particular, on the Iberian colonisation of the Canary Islands that began the globalisation process for La Gomera. We view its development as concurrent with the development of the world system described by Shannon (1989: 20) as

> [t]he set of relatively stable economic and political relationships that has characterised a major portion of the globe since the sixteenth century. Initially the system was limited to Europe and South America in the sixteenth century. Since that time it has expanded to include all areas of the world.

The period following the industrial revolution, with its impact on travel, trade and technology, referred to by Robertson (1990: 19) as the 'crucial take-off period of globalisation' begins the most recent phase. This has accelerated over the past decades with computerisation and, in the specific case of La Gomera, has increased since the mid-1970s as a result of political and economic factors, especially tourism. Wahab and Cooper (2001: 4) give a description of globalisation as it is understood in current times, one that coincides with many popular interpretations:

> Therefore, globalisation is an all-embracing term that denotes a world which, due to many politico-economic, technological and informational advancements and developments is on its way to becoming borderless and an interdependent whole. Any occurrence anywhere in the world would, in one way or the other, exert an impact somewhere else. National differences are gradually fading and being submerged in a homogeneous mass or a single socioeconomic order.

There are numerous understandings, some more abstract than others, which point to the perceived outcomes of globalisation. These include the creation of cultural homogeneity, as suggested here, or contrastingly the increased perception of heterogeneity; the resulting awareness of the finitude of world resources and the assimilation of previously separate groups into a larger whole, with the consequent sharing of experiences (Featherstone & Lash, 1995). These broad issues will form part of the background to investigations in this book with its focus on cultural change.

Although the word 'globalisation' has been with us since the 1960s, according to Cheater (1995: 124) it is only since the late 1980s that it has received attention from social scientists as a serious concept. Similarly, due partly to its recent growth as a social phenomenon and partly to the attitude of many academics who were not convinced of its relevance, the subject of tourism has also been slow to receive serious attention. Things, however, are changing, and globalisation is currently a popular topic of study and discussion, whilst social scientists are also choosing to research and publish papers on tourism in increasing numbers.[4] Yet the two topics have rarely been deliberately combined in an ethnographic monograph.[5]

Tourism is regarded as part of the process of globalisation: in order to appreciate this more deeply, we need to examine the concept of tourism as well as theoretical issues that have been developed relating to it. The tourist has been described as a 'temporarily leisured person who voluntarily visits a place away from home for the purpose of experiencing a change' (Smith, 1989c: 2). This presumes that the tourist has leisure time, discretionary income and positive local sanctions, all features which characterise the ideal lifestyle in westernised industrial societies. Just as globalisation reaches out to others, resulting in the exchange of money, items and information, encouraging trade, travel and communication, so does tourism. In terms of exports, the tourist attraction is simply another commodity embedded in a network that spreads overseas. The globalised world of communications, advertising and travel enables customers to participate as tourists – consumers of export commodities on the salesman's doorstep. Images, dreams and expectations are 'sold' for future consumption as the media attract the clients. This book shows how the island of La Gomera has been part of a global trading network and hence, part of a very powerful geopolitical system since its colonisation by Europeans: it continues this pattern by exporting its assets for tourism. However, the arrival of tourists who consume their purchases on the island sets up a totally different relationship between vendor and purchaser.

One way in which we may think about the situation and events in La Gomera is to use the concept of world-system theory (Wallerstein, 1974; Shannon, 1989) as a means of understanding events both historically and as they continue today. The central theme is that there is a core that controls capital, with political power and cultural dominance in relation to a periphery that is part of the economic system and exploited for its resources.[6] This enables us to comprehend the Canary Islands' relationship as a peripheral region to the core of urban continental Spain. On an even smaller scale, there remain core and peripheral sections of society within a peripheral region, just as there are workers as well as capitalists in the core region. In fact, it may be fair to say that there will be a network of politically and economically influential people overseeing the whole area embracing both core and peripheral regions. Wolf (1982) argues that societies are not isolated or self-maintaining systems and that there are cultural sets of practices and ideas that are continually changing. Wolf's ideas together with the concept of a world system give us a basic model with which to approach the problem of theoretically interpreting and comprehending the ethnographic data within this book and, in turn, relating it to the process of globalisation.

The term globalisation is a means of describing a process: it does not offer any explanations. World-system theory analyses and offers an explanation of the historical and social development of a process and a system – a system that may itself be described as an example of globalisation. As suggested earlier, La Gomera became part of a developing world system after it was colonised by Spain and it has remained a peripheral region, exploited as an agricultural exporter throughout its history up until the present day. A new export product, tourism, is replacing the older commodities – fish, tomatoes and bananas. The core area has changed and includes the metropolitan areas of Spain, Germany and the UK, with the European Union (EU) being a developing conglomeration of political and economic power that has already had a major impact on the island. The EU's impact includes economic funding for building and infrastructural work, with a resultant political entrenchment in VGR and the possibility of radically changing the future of the island through its heavy investment in an airport and tourism. In fact the EU's development program for La Gomera may be read as a form of cultural hegemony (akin to the 'modernisation' ethos) and VGR is now on the cusp of a transition from being a locally run small-scale tourist economy to becoming subordinated to a capital-intensive tourist industry. The funding, which was intended to encourage equality between islands and within the island, may ultimately benefit big business alone.

Whilst world-system theory gives us a means of analysing macro-economic and political events, it also allows us to interpret the micro-changes that happen in terms of the grass-roots interaction between people from the core regions (urban European tourists) and the local population of this peripheral region. Thus, the metropolitan wealthy or those rich in intellectual capital (in terms of a metropolitan-oriented education and experience) may mix with local people and influence their morals, ideas, social and personal behaviour, work patterns and fashion amongst other things and be influenced, in turn, by the local people. Some observers of tourism processes have described the arrival of tourists as an invasion or colonisation and there are parallels with imperialism. Even though the tourists may not perceive themselves to be exploiters of the resort population, they may be gaining comparative economic advantage and they represent the core regions – if only unwittingly – as they inevitably contain aspects of that culture. And it is this limitless interaction and communication between people, be they tourists and locals, business partners, politicians or fishermen, that is globalisation in the flesh.

We must not forget that these processes are grounded in the action of individuals and that people are the drivers of development. The key involvement of people in this process makes our research important and revealing. The world is expanding not shrinking because of globalisation. An increase in communication, ideas, possibilities, travel, knowledge, capital, construction, associates, relationships and so on means that many people's worldviews incorporate more items than before: their knowledge horizons have expanded. Nothing has shrunk but the time it takes to obtain information or to get from 'a to b' and this may even have increased due to heavy traffic – try London. This highlights the fundamental perceptual context of globalisation and its location in the minds of people – which is why an examination of cultural contact and change is so relevant.

It is with this acculturation that most of this ethnography is concerned – the contact and interaction of people from different cultures which results in sociocultural change. Albeit the cultures concerned are not totally different, there is sufficient difference to make it an interesting and valuable exercise. Nash (1996: 21) in a discussion of 'tourism as acculturation or development' draws attention to the predominant tendencies of writers embracing an anthropological viewpoint to adopt the 'cautionary platform':

> Loukissas [1978] points to the degradation of the environment on Myconos. Lee (1978) views tourism as enhancing the position of an entrenched élite in Yacatan. Jordan [1980] sees it undermining and distorting traditional values in a vacation village in Vermont. Pi Sunyer [1977b] studying mass tourism on the Costa Brava, thinks that it promotes stereotyping. Kottak [1966] sees a general deterioration of the communal life of a Brazilian fishing village brought about by the influx of second homes, sport fishermen and hippies.

Of the more positive opinions, the 'advocacy' stance, there are, according to Nash, the following examples: McKean (1976) in Bali, Cohen (1979a) in Thailand, Boissevain (1978) in Malta and Hermans (1981) on the Costa

Brava 'who found tourism to be a benign and possibly beneficial agent of change' (Nash, 1996: 22).

Here we will see a very broad set of influences, which may be regarded as positive or negative according to the position of different observers. To decide in a judgemental fashion on the general outcome is often unwise and unrealistic: there are various impacts and many outcomes cannot be truly gauged over a short time period. Nash (1996) is in favour of a dispassionate, objective analysis: this is a worthy but particularly difficult task for an ethnographer deeply involved with a community. It is hoped that the changes examined in this book are assessed with a reasonably fair touch, although an inevitable occasional bias is not denied.

The research seeks to discover the actual influences that tourists have on local people and uses specific concepts including 'role', which is held to mean publicly acceptable ways of behaving in accordance with a socially recognised position. These roles are not those envisaged by functionalists (see Linton, 1936) who associate them with social status and the passive acceptance of actors (a static quality) but rather they are roles which are various and changing, with actors making deliberate alterations to them and social actions influencing and developing them. They include roles attributable to gender, such as wife, girlfriend, father; roles related to status, such as official or fisherman and general roles recognised in social life, such as friend or tourist. And they all involve the conscious behaviour of the participants who have a mental conception of the expectations of others as they perform their role.[7]

Together with role, the concept of 'agency' is utilised: the active and deliberate action to achieve a specific purpose. People are, therefore, regarded as actors within a social role or as personalities making their own decisions. This allows for a description of people as making their own impression on the general environment, self-consciously deciding to act. For example, much of the tourist development has been created through the agency of local people – fishermen and agricultural workers – who decided to build apartments. This use of agency and freedom to operate leads to the issue of choice, by which it is meant that there are greater opportunities for action, a diversity of paths to be taken, as a result of the growth of tourism. Choice, however, expands with knowledge as well as economic opportunities and areas of social life have increased in which individuals can actively choose from a wide selection and determine part of their future, such as employment opportunities, consumer goods and sexual partners.

Such changes that happen on a micro-level are largely due to communication – the exchange of ideas between different individuals and groups – and the extent and degree of change is also proportional to the amount and type of communication and exchange between groups. Consequently, the type of tourist visiting La Gomera, 'alternative' backpackers, will, because of their tendency to communicate on a personal and informal level, have a considerably different influence from that of the package tourists who choose to remain more isolated from local people, interacting only occasionally in a formal situation.[8] The mechanism, degree and extent of change is the major enquiry of this book. Ethnographic fieldwork provides an excellent opportunity to research this phenomenon, with the meeting between tourist and locals being a uniquely representative example of such intercultural interaction, where either side is more at liberty to give and take than in other cultural group encounters such as migration, wartime invasion and colonisation.

Smith (1989c: 9) sees tourism and 'modernisation' as separable, with modernisation being the predominant influence. However, it is argued here that by recognising tourism as part of a greater globalisation process which includes modernisation, caught up in a world system, we acknowledge that it is but one particularly salient facet of this process[9] – and one which can be studied with a degree of isolation because of the blatant human interaction involved and other consequent explicit events. Here are some examples from VGR in which tourism as a specific part of globalisation and not merely 'modernisation' is responsible: marriages between local people and foreign visitors, beach developments and apartment construction, employment in hospitality services and local people learning the German language. And so we seek to place the study of tourism firmly within the corpus of research into globalisation and world-system theory, whilst recognising that tourism has unique qualities that are worth investigating in their own right.

Many discussions of world-system theory are based on the notion of power centres, usually metropolitan cores, which, in turn, influence ideology and cultural values: such values influence the way in which the natural environment is perceived. The difference between the way a business speculator, a tourist and a fisherman will see a beach – their various 'gazes' – gives us a clue as to the importance of experience, cultural background and current activity in relation to their interaction with the environment. On La Gomera, there are serious disagreements about how the natural environment should be utilised. Natural resources have been exploited historically as export products and subsistence products (plantations, smallholdings, goat-herding and fishing). With the arrival of tourism, the resources can take on different qualities – aesthetic assets, leisure zones and speculative commodities: thus, the sea and the land have been dramatically transformed in terms of their social usage and value. In this sense we have a situation that may be understood in terms of political ecology, that is the examination of relative power at many levels of environmental or ecological analysis. There are numerous groups competing over the resources of the island, each with their own agenda. Their understanding of and their relationship with the environment is determining the lifestyles and future of the inhabitants in a powerful drama, an example of which – the protest against a proposed beach development scheme – is given in this book.

Identity, authenticity and the gaze

Just as the issue of power seems to penetrate most areas of this research, so does the issue of identity. This research relates it to aspects of public and private life as social identity. It examines areas that have been popular within recent anthropological studies, including national, regional, local village and family identity, touching on everything from the EU[10] to the significance of parents and profession. These are social identities and related aspects of research include boundaries and differences, which are especially prominent in a situation where tourists sometimes outnumber local residents. Linked to this are professional identities and interest groups, which inform relationships with natural resources, amongst other things, and the rural–urban dichotomy, accentuated by cosmopolitan arrivals, which give us an insight into the core–periphery relationship in a face-to-face situation. Ultimately, identity in terms of public information is socially constructed and the tourism industry is particularly attuned to creating and marketing identities, just as political interest and historical relationships go towards creating acknowledged identities for places and groups. This ethnography gives examples and analyses the professional construction of images.

Some of this discussion involves individual identity and the personal observation of identity in terms of stereotypification and self-consciousness. It is argued that personal identity is a complex array of factors that are always subject to change and examples are given from tourists and fishermen among others. The basic element of this study is the individual and, throughout this text, attention is drawn to different personalities, their histories and views. Identity is perceived both within and outside a person. It can be viewed in a personal and a public light. Concentration on identity as a tool of research is fruitful as it helps us to understand the behaviour and reactions of people and groups.

Scholars of tourism have looked at the motivation of tourists and their impact on their destination but have rarely placed tourism squarely within the globalisation process – although the emphasis on tourism as imperialism recognises it as a neocolonial process. These studies include the work of MacCannell (1976) who considers the tourist to be a product of modernisation, someone searching for 'authenticity', with the resultant creation of an 'authenticity' staged by host cultures to attract tourists. In this book we see incidents where the concept of authenticity has relevance whether it be the tourist's desire to meet the real untainted islander or the depiction of the island as an unspoilt rural idyll. Nevertheless, the term is deconstructed and it is argued that it has multiple applications and needs to be strictly defined in relation to the context of its use.

Similar to the search for authenticity (in that it becomes both an escape from the home surroundings and a search for something else) is the concept of the tour as a 'sacred journey'. Graburn (1989) argues that vacations within secular societies are the equivalent of traditional religious festivals: the profane or, in the case of vacations, a non-ordinary experience replaces the sacred experience. Contemporary touring has also been likened to a 'profane spirit quest', in which culturally specific values determine the goals of travel. These notions allow Graburn to place tourism in the context of historical human ritual activities, by slotting it into a more anthropologically acceptable mosaic of universal cultural manifestations. However, the religious analogy might be unrealistic, whereas the idea of a quest, which fits in with the search for authenticity and the need for a break from ordinary life for rejuvenation purposes, agrees with the research findings. These aspects are dependent on individual tourists whose motivations inevitably vary widely and many have a number of different reasons for taking a vacation. One aspect of this, uncovered during research, is that the holiday may be a quest for personal truth, a chance to get away from work and social pressures to rediscover or recover one's personal space and peace of mind. Tourists often resolve personal problems, find answers to difficulties in their lives and make tough decisions during the holiday period. Even though the journey may not be a conscious quest for self-discovery, it can certainly end up that way: in fact, the exterior physical journey may become eclipsed by an interior psychological one.

This concentration on the individual, personal, subjective experience and motivation of the tourist leads us to consider an influential means of analysis developed by Urry (1990) which is the notion of the 'tourist gaze', an idea based on Foucault's 'medical gaze'. Urry's point is that the tourist's gaze on different settings is as socially organised and as systematised as the gaze of the medic and he gives examples of historical changes and the diversity between social groups – all of which are constructed through difference. An interesting example of the transforming gaze upon an object is that of the English seaside resort which was originally perceived as a place of 'medicine' rather than 'pleasure' (Urry, 1990: 17). The concept of the gaze as organised by interested professionals or as the predominant means of perceiving an object is something used in the analysis of change on the island. It is particularly insightful when considering the changing use of resources – notably the seafront and the sea – and the conflicts that have arisen over development. The differing gazes of developers, fishermen and tourists enable us to assess how change may be comprehended as well as to appreciate how different people view the same object. More specifically, the gaze of tourists visiting the island varies across groups and over time; thus, there is a marked difference between Spanish and German tourists and between 'alternative' tourists and those on a package tour.

A consideration of the various gazes leads us to one of the major issues dealt with here: the impact of tourism. It is argued that the type of tourism which La Gomera experiences – 'alternative' and backpacking tourism – can have a greater influence on the local community than mass charter tourism. This is because of the propensity for alternative tourists to mix more with local people, communicate with them, meet them on an equal level (not customer to servant), spend money on services provided by local people (not owned by big business) and enter into emotional relationships with them. This contrasts directly with the views of Smith (1989c: 14) and Graburn (1989: 35) who attribute the mass charter tourists with having the greatest impact because of their greater numbers and economic clout and tendency to expect western amenities. Graburn (1989) describes them as carrying a 'home-grown 'bubble' of their lifestyle around with them' in which they can live whilst on vacation. Of course, these are generalisations and there will always be examples contradicting them but this research points to a serious omission on the behalf of many writers on development and tourism impact who do not consider the consequences of communication between visiting people and the local population. Also, some do not appreciate the different economic impacts of different types of tourism upon the indigenous population who provide services for them. This book examines in detail the various influences of the tourists upon the local population and highlighting the variety of ways in which tourists and host population interact and affect one another, challenges the views of Smith and Graburn.

Intrinsically linked to the discussion of impact is the notion of tourism as 'imperialism', which Nash (1989) defines as the expansion of a society's interests abroad – economic, political, military, religious etc. – either imposed on or adopted by the host society. This seems to cover almost any situation that can arise and thereby effectively weakens the term as an analytical tool. A more interesting approach is to examine situations for evidence of outright exploitation or unwanted occupation, which leads to the discovery of which party's interests the development and tourism are actually serving. Élite groups within the host country may be benefiting from the business or a transnational group could be overseeing development, in opposition to the wishes of many local people. Such diverse scenarios are occurring on La Gomera and this study gives details of these processes, attempting to understand their significance, drawing attention to new forms of imperialism.

The subjects of imperialism and transnational groups bring us back to the concept of globalisation, and reaffirm the tourist industry as being one facet of an ongoing global process, currently dominated by western industrialised countries from whom the vast majority of tourists derive. Thus, the tourist becomes a representative of the culture that has promoted globalisation, as well as being a symbol and an intrinsic part of that culture, in the role of tourist and as a productive agent or a passive recipient of western wealth and ideas (see Macleod, 1999). With the example of La Gomera, we see tourists arriving and their economic impact increasing in importance. This is compounded by a transnational geopolitical organisation, the EU, donating funds thus ensuring that their presence will have a significant impact on the environment in terms of the construction of amenities and the employment of local people in construction and service industry jobs. Yet more interesting is the gradual growth in the number of foreign settlers (ex-tourists) who have set up shops and services and with their broader experience of tourism and knowledge of the tourists, together with access to capital resources, are able to succeed and flourish in relation to local entrepreneurs. Thus, a foreign country's interests have increased on Gomeran soil and the global network strengthens.

Islands and tourism

Numerous writers have produced definitions of islands and listed their common qualities.[11] Some of these defining factors include their small scale, isolation, weak economies, separateness, difference in terms of politics, climate, geography, biodiversity and environment, their vulnerability to the vagaries of the market and, hence, dependency. Tourism often forms a proportionately larger or more significant element of an island's economy. It may also have a more pervasive impact on an island community because of the community's small size and, hence, higher levels of sociocultural interaction: 'In an island context, it is difficult to discuss any aspect of tourism without involving most aspects of the community's economic, cultural and social life' (Conlin & Baum, 1995: 7).

Islands tend to rely on one or two products: they are usually minor players on the world stage and tourism often sustains their economic development (Briguglio *et al.*, 1996). Tourism is normally based on the island's natural attractions (often being remote, attractive scenery and wildlife) as well as on a distinct cultural heritage.

In the current world economic system it is simply unreasonable to expect islands and small states with few natural resources and poor prospects to 'go it alone' and arrange their affairs in isolation. Tourism, as many writers have noted, has become more and more international and global in scope. (Conlin & Baun, 1995: 9).

Islands often face structural handicaps because of their isolated, peripheral locations as well as their small size in area and population. They possess a limited resource base, tiny domestic market, diseconomies of scale, poor accessibility, limited infrastructure and institutional mechanism and a high degree of dependency on external forces (Ioannides *et al.*, 2001). Such disadvantages, the 'handicap of insularity', have been seen as a reason for giving residents special compensations (discounts on travel, imports and so on). The cost of insularity was calculated for Majorca at 1.3% of GDP in 1993 (Bardolet, 2001). Writing about the Balearics, Bardolet sees the main problem caused by insularity as qualitative handicaps arising from the absence of non-tourism-sector investments – due to transportation costs. Even tourist investment capital in such projects as theme parks is discouraged by the lack of a major transportation node. Furthermore, sustainability in the Balaerics is 'held hostage' by the furious growth of tourism demand that exceeds the natural resources and actual size of available territory (p. 210).[12] Not only do islands become dependent on tourism in an economic sense but the use of tourism as a 'monocrop' draws islands into a type of dependency on centres elsewhere. Selwyn (2001: 23) notes that the landscape, no longer shaped and reshaped by farmers and pastoralists, has become increasingly objectified and aestheticised because of its transformation into a tourism product.

Problems faced by islands are commonly related to finite resources that impinge on the sustainability of the tourism economy. This is a subject addressed by numerous writers and, in an examination of a Greek island (Hydra), Butler and Stiakaki see overcrowding affecting the quality of the destination and, therefore, the visitor experience. The geography of a destination can play a major role in tourist activities and their consequent impact on resources and attraction, for example town-centre overcrowding. 'The concentration of visitors and popular attractions in a very limited area is a common feature on many small islands, not just in Greece, but throughout the Mediterranean' (Butler & Stiakaki, 2001: 294).

Sharpley sees the relatively small size of islands, their distance from main tourist markets, their limited economies and lack of resources as contributing to an inevitable dependence on dominant tourism sectors.

Indeed, there can be little doubt that the political economy of many island micro-states is characterised by dependency on the core, manifested in a dependence on specific tourist market and trans-national corporations and a relatively high level of leakage. (Sharpley, 2001: 243)

Because of the difficulties and expenses entailed in travelling to islands, they need to make a special effort to create a positive image and provide added value. Special events are able to give such a boost to their image, however, their carrying capacity (related to physical space, services and basic resources) limits the size of such events (Getz, 1995). Getz (pp. 151–8) notes that island cultures can be especially susceptible to cultural commodification and the demonstration effect: this is particularly important when we consider that an island's 'culture' is often a major attraction for visitors. He lists a number of factors related to special events where islands have particular problems: capacity, organisation and leadership, marketing management (more diversity needed), quality and support services.

> There are a number of potential obstacles when developing event tourism in islands that must be considered, most notably the difficulty of hosting mega-events which depend on high accessibility and require considerable infrastructure and space. But through community-based events, cultivation of high-profile Hallmark events and creative marketing using the image-enhancing power of events, even the smallest island can employ event tourism successfully. (Getz, 1995: 164)

When considering the appeal of islands, there are a number of salient elements: remoteness, insularity, cultural traditions, 'otherness', unique environment and character. King (1997) considers the attractions of an island and believes that, to the European mind, they are beautiful places that offer the traveller an escape from daily reality, providing the 'good life'. He traces the image of the tropical island to associations made in literature of the carefree, romantic and adventurous destination, which has now been supplemented by deliberate tourism marketing.

We can note that those same traits that allure tourists are equally ones that create problems for the islands as discussed earlier. Islands are no longer so isolated from the mainland because of improving communication: those that encourage tourism are integrated into the travel network and have become firmly linked. The factors that cause most problems relate to their size and finite physical and, occasionally, cultural resource capacity to withstand large numbers of visitors. Controlling tourism and reaching decisions on the type of tourism to be encouraged is, therefore, of vital importance to all sensitive regions, particularly islands. In our examination of La Gomera, we will observe these issues in great detail and witness the development of tourism and its consequences for the local community and the environment, a process that has particular resonance for other islands involved in tourism.

Accounts of history

History remains a major theme throughout this study, whether in the form of written texts used as sources, the spoken narrative of a fisherman, the changes perceived by the author and others over the period of field research or the broad history of political and economic events which support theoretical models. History forms a backdrop to events and gives an important dimension to the current investigation. A historical analysis places the fishing lifestyle and the tourism phenomenon into a temporal perspective of colonial trading and resource exploitation: it also serves to introduce different individual narrators into the text. Changes in the modes of livelihood of the islanders are noted and the importance of economic mainstays to social organisation is revealed. The 'historic' event of the EU after 1992 and the consequent removal of trade barriers for EU member states is recorded – with local people making comments both before and after the event. This ties in with the work on EU funding and its serious implications for the island's future.

The implicit bias in making observations, whether for specific 'historical' purposes, general comments or official records, and the potential subjective usage of any such material is recognised throughout this book and no pretence is made by the author of being a totally objective observer. Instead there is a conscious effort to make a fair assessment of material and give voice to a variety of opinions. Therefore, this book attempts to be multivocal in its usage of a variety of sources – including written texts from local records, academic works, popular works, periodicals, brochures and propaganda broadsheets. Similarly, numerous individuals are allowed a voice: conversations with diverse sources, men and women of all ages, local people, tourists and foreign settlers are recorded. Of course the editorial presence of the author's voice pervades the text and is undeniably influenced by background and intentions.

If postmodernism is to be understood as a dismissal of the meta-narrative, with a desire for democracy of opinion, the giving of equal status to different voices, then, to an extent, this book is in accordance with postmodernist intentions (see Marcus & Fischer, 1986). However, I cannot deny any attempt to influence the text: it is a fallacy that an ethnographer is scientifically neutral: in fact to be 'neutral' is a stance – an intellectual concept. Models are used to theorise about the material and it is not presented as if it were a pristine picture of a culture; rather, certain aspects of the material are highlighted as they tell us a story worth considering. This reflexive approach enables the author to interpret and understand the stories that have been told with a greater critical awareness. 'History' as an object is similarly used for effect, in that people can utilise it for their advantage constructing events, repeating stories, elaborating on their memories, and it may be seen as something which is in a continually prob-lematic state, where opinions will be divided, events questioned and versions recreated. History, after all, is a human interpretation and con-struction of experience subject to bias: there is no purely neutral, omniscient human narrator.

So we are alerted to the human potential for using narratives of history for particular purposes and here there are numerous examples of individu-als and groups employing historical accounts to further their interests, explain their situations, entrench their political position and elaborate their identities. Such examples include the stories and ideas circulating about the Guanche (pre-Hispanic) people and their culture, the Spanish colonis-ers and Columbus, the days before the tourists arrived and the days of hunger during the 1940s and 1950s. Postmodernist thinking alerts us to the dangers of listening only to powerful voices and offers a critique of over-confidence and hegemony: in a way it encourages us to treat all accounts with scepticism – a democracy of criticism.

The account of a protest, which follows later, illustrates the utilisation of history as a cultural asset, a means of organising sentiment when the 'Guarapo' group of protestors (against a beach development) point out that their cultural heritage is being lost amid the construction and development mania. The protest event itself was regarded by observers and the media as an historical moment – a watershed for democratic public protest – and it encapsulates many of the theoretical concerns elaborated here, as well as providing an example of some of the major issues dealt with here.

The Fieldwork Site

The Canary Islanders have been involved in human networks beyond their geographical limits for many centuries. Originally populated by people arriving from NW Africa around 3000 years ago, the islands were invaded and eventually colonised by Iberian powers during the 14th and 15th centuries AD. Spain became the ultimate victor and the islands were claimed for the Spanish Crown. La Gomera was eventually subjugated after a long struggle and it was from this island that Columbus set off on numerous voyages of discovery. So began the history of the islands as the first overseas colony of Spain, the stepping-stones to America and the prototype slavery-based plantation economy for the New World.

Throughout the period since the Spanish colonisation the Canaries have served as exporters, producing such goods as sugar, wine, orchil (a purplish dye obtained from lichen), tomatoes, bananas, as well as supplying labour for overseas markets. More recently, they have added tourism to their list of exports. Caught up in a web of trade and dominated politically by a distant centre, the islands have experienced the expansion of capitalism and European culture, in other words globalisation, over the past 500 years. La Gomera is one of seven islands that have a total population of around one and a half million permanent inhabitants and are situated between latitudes 27 and 29 north (subtropical) and longitudes 13 and 18 west. The nearest island is only 100 km from the African coast and 1000 km from the Iberian Peninsula. They are now an autonomous region of Spain, a member of the EU, whilst at the same time they retain strong links with Latin America and less tangible roots in Africa.

Recent returns to the field have allowed detailed observations of change since 1991 to be recorded. This is important for a study of this rapidly changing site, a fishing settlement that has become a popular tourist destination. Fishing had been the dominant means of livelihood for the village. Developing from a primarily subsistence activity at the beginning of the 20th century, it evolved into a successful export business in the 1970s but it has since waned, due to world market pressures, and is now being eclipsed in terms of income by tourism.

Vueltas, the community at the centre of this research, is bound inland by a sheer rock-face some 1000 m high and faces the might of the Atlantic Ocean which crashes at the rocks and manmade barriers forming its coast. It is possible to hear, smell and probably see the ocean with its deep shades of blue and green from any window. This is a fishing settlement and most men at the port will know the sort of fish being caught on the day and where the fleet is heading. *'Todo el mar'* (The sea is everything) is the phrase used to describe the preoccupation of the people of Vueltas. The settlement, which has a population of around 350, is part of the municipality of Valle Gran Rey (population – 4200 in 2002) developed during the 20th century on the scrubland edge of a broad floodplain and beach. It housed the fishermen and their families who came from other islands and different parts of La Gomera to settle and take advantage of the good fishing and opportunities offered by a nearby fish-processing plant. And so the story has continued up until the 1980s when something began to happen which is radically altering the place – tourism.

This is one of only a few ethnographies to take tourism and tourists as a central theme and it is also the first full-length English language ethnography of a Canary Island community. As well as the indigenous inhabitants and tourists, it examines the foreign settlers, often ex-tourists, who have made the village their home. So, the theme of identity becomes of major importance given the continual interaction of people possessing widely different experiences, backgrounds and outlooks and this relates to the corresponding theme of conflict and differing perspectives. When a middle-aged resident of Vueltas was asked whether she thought that there had been much change over the past couple of years she replied '*Casi igual*' (It's almost the same) and yet for many other returnees (this writer included) and other members of the local community, there seemed to have been great transformations. This highlights the relativity of perception that makes for the dynamics of conflict and change examined here.[13]

Since the early 1980s, the municipality of Valle Gran Rey (henceforward VGR) in which Vueltas is embraced has been on the threshold of dramatic changes. It has transformed from a quiet valley full of agricultural workers and fishermen into a thriving tourist centre. It still retains its former rural qualities which first made it so attractive to visitors: a raw beauty, magnificent beaches, impressive terraced fields, a bamboo-covered river-valley and a rich carpet of banana plantations. However, its isolation due to the poor road system has been ended with the increased construction and improvement of roads and tunnels. Together with the shift of employment away from the primary industries of agriculture and fishing towards the tourism sector this has meant that the place is transforming rapidly and is in danger of losing its unique character. An island of unspoilt volcanic sand beaches, where fishermen capture tuna with bamboo rods and farmers whistle sentences to each other across ravines, may well disappear (Macleod, 2002).

There are groups of people that are well aware of the importance of these dramatic changes, and the issue of growth and planned construction is a hotly contested one. It is a debate that is of relevance for many places experiencing expansion at the expense of the natural environment and traditional lifestyles around the world. And it is one of the crucial global issues facing the world today in its struggle to retain an ecologically beneficial equilibrium and an environment fit for future generations striving to achieve cultural sustainability. In this sense the research in this book is of relevance to all those concerned with the future of tourism and the destinations receiving the tourists.

Notes

1. Anthropologists have proposed various and changing definitions of culture: here are some examples to give the reader an idea of their breadth. Tylor (1871) described it as including 'knowledge, belief, art, morals, law, custom, and any other capabilities and habits' of a society. Geertz (1973) famously described people as being suspended in webs of significance they have themselves spun. He wrote: 'I take culture to be those webs, and an analysis of it to be therefore

not an experimental scheme in search of law but an interpretive one in search of meaning.' Other anthropologists see culture as a system of ideas, belief and behaviours. In this book culture is regarded as embracing all of the these facets of human experience and located within contextually defined groups of people.

2. See Cheater (1995), Appadurai (1995), Hannertz (1992), Ekholm-Friedman and Friedman (1995), all of whom mention tourism as an important aspect of the globalisation process. Cheater (1995:125) writes: 'Tourism, of course, is the world's fastest growing "industry", with an immense potential for affecting global relations, sociopolitical as well as financial and ecological.'

3. Burns (2001: 292) draws attention to the 'monocentric' views of élites in the descriptions of globalisation and the so-called 'global village'.

4. Jafari (1980) was one of the pioneers of the anthropology of tourism. Wilson (1993) gives an overview of the subject, as does Nash (1996) and anthropologically oriented publications on tourism include Smith (1989a), Urry (1990), et al. (1993), Crick (1994), Abram *et al.* (1997), Boissevain (1996a) and Fsadni and Selwyn (1996).

5. It is unusual enough to find an ethnography dealing seriously with tourism – Crick (1994) being an outstanding example. This book is, therefore, breaking new ground in its subject matter involving globalisation and tourism.

6. According to Roseberry (1989: 110), the basic assumptions of a world-system perspective include the following. (1) It is integrated economically rather than politically. (2) It is economically differentiated, composed of (a) core states at the developed centre of the world economy (USA, UK), (b) peripheral underdeveloped states (Dominican Republic, Bolivia) and (c) semi-peripheral states – buffers, exercising some influence (Mexico). (3) The international inequality is a deeply rooted historical product dating from the formation of a capitalist world economy in the 16th century. (4) Social processes should be understood in terms of the place and function of those regions within the larger world system. Problems may often be explained by considering developments occurring at the core and the maintenance requirements of the system as a whole.

7. Goffman (1969) studied people creatively dealing with roles within social establishments, emphasising the manipulative 'impression management' which they utilised. He focused on relatively fixed scenarios however, for example the working environment, defining the role as 'rights and duties attributable to a given status' (Preface), whereas this research uses the term to describe a set of socially recognised positions which are loaded with assumptions regarding behaviour and are subject to change from all directions.

8. Long and Wall (1995) argue that alternative tourists are more intrusive than package tourists, and Selannieni (2001) mentions the minimal cultural impact of package tourists because of their minimal contact with the host community.

9. Harrison (2001: XI) in his preface makes a similar point: 'And the main argument is very simple: international tourism in Less Developed Countries at the beginning of the third millennium is the extension of a process of globalisation that was well established by the middle of the 19th century, and must be understood within this historical context.'

10. Throughout this book I refer to either EU (European Union) or EC (European Community) depending on the context, usually whether it is pre- or post-1992 and the Single European Market.

11. Definitions and common characteristics of islands can be found among the following writers: Conlin and Baum (1995), Briguglio *et al.* (1996), Ioannides *et al.*

(2001), King (1997), McNutt and Oreja-Rodriguez (1996), Bardolet (2001), Selwyn (2001), Boissevain (1996b), Getz (1995), Pearce (2001), Sharpley (2001) and Selannieni (2001).

12. See also Rozenberg (1995) on international tourism in the Balaerics.

13. As Marcus and Fischer (1986: 107) point out when discussing change and history: 'Change entails competing interpretations . . . '. They also draw attention to the slow, almost imperceptible pace of change: 'As Todorov concludes (1984: 254), 'to become conscious of the relativity (hence arbitrariness) of any feature of our culture is already to shift it a little . . . ' [history] is nothing other than a series of such imperceptible shifts.' It is the task of a historically sensitive ethnographer to perceive structural shifts in the details of everyday life, which are the primary data of fieldwork and the raw materials of ethnographic representation' (pp. 106 –7).

Chapter 2

Valle Gran Rey: A Changing Destination

La Gomera in Context

The Canary Islands, as part of Spain, have shared certain experiences relating to the development of tourism but the Islands' peripheral maritime location has meant that it was only after the introduction of package tours involving air travel that the mainland and the Islands followed a similar path. For mainland Spain, tourism first began to flourish when, during the 18th century, the Romantic Movement captured the North European imagination and the popularity of rugged natural scenery and exotic cultures increased. Visitor numbers increased dramatically during the 20th century with improvement in transport routes and the introduction of air routes. Spain had created a national tourism agency by 1905 and offered a network of state-run hotels and inns. Package tourists arrived from London in the 1920s and, by the 1930s, some 260,000 people visited Spain annually. After the Second World War visitors increased rapidly and 'mass tourism' started in the 1950s with numbers exceeding one million by 1951 and three million by 1958. Visitors increased immensely with cheap air travel: 30 million in 1970, 40 million by 1980 and around 52 million by 1990. Catalonia, on the mainland, received around 15 million in 1990 and the Balearics experienced 10.1 million arrivals in 1998, 12% were Spanish, with the rest being European (Barke 1999; Bote-Gomez & Thea Sinclair, 1996).

Tenerife, the largest island in the Canary archipelago and the dominant neighbour to La Gomera, hosts the international airport for both islands. It has an area of 2026 km^2 and a population of 648,000 in 1989 (McNutt & Oreja-Rodriguez, 1996). It also has a longer history as a major tourism destination than La Gomera, receiving some 189,000 tourists in 1967, one million in 1975 and 1.6 million in 1984 – whereas until the early 1980s tourism in La Gomera was regarded as relatively negligible (Hernandez-Hernandez, 1986). In 1991 Tenerife received 3.3 million visitors, 95% of whom arrived by air, the remainder by sea. Tourism has been the mainstay of its economy since the 1970s and, by 1989, tourism represented 45% of the GDP of the entire Canary Island archipelago.

La Gomera is much smaller than Tenerife, being 369 km^2 in size, with a population of some 18,000. It also receives fewer visitors: during the early 1980s estimates give average annual figures of 25,000 tourists staying overnight. In 1983, there were 170,000 people journeying by ferry from Los Cristianos to San Sebastian, of these 35,000 were residents of La Gomera, 58,000 were day-trippers in coaches and cars, 44,000 were Gomeros resident in other islands and 33,000 were tourists staying overnight (Ministério de Obras Publicas y Urbanismo). By 1999, Fernandez-Lopez[1] was able to write that the island received 600,000 visitors (including day-trippers) during the year. In terms of accommodation, it is estimated that, in VGR in 1983, there were 800 beds available for tourists, with an average occupancy of 46%. These figures have expanded dramatically to 3500 beds in 2002.

The Physical Setting

VGR is a valley in the south west of the island of La Gomera, itself one of the seven islands that make up the Canary Islands archipelago. These islands are situated some 1000 km from the Spanish Peninsula, and some 100 km off the North West African coast (see Map 1). They are in the sub-tropical belt and strategically placed for the sea routes between Europe, West Africa and America. La Gomera is famous for being the island where Columbus prepared to face the journey across the Atlantic. The Canary Islands were produced by volcanic activity from the ocean floor, which began during the tertiary era and continued until as recently as 1971 on the island of La Palma; however, La Gomera has had no volcanic activity for millions of years. The volcanic origins are reflected in the topography, with a conical shape forming the central feature of most islands, together with the presence of calderas. Volcanic activity also led to a soil that is rich in trace elements, important for the growth of vegetation.

Even though the islands are relatively close together, their respective micro-climates vary considerably: they are all subject to the 'Alisios', winds from a northerly direction, and their altitudes determine such factors as rainfall and temperature. At sea level the average annual temperature fluctuates around 20°C degrees centigrade throughout the year, with certain months experiencing high temperatures of 30°C plus on occasion. Conversely, the highest peaks will experience freezing temperatures during the winter season. There are also *brisas* (breezes) between the sea and land, as well as between valley and mountain, while each island may suffer local

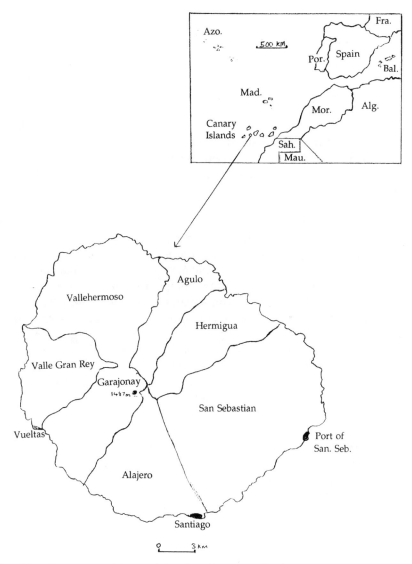

Map 1 La Gomera and its position in relation to Spain

irregular wind systems. The islands have been divided into three distinct climate types based on altitude:

(a) low islands – Fuertaventura and Lanzarote, below the level of cloud formation and consequently dry, with between 100 and 200 mm of rain

per year; (b) intermediate – La Gomera, and Hierro, reaching the level
of cloud formations; and (c) high; Tenerife, La Palma and Gran Canaria
rising above the cloud level, receiving rain except at high altitudes.

Heights vary between Lanzarote at 670 m and Tenerife at 3718 m; La
Gomera reaches 1487 m on the peak of the mountain 'Garajonay', in the
national park.

It is clear that the islands vary considerably in shape, elevation, climate
and overall character: the island of La Gomera receives abundant rainfall, is
verdant, has a large forest, and contrasts starkly with Fuertaventura, which
is predominantly bare rock, with its sandy coastline and minimal rainfall.
Another factor which affects the climate and profoundly influences fishing
is the behaviour of the sea: the Gulf stream from Mexico passes the western
side of the islands on its journey north bringing warm water and returns
down the eastern side, colder. Other currents come down from the Mediterranean and together they form a complex mix of currents that give the
islands a large diversity of sea life and a complicated seasonal pattern. The
sea itself also serves as a regulator of temperature for the air masses.

Below the sea level, there are other variations between the islands due to
the different erosional patterns and geology. Thus, La Gomera, having
experienced 15 million years of erosional activity, has a large sea platform,
i.e. it remains shallow around the coast for a considerable extent, thereby
allowing the growth of sea vegetation and the survival of certain types of
sea creatures. In contrast, Hierro has a more profound drop from the
island's coast, creating quite a different oceanographic ecology and,
therefore, fishing potential. All the environmental factors mentioned here
have a direct relevance to the industries of fishing and tourism and imply
the close relationship that these human activities have with the environment, indicating their subtlety and complexity.

La Gomera itself, with its circularly shaped, peak of 1487 m near the
centre and huge *barrancos* (ravines) running towards the periphery, has
been likened to a gigantic lemon-squeezer. It is fortunate in its flora, much
of which is unique to the island and there is sufficient elevation to profit
from the moisture-rich winds which come from the north, giving a sea of
clouds over the uplands which the forest covering is able to absorb. The
deciduous forest, which occupies 10% of the island's surface, has been
recognised as unique and was declared one of the world heritage parks by
UNESCO in 1986. There are four other national parks on the island and
nine natural areas of landscape recognised as worthy of protection by the
government of Spain. La Gomera is therefore, of great ecological importance and the Institute for the Conservation of the Environment (ICONA) is
active in maintaining and protecting it. The forest cap not only serves to

support many rare species of flora and fauna but also absorbs moisture that eventually runs down to create the water supply for the lowlands. Maintaining this ecological equilibrium is of interest to everyone.

The beauty and uniqueness of the landscape and vegetation is something that is promoted by tourism literature, as is the potential for walking along the island's mountain routes. There is then a potential for eco-tourism, which has been only partially realised by the island's developers, and this asset complements the island's pleasant climate and volcanic sand beaches that serve to attract the North Europeans.

Vueltas is a port and one of 15 *barrios* (hamlets) in the municipality of VGR, which contained a total population of some 4200 in 2002 (3000 in 1991). Vueltas itself had a population of around 350 people in 1991 (electoral role of 314 in 1990, plus minors and foreign residents). The large *barranco* from which VGR ('Valley of the Great King') gets its name runs for more than 5 km from the interior of the island to the coast. It is flanked by steep-sided mountains that reach heights of between 1000 and 500 m where they stop abruptly, shelving down to the fluvial plain or coast. To the north the mountain is known as La Merica and, to the south, as Teguergenche. The rock itself being of volcanic origin is predominantly basaltic. These mountains have acted as barriers to travel for many years and some locals express antipathy towards them, blaming them for the community's isolation.

VGR is on the south west coast, facing in a WSW direction (see Maps 1 and 2) and, thus, gains some protection from the north winds, an important factor for the fishing fleet. The change in altitude, soil, aridity, exposure to the sun and other environmental factors affect the land-use along the route of the valley. Thus, in the upper part, the steep-sided terrain necessitates the construction of terracing to contain soil for agricultural use: the crops grown include potatoes, sweet potatoes, maize, beans, tomatoes, lettuce, cauliflower, pepper, onions, avocado, mango, papaya and bananas – potatoes occupy most area. Smallholdings are generally used to produce a secondary means of income, with crops supplying a portion of the household's consumption. The occasional surplus of potatoes will be sold to local shops and restaurants or friends and family. This is clearly not an organised large-scale agricultural concern (*latifundia*) but a series of small plots owned and worked by separate family groups whose main breadwinner would be employed on plantations.

The small-scale agriculture of the upper valley contrasts with the plantation activity on the fluvial plain and the coast. As for the river, it no longer runs its entire course to the sea having been diverted to supply irrigation tanks. However, during the winter storms the whole course becomes flooded – a phenomenon known locally as '*el barranco*': at this time it may be

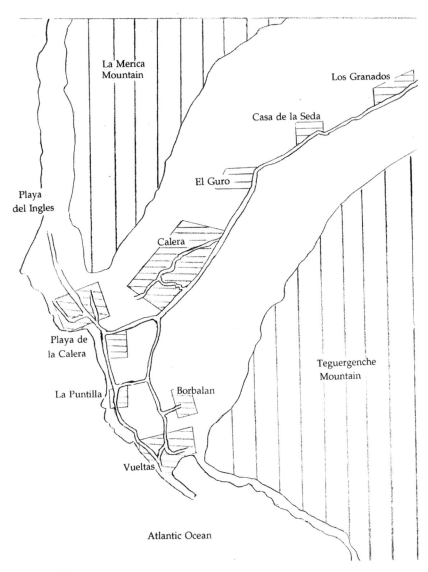

Map 2 Valle Gran Rey

impossible to ford for days at a time. Map 2, drawn in 1991, shows the middle to lower section of the valley with a dry river valley. In the upper valley the river is surrounded by a dense growth of bamboo, not currently commercially utilised, although at one time used amongst other things as supports for tomato plants in Tenerife. The mouth of the river then meets

Plate 1 Elevated view of the valley towards the port of Vueltas, 1970

the sea where the flood plain opens out and spreads across the coast to provide an area of beach and plain approximately 3000 m long and, at some points, 500 m in breadth (see Plates 1 and 2). This considerable area, up to 100 m above sea level, was until 150 years ago covered by scrub, brush and other rugged coastal vegetation. It was regarded as unworkable, the soil being unproductive; however, various businessmen saw the potential for working the land and producing plantation crops with the result that from the late 19th century tomatoes and bananas have been cultivated on this coastal zone.

Relatively unworkable areas remained up until the late 19th century, one of which is now occupied by Vueltas. After the turn of the 20th century, fishermen settled because of the good local fishing. Most came from Tenerife and a few from other parts of La Gomera, notably Santiago. Thus, the people of Vueltas developed very strong ties with the sea in contrast to other parts of the valley where people had stronger links with the land. However, the division between fisherman and farmer has not always been

Plate 2 Elevated view of the valley taken in 2002 towards Vueltas, showing enlarged roads, port harbour wall, new houses, the hotel and abandoned banana plots

as profound as it became in the 1960s. Many men from other parts of VGR were able to participate in fishing whilst retaining and working their smallholdings, a relatively common phenomenon (see Acheson, 1981; Palsson, 1991). The division of labour is sharper now in some respects than it was 50 years ago.

Political, economic and ecological factors within the valley have influenced the modes of livelihood of the inhabitants and created a number of clearly differentiated lifestyles based on primary forms of livelihood such as smallholder, fisherman and plantation worker (often share-cropping). Yet the complexity of economic and social survival has meant that the exchange of goods, the flexibility of labour and social ties such as marriage have created a multitude of links between the various *barrios*. As a consequence this study, whilst focusing on the predominantly maritime oriented coastal settlement, will include observations on the surrounding communities. It remains to be said that the fishermen's work at sea and their association with other ports, particularly Santiago, leads them to form a social network with other sea-going people that is occasionally richer than that with their land-based neighbours (see Lienhardt [1964] on social and physical distances).

Plate 3 Vueltas from the sea wall showing the port boundary, the chapel (*ermita*) and the numerous apartments

There is also another major factor that has profoundly influenced the economy and the environment –tourism. As a result of local responses to tourism and the subsequent construction to encourage it, the landscape, land-use, skyline and village layout have all been rapidly altered. The building of apartments in Vueltas, usually on the site of houses as extensions or as separate blocks on family land, has created a multi-storey network of buildings making demands on the infrastructure, resources and land (see Map 3 and Plate 3). A road runs alongside the valley floor from the uppermost region of the municipality by Arure, the ancient seat of the local council, down to the beach; smaller connecting roads and paths serve to link up the *barrios* with this arterial route. The renovation and reconstruction of this road has been funded by the national coffers and the European Community. It has importance both as a means of communication and currently as a means of employment. The first road replacing a path, was built around 1965, and this was then linked to Arure by a metalled road in 1977. This early lack of easily manageable land routes inhibited the modernisation of the valley, which received electricity after the creation of the road in the late 1960s. Plates 1–4 illustrate changes in the valley since 1970.

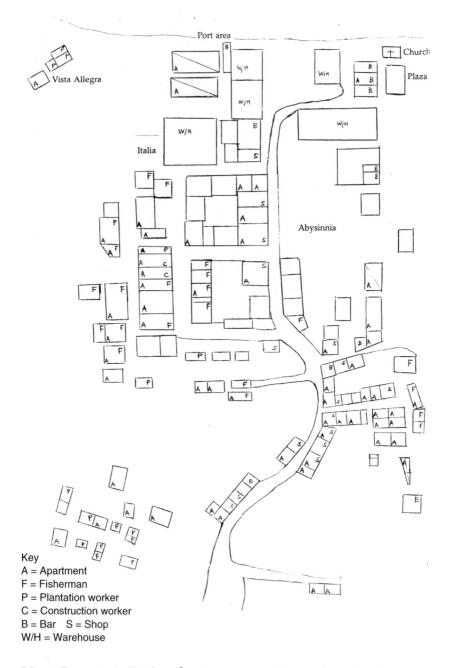

Key
A = Apartment
F = Fisherman
P = Plantation worker
C = Construction worker
B = Bar   S = Shop
W/H = Warehouse

Map 3 Property in Vueltas showing usage and owner's profession

Plate 4 View towards La Playa at Calera beach, 1975

Vueltas: The settlement

Vueltas is linked to the *barrio* Calera (the current seat of the council situated 0.75 km inland) by a smaller route, which was being metalled, widened and generally redesigned for parking and pedestrian walkways in 1991. Apartment buildings up to four storeys high rise above the coastal plain, and with their whitewashed breezeblocks and aluminium metal-work they look ready for business. Vueltas occupies an area approximating to a square 300 m × 300 m, bounded by the inland rock-face and the sea. A coastal pathway runs from Vueltas via another *barrio*, Puntilla, to the beach area and settlement. In 1991 the border of Vueltas was defined by an area of plantation; however, the building of houses and apartments has since created a sort of ribbon development, an 'urban sprawl' linking it to the next inland *barrio*, Borbalan. In 2002, there are no obvious gaps or changes in territory-defining boundaries. The banana plantation has been reduced by up to half its size in 10 years, enabling residential flats and tourist apart-ments to be built.

Map 3 illustrates the layout of Vueltas in 1991: it comprises a cluster of fishermen's houses in the central and coastal part of the settlement, with plantation workers housed on the periphery in more recently built dwellings. Large warehouses dominate the port frontage occupying prime

Plate 5 View towards 'La Playa' in 1991 showing the development of apartments and shops

land and shops line the arterial route, whilst apartments are ubiquitous. The abandoned warehouses have since been demolished to make way for residential housing blocks.

A road divides Vueltas. It meanders through the buildings and is metalled in its entirety serving as the arterial route from which other paths lead off to alleys and thoroughfares. In 1991 the construction programme organised by the local council was re-paving or constructing paving for various interlinking passages in the neighbourhood, giving the place an air of busy activity, renewal and change. Such a passage was under construction outside the apartment of Manuel Barroso, who was the man in charge of the building company undertaking the work (see Plate 6). This is an example of one man using his influence to improve his home environment. The workers effectively levelled the previous rough pathway, removing a huge boulder 2 m in diameter, creating two distinct levels of path linked by cement steps. They also constructed raised steps for entering the front doors of the on-looking houses and steps down towards those at a lower level than the new path. For some observers this took away much of the character and attractiveness of the earlier pathway. A lemon tree was cut down and a flowering shrub taken out: the new path gave a uniform monotony to the route simply conforming with other redesigned back

Plate 6 Creating a new path in Vueltas. The heavy rocks of the old pathway are removed to make way for a new smooth and tiled surface

alleys; it lacked authentic rustic idiosyncracy. Yet the local inhabitants seemed to be in favour of the change.[2]

Vueltas, being divided by a road, has two sections known by the locals as *Italia* (inland of the road) and *Abyssinnia* (on the seaward side). These names are derived from the conflict between the two countries in the 1930s and, hence, symbolic of the one-time antagonistic relationship between the two zones of Vueltas. There is also a third peripheral area known locally as *Vista Allegra* (happy view) that is formed by four separate houses and a collection of buildings overlooking the port at the foot of the mountain slope. It is also known as the 'Chinese barrio', a local derogatory term used because of the large number of people living in the households.

The coastal path and nearby buildings have the protection of huge concrete blocks which run along the vulnerable coastline developing into a sea-wall continuing for 200 m. This wall, about 5 m high, has allowed the natural bay to become a safe harbour for the fishing boats and yachts. The development of the port area at Vueltas began during the early 1980s with the wall finally being finished in 1985. Before this, a small jetty with some lifting gear served the fishing boats and cargo ships. The port area occupies some 20,000 m², most of which is public land, used for parking cars, walking, playing, loading fish and all the associated activities of a small port.

There is a building within the port area that houses the office of the *guardia muelle*, the official who ensures that the fishermen and yachtsmen abide by the martime regulations. It also provides a large storage area. Another new building offers residential quarters for the officers, as well as the potential to operate as a ticket office for marine transport. These two large buildings dominate the port area but play a small part in the lives of the local people, whereas the *muelle* (quay) area is a meeting point for socialising and generally relaxing. The fishermen tend to gather around their boats that have been hauled up for repair: the boats rest on a concrete runway at the top of which is a small building housing a redundant hauling machine.

The land at the foot of the mountain behind the settlement has been terraced and a substantial area running the length of the settlement was, at one time, agriculturally productive. In 1991 only a few hectares remained cultivated, the other terraces and allotments having been abandoned. Two distinct plots remained: one covering an area of 50 m × 30 m, was owned by a family living in Vueltas and worked by an employee who put in 40 hours a week for £100.[3] He explained that people no longer wanted to work as agricultural labourers because there was a greater choice of employment due to the expansion of tourism, which also led to the eventual abandonment of terraces. The owner of the other plot worked on a banana plantation for his main source of income and tended his plot at weekends helped by his son or a paid worker. He also rented out three apartments and owned a 7 m boat, fishing occasionally for household consumption. Further along towards the sea, in *Vista Allegra*, there was a goat enclosure owned by the nearby household. The owner himself worked on the banana plantation and often fed the goats on any unwanted foliage and fruit. These goats were periodically tethered amongst a group of rocks overlooking the port beach and were occasionally tended by his children. There was also a pig enclosure behind the group of houses that belongs to the family. This man and the one in the previous example both supplement their meagre earnings from plantation work through producing food and renting out rooms to tourists. By 2002 the agricultural plots had been abandoned and the goat enclosure had disappeared to make way for a crane based near the construction site.

The developing uniformity and constant construction taking place in the residential area of Vueltas contrasts strongly with the ramshackle and abandoned aspect of the old agricultural zone described earlier. This graphically illustrates the change in working patterns experienced by the villagers in recent times. One striking aspect of the port is the attractiveness

Plate 7 The *falua* returns to dock in Vueltas after a fishing trip, with the smaller fishing boats neatly moored in the bay

and uniformity of the fishing boats (see Plate 7): these are moored in three lines of up to 14 boats, their red and white hulls gleaming in the sun. Varying in length from 5 to 11 m, they dominate the view out to sea. Furthermore, alongside the harbour walls, up to a dozen yachts of all shapes and sizes are also moored. All these vessels, together with the two large *faluas* (tuna fishing boats) coloured red, white and blue, make the port a place awash with colour and activity.

In 1991 there were two large ex-packing stations next to the port, serving as reminders of its original purpose. This was to provide a docking area for cargo ships from where plantation products (tomatoes and bananas stored in the warehouses and packed into boxes) could be taken away and incoming goods offloaded. These buildings now act as garages, general storage areas and machine workshops: one also served as an art gallery and sculptural workshop for an Austrian and a German who have settled in the valley. There were plans to turn one warehouse into a discotheque but it has since been demolished in 1999 to provide space for a shop and apartment complex.

Other buildings of interest in Vueltas include the *Ermita* (Chapel) '*Nuestra Señora Del Carmen*' where masses are usually held monthly and where a mass for the Virgin Carmen (who protects those at sea) on her saint's day is celebrated. This was built in the 1980s with the help of the local people who contributed towards some of the costs: it has stained-glass windows depicting fishermen, fish and other maritime themes and it possesses a lectern in the shape of a boat. The plaza behind the *ermita* is utilised for fiestas as well as serving as a meeting place for mothers and their children in the early evening. A bakery is operative in Vueltas, being annexed to one of the oldest (at some 80 years of age) houses in the village. This is run by Ullyses, whose father before him ran it, producing a variety of bread baked during the early morning hours. Other businesses in operation during September 1991 in Vueltas included: two car-hire firms, six supermarkets, one hardware shop, one clothes and gift shop, one florist, one T-shirt shop, one photograph and poster shop, one carpenters yard, one furniture shop, one discotheque, one meditation centre, one fishing tackle shop. In addition, there were also seven restaurants that have bars, four bars that may serve tapas, one restaurant, and one cafe that also serves food. This gives a total of 13 outlets for food and/or drink: each of these catering outlets has unique characteristics attracting a particular clientele. By 2002 the number of businesses operating as traders had grown from 33 to 52, with a distinct increase in foreign-run, tourist-oriented shops (analysed in greater detail in Chapter 4).

In 1991 two large apartment blocks dominated the port beach: they both had five floors and each contained up to 24 separate apartments. Another block with four floors overlooks the sea at the northernmost corner of Vueltas. These three blocks and the new block mentioned earlier, were the only non-household apartment blocks in Vueltas; the other apartments being extensions of houses or purpose-built blocks also housing members of the family, usually children of the owner. The private household apartment blocks numbered at least 36, and were separately named, usually after the owner or a member of the family, such as 'Apartmento Abraham', 'Humberto' or 'Miguel'.

In 2002, some 47 sets of tourist apartments were acknowledged in Vueltas, comprising 228 rooms (as recorded in a Tourism Office brochure). Further developments in progress include three huge blocks of residential apartments (ground plus three floors) being built next to the original two blocks by the port. In addition, private building has added tourist apartments to other dwellings in the village.

These apartments range from single-room *habitacions* with one or two beds and use of shared toilet facilities to two-bedroomed apartments, fully furnished with bathroom, kitchen, dining room/lounge, veranda or rooftop terrace. In general, the apartments cater for two people, with kitchen and toilet facilities and a bedroom/lounge. This style of self-catering set-up influences the type of tourists who visit, i.e. those who prefer to stay in places where they are free to move around without the bother or restraint of reservations. There are opportunities to meet the local people who own the apartments and it is possible to cook in the apartments, allowing the tourists to sample local food and products in an environment other than a restaurant and giving them a place where they can entertain friends. The apartments developed in response to the type of tourists who first visited VGR: mostly backpackers and self-styled hippies, originating in the late 1960s and early 1970s as a trickle of travellers, people who were prepared to brave the comparatively rough journey to this region. By the 1990s the tourists were predominantly Germans, in general well-educated backpackers between 20–45 years of age, prepared to search out accommodation on arrival. This type would be classified as 'unusual or off-beat' by Smith (1989c), although they are generally regarded as 'alternative' by themselves and sometimes as 'hippies' by the local people. Here we will refer to them as 'alternative' tourists and discuss their qualities in later chapters.

Originally, private apartments reached a maximum of three levels above ground in 1991, with occasional rooftop rooms for rent. A planning restriction imposed by the local council halted further vertical construction. A number of households were awaiting a possible change of political party which would enable them to start building more apartments. One landlady said that she hoped her socialist relative would gain a seat in the forthcoming elections and allow her to continue constructing another level for her apartments: everything was prepared for further extension. Eventually the building restrictions were relaxed and the construction of additional floors continued. The number of rooms / apartments available in each private property ranges from one to 20, with the mode being six. An impression can, therefore, be had of Vueltas with its abundance of apartments, cheek to cheek, bearing familial names, all extensions of the original *casa* (home).

The *casa* in Vueltas comes in many forms: old-fashioned traditional Gomeran types dating from the 1920s; more recently built ones with the same basic design; and flats. The original houses are built of solid stone and cement in a rectangular shape that varies in size and may also shelter a small courtyard. The interior of the single-storey building may be divided into two or three large rooms: one or two rooms serving as bedrooms, the other serving as the sitting / dining room – in some instances it also doubles as a bedroom. This sitting room usually houses the television, radio and hi-fi if there are any. The kitchen and lavatory are built as extensions at either end of the length of the building. The external walls are usually white-washed or may be coloured green or blue; occasionally they are not painted at all. The windows are oblong in shape, double and usually have wooden shutters which are coloured differently to the external walls, the wooden frames being painted either blue or green for example. Roofs in the very old houses are tiled with red clay tiles making an attractive sight. However, most currently have flat concreted roofs which form storeage areas for building materials, nets, wire fishing cages, fishing rods, water tanks and other large items: they are rarely used for relaxation by the locals, although they are often converted into sun-terraces for the tourists.

In 1991 there were 14 of these traditional houses in Vueltas. Two have since been demolished and replaced by apartment blocks and another group along the coastal path was demolished for the new roadway. This group of old houses has been particularly admired by visiting tourists who take photos of the quaint buildings painted blue and green. In contrast to their attractive exterior, such houses have severe problems inside and locals pointed out the difficulties that the tile-roofed old houses have with dirt that enters through the tiles. Most people prefer to live in the cleaner new buildings with their efficient plumbing and electrical fittings.

Some of the houses have gardens or small yards adjacent to them, in which their owners sometimes place potted plants and shrubs to add colour and greenery: plants are also placed outside the houses alongside the walls to give an attractive appearance. There may be small fruit trees such as orange or lemon, papaya or even mangos in the gardens and, where possible, planted crops. Often, however, the yard is just concreted and possesses a table and chairs neatly placed to allow the family to sit, eat and chat at their leisure in the shade. In some, a caged bird such as a canary or parakeet is kept and others have pigeons. Normally a hose hangs outside and this is used to water the plants, dampen the dusty soil and wash off dust and seawater from members of the family. There is usually an outside washbasin, allowing for the scrubbing down of clothing. These gardens, backyards and front yards are very small, about 100 m^2, and cannot be thought of in the same way as an English garden. There are no lawns due to the dry, rocky soil and only the older houses actually possess gardens, whereas the people who live in flats make do with small verandas.

Houses that have been built since the 1960s are constructed from breeze-blocks made out of locally quarried gravel mixed with cement: these blocks were manufactured by a local builder until they began to be imported from Tenerife. Such houses usually take the same form as the older ones, i.e. rect-angular bungalows, although most have a central hallway leading to individual rooms. The design and flat roofs make it straightforward for the building to be extended vertically giving an additional floor or more. This is very common and with the popularity of rented apartments due to tourism, many single-storey houses have built upwards, some adding three new floors.

Flats vary but most have one or two bedrooms, a sitting/dining room, a bathroom and lavatory and possibly another room. Some families live in apartments that may also be rented out to tourists in their absence: others live in flats built on top of their parents' home. One couple and their child lived in what looked like a converted garden shed, in the garden of the wife's parents. Another couple lived directly above the wife's parents in an apartment, one of several within the parental building, which is now a common situation in VGR. One retired fisherman, who lives in his own bungalow with his wife, possesses another two-storey house and apartment in which his married son and family live and also two separate blocks of apartments, each of which also houses a married daughter and her family. The tourism-driven apartment boom of the early 1980s has enabled many young couples, children of the villagers, to remain within the village, housed near their families, without the problem of finding and financing a new home. Couples in this situation often pay rent, although their parents are usually sensitive to their financial problems. The tourism industry has meant that many have been able to find some type of employment locally: out of five such couples in Vueltas, at least one partner in each relationship worked in a job involved with tourism

Perspectives on History

Recorded history

Vueltas is a relatively recent settlement dating from the beginning of the 20th century. However, the valley in which it has grown has a far longer history, mostly unrecorded, but nevertheless partly known through archaeological work and travellers' accounts, as well as oral history. Before the conquest of La Gomera by the Spaniards in the 15th century, VGR formed one of the four demarcated regions of the island and was known as the *Bando de Orone*. This region occupied what is now the municipality plus the southern part of Vallehermoso, the adjoining municipality in the east. The aboriginal people, known by the contemporary Gomeros as 'Guanches', are believed to have settled the Canary Islands between 2500 and 1000 BC. Abreu-Padión (1986), a professional historian from the Canaries, writes that they had a monarchical system and practised sophisticated ceremonies which included the mummification of the dead. They are believed to have crossed from Africa and to have entered Africa from Europe via Italy and the Sinai Peninsula. Many questions remain unanswered about these original settlers but they exercise an important influence over the imagination and identity of the people today who retain an interest in their past. Some elements of the Guanche peoples' culture remain in use, including their music and dance, culinary habits, agricultural methods and the famous silbo whistling language.

European slave traders 'rediscovered' the islands in the 14th century and this led to the eventual claim on the land by Pope Clement the Sixth in 1344. Luis de Cenda, a scion of the Spanish royal family, was later appointed 'King of the Canary Islands' bringing them into a broader (and eventually global) trading network. Jean de Bethencourt began the conquest of the islands in 1402, occupying Lanzarote, and later Fuerteventura and Hierro in 1405. He was then granted the title 'King of the Canary Islands'. Possession of the islands became confused as Portuguese nobles purchased office and in 1445 Hernan Peraza the elder established his authority on La Gomera, residing in San Sebastian, from where he vainly hoped to conquer the islands of La Palma, Gran Canaria and Tenerife. In 1478 the sovereignty was sold back to the Spanish and the Treaty of Alcacovas recognised the island as belonging to Spain.

The grandson of Hernan Peraza inherited the title of Count of La Gomera and became hated by the Gomeros because of his cruelty and his sexual abuse of their women. There were numerous uprisings and eventually a shepherd (named Hautacuperche) killed the grandson when he went to visit a local beauty named Iballa. This episode forms the basis of many folk stories, one of which relates to a rock, still known as the 'rock of secrets' just off the coast at Vueltas, to which fathers would row their sons to tell them 'the secret': the fact that they were plotting to kill the Count. If anyone revealed the secret, he would be killed. Unfortunately one young boy did reveal the secret and was consequently dispatched by his father. After this disclosure the men set about the task of murdering the Count.[4]

The assassination of the Count led the islanders to attempt to expel the conquistadores; however, the Governor of Gran Canaria was alerted and arrived with soldiers to quell the insurrection. He offered to pardon the remaining forces that were in hiding, but when they gave themselves up he went back on his word and hung many, sending others off to slavery. This story, well known to the islanders, reinforces the notion of the Gomeros being a colonially subjugated people capable of revolution: a people able to act for themselves as agents of their own destinies.

A more globally famous historical event was the arrival of Columbus, who put in at La Gomera, where there was abundant freshwater, on his first voyage of discovery in 1492, returning on subsequent journeys. There is a tower and a house named after him in the Port of San Sebastian, the island capital, and La Gomera is also known as *La Isla Columbina* (The Island of Columbus). It hosted a major celebration in 1992 when boats docked at the port, breaking their journey to the Americas as part of the 500th anniver-

Plate 8 A pavement mosaic in San Sebastian showing the journey of Christopher Columbus: from Spain to La Gomera and onwards to Hispaniola (Dominican Republic and Haiti)

sary of their discovery by Columbus. Travel promoters for La Gomera have made its connections with Columbus a tourist attraction and make references in guidebooks to its earlier status as a one time major port for transatlantic travel. EU funds have helped to preserve a building in which Columbus is thought to have stayed and a large mosaic on the newly built promenade celebrates the journey across the Atlantic from the Canary Islands to Hispaniola – what is now the Dominican Republic and Haiti (see Plate 8). However, the quintennial celebrations are the subject of critical debate amongst some academics and politicians on the islands and the arrival of Columbus remains a controversial part of history. He is not a part of popular folk memory among the people in VGR.

The Spanish Crown, which had sovereignty over La Gomera, Hierro, Lanzarote and Fuerteventura in the 15th century, granted rights of possession to nobles and ecclesiastics, subject to payment of duties to the island and the Crown. Gradually, the indigenous population became assimilated into the Spanish settlements through a policy of enforced relocation. Over time they were joined by migrants from Spain, Portugal, England and France, all attracted by the fertile islands. Much of the land was utilised to produce plantation crops for export and only a minority of the indigenous population were able to continue their pastoral lifestyle, notably those who had retreated to the hills. Those who had helped the conquerors were integrated into the organisation of social life, many as slaves or servants. One Canarian writer, Concepción (1989), draws attention to this and promotes the idea that the original 'Guanche' inhabitants are still the 'dominant race' in the Canary Islands: he claims that some two-thirds of the population of the islands have Guanche blood. These claims are supported by academic findings and his books sell very well on the islands. The importance of the Canary Islands to Spain's colonial history is immense – their conquest represented Spain's first overseas venture, which became a precedent for the colonisation of America. The Islands became, in effect, a testing ground for colonial administration including the enslavement and evangelisation of an aboriginal population.[5]

A long history of exploitation began for the Islands. They were crucial in the establishment of the New World, creating a network from which the modern world system developed (see Shannon, 1989: 21). Sugar cane provided the main source of income until the 1650s when competition from the Caribbean grew strong. Wine was then produced, this industry being dominated by British owners until tastes changed in the 19th century. The cochineal beetle began to be cultivated to provide dye, although the introduction of synthetic dyes ended the demand; the cactus on which they were reared is still to be found in abundance in VGR. It was the bananas, brought over from Indonesia, which were to become the successful export product of the early 20th century: they are still grown on a large scale on Gran Canaria and the Western Isles although global competition has led to their recent demise as a viable export product. Banana plantations take up almost half of the coastal lowlands of VGR, and the fruit is sent to mainland Spain for consumption. The Spanish Government agreed to purchase the bananas from the producers until 1996 and the insecurity over the future market for the crops together with the difficulty of getting labour has led to uncertainty over land-use in the near future. Nevertheless, by 2002, the bananas were being exported by the company 'Coplaca–Eurobanan' as '*Platanos de Canarias*'.

Other crops cultivated for export in the past include orchil (a red / violet dye made from lichen), tomatoes and silk: there is still a hamlet in VGR known as Casa de la Seda – the House of Silk. VGR, a fertile valley, was regarded as one of the best estates owned by the Count of La Gomera (see Armas, 1990)[6] and land was intensively cultivated with upland plots being divided amongst local families people. They often subsisted on such crops as potatoes, sweet potatoes, maize, beans and fruit as well as rearing goats, chickens and pigs. They also went fishing in small boats using a rod and line. Local men say that the people of VGR have fished for over 200 years, with many combining fishing with work on the land. This indicates the historical depth of fishing as a way of supplying food for auto-consumption and exchange: it also demonstrates the practice of indulging in diverse activities to supply the household, a prototypical form of plural employment in a number of different work areas. In later times, many people combined farming with work on plantations to acquire cash or credit to pay for basic necessities. They were a form of semi-proletariat and, as such, were super-exploited in the sense that their private activities subsidised their employers indirectly by helping to pay towards the reproduction of their labour.

The fishing activity in VGR attracted the interest of Pastor Casanova Miravent at the beginning of the 19th century. He was a businessman from the Peninsula, operating in Tenerife, with knowledge of fish processing and he established himself in VGR, building a salting factory for fish, which employed local people. He also obtained land on the alluvial plain that was regarded as unworkable, and grew tamarisk, transforming the soil into a productive state. His family later built a bulwark to contain the potential floodwater on the south-east side of the estuary which allowed the land to be developed into agricultural property. This example illustrates on a micro-scale the entrepreneurial activities on the island involving the exploitation of produce and the working population. Casanova, an important actor in this sense, created a business venture and, in so doing, became relatively rich and influential. In this way, he developed into an agent within a strong interest group which forms part of a class of powerful families.

A direct descendant of the pastor, Jaime Casanova, still lived in VGR in 1991 and sat at his desk in an inoperative shop talking to his friends and passers-by. He talked proudly of his ancestors' business activities and sometimes showed visitors some old photos that he had taken of the valley and the port more than 30 years previously. His son Jaime was deeply involved in the protest against the beach development and ran for the post of mayor with the socialist party in the local elections: Jaime's family connections became an important element of discussion throughout the election in 1991 which centred on the Casanova family as *caciques* (bosses, the ruling élite). It will be helpful to examine this term, which has historical and sociological connotations and is used to describe the land-owning families amongst others. Hernandez-Hernandez (1986) identified the Spanish conquerors as *caciques* and the subjugated native population of the Canary Islands as *magos* (rural peasants): this ethnic division is not apparent now but the two-tiered system of master and servant is still perceived by many inhabitants as forming the class system of VGR.[7] The people talk of the *caciques* as a group and the powerful families certainly

tended to intermarry. In the film *Guarapo* (1988), which was based on life in
La Gomera in the 1940s and 1950s, the plantation owners are portrayed as
abusers of the workers and violent masters. This film was sympathetic
towards the La Gomeran workers, emphasising the division between the
peasants and the rich landowners who were allied with the Guardia Civil,
agents and symbols of a distant metropolitan Spain. Many of the local
people in VGR believed that it gave an accurate representation of life then
and that *caciquismo* continues to influence contemporary society.[8]

The *cacique* is often a patron who needs clients and who can use his links
in the bureaucratic chain. It is relevant to observe that, at one time, a
member of the Casanova family handled the social security documentation
for the fishermen of VGR and other members of *cacique* families were
medical doctors, pharmacists and merchants. The *caciques* were the bourgeoisie and the *magos* the proletariat in this scenario of class division. These
wealthy entrepreneurs seem to be the inheritors of the *señorial* (baronial)
mantle: those men granted rights over land, latter-day feudal lords who
lost their control of the land after the court of Cadiz called for the return of
the land to the common people in 1812. This period marks a decisive sea
change in the relationship between the Spanish court and the Canary
Islands. Hitherto, since the conquest, the islands had been regarded and
governed as colonies – with aristocrats being answerable only to the
Crown. After 1812, and notably with the court decree in 1823, the Islands
were considered as a province of Spain, with their capital being Santa Cruz
de Tenerife.[9]

After 1812 the new entrepreneurs and wealthy families in La Gomera
were still able to exercise a powerful control over local people who
depended on them for cash income and work. This big divide between the
rich and the poor has diminished rapidly since the 1970s, largely as a result
of wealth acquired from a successful fishing industry and, more recently,
tourism. VGR had a below average migration rate within La Gomera due to
the intensive nature of land cultivation and the pattern of ownership at the
beginning of the 20th century. At the same time as the development of the
banana plantations, the fishing sector expanded with the arrival in 1918 of
Jacinto Lloret, who built a fish-processing factory at La Rajita, a village a
few miles along the coast from VGR. Factories were also established on the
island at Las Canterras and Santiago. The fishing industry of La Gomera
consequently expanded very rapidly and this was reflected, amongst other
things, by the growth of the settlement at Vueltas. At the beginning of the
1920s Vueltas contained only one house according to testimonies, whereas
by 1930 it possessed 168 inhabitants registered by the national census. The
growth in agricultural work boosted the population of other settlements in

VGR, specifically Calera, Guro and Casa de la Seda, in the lower valley: VGR experienced a doubling of its population during the 1920s.

Work on a road was begun between Vueltas and La Calera during this period of growth and continued along the route up to Retamal: people say that there was only one vehicle, a lorry, operating in those days. In the 1950s, the road was extended to Arure, the original administrative centre of VGR in the mountains. There was, however, maritime communication, with the boat 'Junonia' making the trip from Vueltas to San Sebastian twice weekly. Two small sea walls were constructed in Vueltas at the end of the 1920s and a platform, built during the 1930s, enabled dock work to be undertaken. We can see that the demands for transport related to economic patterns and this has continued to the present day, with the needs of the tourism industry requiring infrastructural improvements. Historically, the arrival of foreign entrepreneurs has made for local changes and the influential fish factory developers were one such example of these agents of change.

The migration of men in search of work has formed a central part of La Gomera's history over the last two centuries.[10] The population grew from 6919 in 1787 to a peak of 28,383 in 1940; and then declined to 17,273 in 1987 and rose to about 18,000 by 2002. Emigration slowed down towards the 1940s, due to the success of the tomato and banana plantations; however, the market isolation of Spain after the Second World War led to a consequent stepping up of emigration. The destination for migrants also shifted in the 1970s from Latin America to Western Europe and many Gomeros moved to Tenerife in search of work where the opportunities offered by tourism allowed them greater possibilities. Numerous families on La Gomera have relatives in Latin America, usually Venezuela and Cuba: some had left illegally in the 1940s and 1950s to escape the period of intense poverty and hunger popularly known as *La Miseria*. One booklet describing the island gives a generally acknowledged opinion that tourism may be able to revive the battered economy (Mora, 1988). Many people still leave La Gomera in search of work and VGR is the only place on the island apart from the capital San Sebastian that has a growing population (see Ministerio de Obras Publicas y Urbanisma, 1988), a fact that can be attributed, in a large part, to the opportunities created by tourism.

Local observations

The historical account that follows describes in detail the development of VGR and especially Vueltas. It has been accumulated from a number of casual discussions and interviews with local people including long-term inhabitants and foreign settlers, being created from oral history, it is subject to the limitations and strengths of personal recollections.

Nicholas 'Rolo' Dorta, a local man from Calera, insisted that Vueltas was named after a lone cave dweller (Juan Vueltas), the first occupant of the area in the 19th century.[11] In those days the area was one of scrubland, which was gradually replaced by a few plantations and eventually boasted three packing stations for the exportable crops, tomatoes and bananas. Pablo Jimenez, some years older than Rolo, arrived with his brother and father from Tenerife in 1910 when he was seven years old. His father was unable to settle in Calera, as the inhabitants did not welcome new settlers, so he moved to Vueltas where he lived in a cave for a while and eventually built a stone house. Jimenez senior was a fisherman, who would fish in the then current fashion holding a rod in each hand to catch mackerel: he knew the coast of VGR well as did many fishermen from Tenerife who arrived seasonally to fish for tuna. Jimenez was, therefore, one, if not the first, of the fishermen to settle in Vueltas, an otherwise uninhabited spot.

Eventually other fishermen arrived, the fathers and grandfathers of the current generation over 50 years old, most came from Tenerife. At this time, in the early 20th century, the fishermen of VGR (including the Ramos family) were settled in Calera and its beach from where they launched their fishing boats. With the construction of the fish-processing plants, the work for fishermen became relatively plentiful and, consequently, Vueltas grew steadily, composed in the majority by fishermen and their families.[12]

The Spanish Civil War led to some of the local men being drafted to the mainland: although there was no action on the island, bitter divisions and reprisals occurred in some parts, particularly in the north. It was after the Civil War and up to the 1950s when the victorious allies snubbed Spain that the Canary Islands really felt hardship. This period, known as *La Miseria* by the local people, is still very current in living memory, being a topic encountered in conversations. The word itself is commonly used as an indication of poverty or bad luck, as, for instance, when there are few fish about and catches are small, the fishermen would say in jest '*Que miseria*'! (What misery!) sometimes with a hint of desperation, the comedy and tragedy juxtaposed. It was in the early 1950s, when men were needed for Spain's economic recovery, that clandestine journeys to the Americas, particularly Venezuela, became a commonplace occurrence due to the difficulty and expense of obtaining legal permits to emigrate. The film *Guarapo* (1988), which depicts such an escape, is based on the true story of a migrant from the north of the island. Pablo Jimenez was another of those who crossed the Atlantic Ocean in a fishing boat with some of his sons: the hardship in VGR at this time was indisputable and *gofio* (roasted maize flour) became the staple diet for the majority of the inhabitants.

With no gas, electricity or running water generally available until the 1970s, much of the women's time was spent retrieving firewood for cooking, collecting water for the day's intake or walking with washing to the local fountain or river. In addition to these hard physical activities, some women had to carry fish on their heads in buckets up the valley for 3 or 4 km in the early hours of the morning in order to exchange them for cash or agricultural products with which they then returned. One woman spoke about her arduous journeys up into the mountains after her father, a fisherman, had returned home with the catch: she would carry 5 kgm of fish on her head to the inland villages where she would exchange them for farm produce and return with the new load. A middle-aged man, now working as a teacher, said that in his younger days the men's working lives were very hard, with plantation workers often working throughout the daylight hours for enough money to purchase basic necessities and little else. Many older men recalled that the first time they wore shoes was when they were drafted into military service. With no main line public electricity or gas, the valley remained in darkness except for lamps in houses and social life, aside from the fiestas, was generally restricted to the house, family and friends. People would chat on their doorsteps or play at dominoes and cards together until an early bedtime. These descriptions show how the opportunities for local people were very limited: their lives were based around manual work. Poor and hardworking in general, they had little choice about employment. The limitation of opportunity and the exploitation is underlined by the great risks taken in trying to escape by boat to South America.

Yet there were some opportunities for entertainment outside the home: Maria, the manager and owner of the restaurant 'Las Jornadas' (known locally as 'Casa Maria'), said that it was opened in 1945 at Calera beach (see Plate 9). The locals would meet there on a Sunday and dance to gramophone music with young people encountering prospective spouses. Another small bar at Calera offered wine and rum in a more spartan environment, whilst the bar 'Puerto' in Vueltas catered mainly for the passing boat-crews and local fishermen. Apart from fiesta days, Sundays were the only days that married couples went out together as entertainment and money was limited. Nevertheless, many recall these times with fondness, saying that the people were friendlier in those days.[13]

In 1963 'Las Jornadas' offered a room to passing travellers, the first of such available in lower VGR: there was one already at the top of the valley in Arure according to local accounts. The 1960s also saw the introduction of gas to the valley and with the building of the road in 1965, electricity arrived in the late 1960s. Some people had bought petrol-driven generators and were able to operate devices off these but they were exceptional. In 1968 the first set of tourist apartments were created out of an old house on the beachfront at Calera (see Plates 4 and 5). It was owned by Rudolfo (a

Plate 9 Tourists sit outside Casa Maria's which is a favourite meeting point, affording an excellent view of the Atlantic ocean and the setting sun

German) and is another example of how foreign ideas and money can introduce new economic possibilities. Agents of economic change from foreign lands have been an important factor in La Gomera throughout its history since its imposed inclusion in an imperial web of trade.

During the Franco years, from 1939 to 1975, many profound infrastuctural changes were implemented in VGR, including the new road, the arrival of main-line electricity, the introduction of piped household water and the building of a small harbour at Vueltas. These years are remembered by some as times when crime on the streets was virtually unknown: one fisherman recalled how a man may be asleep in the road with thousands of pesetas hanging out of his pocket and no-one would touch his money; whereas now, according to him, 'there are *bandidos* [thieves] everywhere'. Another man, Rolo, who is now retired, felt that the Franco regime gave the ordinary man a helping hand, 'limiting potential exploitation by introducing a maximum working day of eight hours, and other social rights including pension benefits and education for adults to combat illiteracy.' In short, Franco was felt by many of the older generation to be a *buen hombre* (a good man), reflecting, to a great degree, their current political persuasion. Whereas, in general, younger people believed that the years under the dictatorship were best forgotten.

It was in the year of Franco's death, however, that one of the greatest factors of change for the island was introduced (aside from the major political and consequent social transformations initiated by the loss of Franco): this was the introduction of the 'Ferry Gomera' owned by the Olsen Company of Norway. It linked La Gomera to Tenerife in a journey lasting 90 minutes, which transformed the communication and transportation networks. Fresh products such as fruit and fish could now be got away quickly and this opened up the market; one such beneficiary was Ramon the fish salesman, who now commands most of the tuna market in La Gomera and Tenerife. He started life as a poor trader from the north of the island, walking for hours to VGR to buy fish that he later sold in the northern villages. After winning the fishermen's trust as a reliable purchaser, he came to monopolise the tuna fish market.

The ferry was to prove a major tool of change in the economy, easing the transportation of natural foodstuffs, vehicles and construction machinery and also, importantly, the carriage of tourists. So the means was established for a potential growth in this slowly developing source of income and soon the trickle of tourists grew in strength: in Vueltas a large block of apartments overlooking the port was built by an Austrian (believed to be an ex-Nazi). This man was a nautical engineer and he designed many of the small rowing boats still used by the local fishermen to reach their larger fishing boats moored out in the harbour. Many of these apartments are now rented long term or owned by foreign families, the remainder being used by tourists throughout the year. People agree that the construction of this block of apartments, plus the regular presence of tourists, initiated the building boom in Vueltas during the 1980s. One of the first fishermen to build apartments, Miguel Jimenez, said that he saw the potential for making money and a good investment for his retirement days, so he built an additional floor on top of the house he inherited from his father to rent out to tourists.[14] Relatives and friends joined in the frenzy of apartment construction that saw entire rows of houses being extended vertically to accommodate the prospective tourists. The activity continues with at least 47 individual groups of private apartments in Vueltas and numerous rooms to let, giving a total of more than 228 apartments for rent.

The 1980s witnessed the construction of apartments and the acquisition of television sets by the general population, as well as such modern electrical conveniences as washing machines. In this way the people were exposed to mass communication: new ideas and attitudes appeared on the TV screens as well as arriving in the flesh in the form of tourists. A branch of a national bank opened in Calera in 1984 offering free television sets to potential borrowers (previously the people had used a travelling bank). The credit culture was made available to the population at a time when many needed just this to become established in the apartment business. This decade therefore saw a huge expansion of the indigenous population's mediascape, finanscape and ethnoscape, all major aspects of globalisation (see Appadurai, 1990). Sadly, there are examples of people who over-extended themselves acquiring crippling interest payments, one of whom killed himself because he was unable to service his debts. A long-term foreign resident thought that this partly illustrates the local people's lack of experience in financial management and understanding of financial institutions and their concept of credit. Many people would purchase things on credit at the local store, settling accounts at the month's end, but they were not accustomed to borrowing large sums of capital and regularly paying a high rate of interest on the principal sum.

Construction in Vueltas during the 1980s was also in progress at the port: a new harbour was in the making, with a large quay protected by a huge sea wall 300 m long and 5 m high. The project started around 1980 and was finished by 1985. It gave the community a secure port, capable of berthing a hydrofoil and there were over 50 yachts moored there for a Labour Day (1 May) regatta event in 1991. The port wall protects the fishermen's boats from the constant pounding of the Atlantic; it allows yachtsmen to weigh anchor or tie up alongside; and permits the offloading of fish. It also gives sufficient road room for lorries of all sizes to move in and out and is now of increasing use to recreational yachtsmen, tour boats and passenger ferries.

Fishing development and decline

Fishing has been an activity performed by the inhabitants of VGR for at least 200 years. Within living memory, the people had both land and boats and would combine the two livelihoods of fishing and farming as well as working on plantations to supply the necessities for living (cf. Acheson, 1981). Fishing was not a profession as such for dedicated artisans but part of a group of economic activities undertaken by individuals. Pedro Ramos, a local fisherman, recalls that his great-grandfather did not specialise in fishing or building boats, as his descendants were to do, but mixed fishing with work on the land. He would have fished with cane rods and hooks for tuna, mackerel, white fish and others, just as today's fishermen do: some men would use two rods, one in each hand, others preferred short rods for particular types of fish. These part-time fishermen were based in the valley at Calera at a time when Vueltas was rough undeveloped coastland.

In the early 1900s some fishermen from Tenerife who hunted tuna off the La Gomeran coast on a seasonal basis decided to settle in VGR but found it hard to gain acceptance in Calera and were forced to establish dwellings near the uninhabited coastline at Vueltas in 1910. With the settlement and establishment of Vueltas at the beginning of the 20th century by fishermen from other parts of La Gomera and Tenerife attracted by the tuna fishing, a more specialised conglomeration of people who were able to rely solely on fishing to support their families began to develop. Some of the first fishermen and their families to reside in Vueltas include the Jimenez and the Gonzalez families; they built their homes out of stones and clay and were self-sufficient, selling fish or exchanging them for other necessities. Many of the settlers, who originally came seasonally to fish, obtained employment at the newly constructed fish-processing plants on the south of La Gomera, which were to strongly determine the development of the area. By 1930 there were 168 people living in Vueltas, many relying on the fish-processing plant for their market.

The company 'Lloret and Llinares' established a fish-salting plant in a bay called 'La Rajita', some miles along the coast from Vueltas, at the beginning of the 20th century. In 1928 they built a conserving factory for tuna and mackerel: this attracted workers and fishermen not only from the neighbouring villages but also from other islands. The population at the plant site grew from 39 in 1920 to 339 in 1970; special housing was built for the workers but conditions were harsh with only one water fountain and the awful smell of the factory. The process of establishing communications by road with the northern villages commenced. This led to the appearance of *furgonetas* (the middlemen who would buy the fish direct from fishermen and sell it in other villages), an example being Ramon Morales currently the owner of the two largest boats. The factory-owners would secure their purchases by saying that if the fishermen did not sell to them alone, they would stop buying their fish altogether. As the fishermen initially desired security, they remained loyal to the factory, however, with strong competition amongst the middlemen, the fishermen eventually found that they could successfully transfer allegiances without risking future sales.

A number of other factories were set up on La Gomera at the beginning of the 20th century, at San Sebastian, Santiago and Canterra that had had a salting plant in the 19th century. The island became a very successful region for the fishing industry (Garcia, 1969). Large boats began to arrive during the 1950s from other regions to fish in the local waters. The factory near VGR had provided its own engine-powered boats for some fishermen and employees. However, with the ability to save the cash they had made from the sales the fishermen were soon able to buy motors from the factory for their own small boats, which up until then were powered by sail and oar, thus enabling them to compete on good terms. This potentially gave them independence from the factory and improved their economic situation.

In 1972 there were 61 fishermen in VGR. From 1975 to 1978 four *faluas* (tuna fishing boats around 20 m in length requiring a crew of five or more) were acquired at Vueltas and, by 1980, there were six in operation employing 65 out of a total of 95 fishermen (Mesa-Moreno, 1982). Agricultural workers and mechanics from different areas arrived to boost the crew numbers. Over the years the fishermen have increased their catch capacity and variety through the enhancement of their equipment, including improved engines, man-made materials and radio technology. Despite this, their methods remain essentially artisanal, i.e. based on a traditional manually operated technique, and they are reliant, as always, on a market for their catch. The 1960s saw good fishing and the pattern continued favourably up until the early 1980s, when the factories closed because of global market economic pressures.

In 1991 there were 23 professional registered boats and around 45 professional fishermen, mostly based in Vueltas. A variety of fishing was practised, with an emphasis on tuna and mackerel, using rods, lines and hooks. The *nasa* (a wire cage), *tambor* (drum for eels), *panarela* net and harpoon were all still in use. The composition of Vueltas remained largely that of fishermen and their families in 1991 as Map 3 indicates – although the working population pursued a wide variety of jobs in the service industry.

By 2002 the situation had not changed drastically with 22 professional boats and 53 men registered as professional fishermen. However, it is said by the *Cofradia* (the organisation for fishermen) that almost half gain most of their income from apartment rent or other forms of work – and many observers suggest that a realistic figure for full-time fishermen is around 20. Some fishermen believe that fishing will disappear as an industry in their children's lifetime.

Individual voices

Space is given here to individual voices in the form of summarised accounts taken from numerous conversations.

Nicholas 'Rolo' Dorta, a man in his seventies, is regarded by the villagers as knowledgeable on local history. He spent much of his time with his cousin in his clothes shop in Calera. He recalled:

> There have been fishermen in VGR for at least 200 years, using the rod and line techniques that are still employed. They fished for mackerel holding a rod in each hand, as well as for *vieja* and *cabrilla*, in fact most of the fish that are caught today, including shellfish. They sometimes exchanged the fish caught for other products such as potatoes, although many also had small plots of land.

I myself worked as a fisherman when around twenty years of age: this was not full-time labour though and I combined it with work in the plantations. This was very common then and there were more people fishing part-time in those days than now fish full-time. The youth don't work much now, not like they used to, they only go out to the bars and disco, although I know that some study for qualifications.

After the Civil War times were hard, and only Argentina opened her doors for Spanish products: the people experienced poverty and hunger. But the relationship between the people of the Canary Islands and the people from mainland Spain is good now, we are more Spanish than the Basques or Catalans.

Many other villagers echoed these sentiments regarding the Canary Islands and mainland Spain, describing themselves and other islanders as *tranquilo* (in the sense that they are not political agitators). Another of Rolo's opinions, which was generally voiced by others, was the belief that the products of the valley were of a superior quality to other regions on the island:

The bananas are more smooth and have more aroma than those from the north, the cheese is more fatty, and the young goats have a better flavour, because they eat the lush banana plants and fruit.

One of the many topics on which Rolo was knowledgeable was the Guanches (the pre-Hispanic inhabitants) and he believed that there were originally three distinct physical types: tall and blonde, short and dark, and some in-between. The islands did not communicate with each other in those days, not having sea-going vessels, although the Guanches did fish from the coast. He also told the story of the picture of the *Virgin de los Reyes*, now kept in the small *ermita* up in the valley:

This portrait was bartered for water by a passing ship as it anchored off the beach. On receiving the water and other provisions they refused to part with the painting. But the weather became completely calm for days and kept them in the bay until they needed more provisions. They then reluctantly handed over the painting, after which the weather changed and they were able to get away.

Rolo had learnt history from reading and listening to others: he said that he did it for his own interest – as a hobby. He had benefited from a school education, albeit poor, to which only men were privileged in his youth and he applauded the Franco regime's efforts to educate the older people: classes were held for adult illiterates in local schools. When asked if he thought that there were differences between the various hamlets, he replied that he felt there were distinct differences between them:

> The people of Vueltas, the fishing settlement, are very different from the farmers of the upper valley, they are people of the sea; they live and work by the sea: '*todo el mar*' [the sea is everything].

This account shows how the history of the valley, in the guise of personal life experience together with pre-Hispanic and mythical history, is maintained by members of the older generation. The sense of identity and pride together with a subtle differentiation between hamlets is apparent and remains very much part of contemporary life in the municipality of VGR. It also illustrates how the plantation workers were engaging in other subsistence labour and fishing to support themselves and their families. Rolo's account of the Guanches, although brief, exhibits an interest in the pre-Hispanic peoples that is common throughout the island and is one of a variety of explanations and descriptions of these people.[15]

Miguel Jimenez, the son of Pablo, worked as the captain of a *falua* for 13 years and is now retired. He recalled:

> My grandfather arrived from Tenerife knowing that the coast here was a good area to fish for tuna, having learnt how to fish for them from the Gomeran fishermen. He spent some time living in a cave in Vueltas, being unable to establish a home in Calera. Eventually he built a house out of stone in the style known as *tosca*, using clay and water to cement the large stone blocks, with the floor remaining as soil, covered with palm leaves.
>
> The house in which my son now lives was the first to have used concrete. Vueltas was the site of a tomato packing station, whilst the main port was at Calera beach, and tuna was sold to the factories at La Rajita, San Sebastian and Canterra. I remember going fishing during the 1940s and seeing Los Cristianos on the south of Tenerife, with its *salvage* (wild vegetation) and single house. Now it is a huge town, with many large hotels.
>
> We were poor when we were young, like the slave 'Kunte kinte' in the film *Roots*. I got my first pair of boots when I entered military service, in my twenties. In 1940 there were about ten houses in Vueltas, and my friend can remember when there was only one house with five occupants in 1920, near where the Columbina apartments are now. We didn't have motors in those days but used oars and sail; the journey to San Sebastian would take four hours. In the 1940s and 1950s times were hard with little food and few clothes, but the people in power had gold. At one time 75 kilos of tuna would fetch only 60 pesetas, now 1 kilo

fetches 50 pesetas. But the coming of the ferry opened up the market for agricultural products and tourism and this has brought a change of fortune to the islanders. We Gomeros are still the best at producing the tomatoes and bananas, and specialists at catching the tuna.

The rich families had bought Vueltas when it was wild coastland but they eventually had to sell most of this unprofitable land to pay for their taxes. Now there's a sharing of wealth, with the tourism boom allowing ordinary working people like me to get richer. Tourism in VGR offers work to the youth in bars, restaurants, discos, shops and apartments, but the big pueblos such as Hermigua, Agulo and Vallehermoso in the north of the island have only agricultural labour or unemployment.

Juan, another fisherman, could see the pros and cons of tourism, and said:

It is good that the tourism is seasonal because it allows time to recover and lead a quiet life. If the tranquil times were permanent it would be boring; whilst too much tourism would be too stressful. Although people earned little in the earlier days, say four pesetas a day, the cost of living was cheaper, whereas now the cost of living has risen with the amount of spending money. In fact, due to the competition from tourism, many items are beyond the pocket of the local inhabitants. But I think that people are quite content now, they have money and the things it can buy; previously no-one had motor-boats, few had cars and everyone had to leave VGR to find work.

Pablo Jimenez, the son of the original inhabiting fisherman of Vueltas, and the father of Miguel, now lives in Tenerife with some of his family. In 1991 he visited his son in VGR and spoke about his past and the changes he had seen, saying:

I first came over from Tenerife aged seven years, together with my brother and father. My mother, surnamed Gonzalez, was from Tenerife as well, and her brothers also arrived in La Gomera establishing some of the families that currently reside in Vueltas. I married in 1925, and my wife's father looked after cows, which are scarce on the island now. I remember the first fish-processing factory on La Gomera, which was the best in the Canary Islands. Another one opened in 1928 at La Rajita, and people walked over the mountain to arrive there in time for work. It employed around 60 women and 50 men, but this factory was a trap because there was no social security and no pension for the workers. I began life fishing with my father; but hard times forced me, and most of my children, to emigrate during the 1950s. We headed for Venezuela in a 13.5 m boat containing 73 people, of which two were women; we survived on only two spoonfuls of soup a day for 32 days, and water was trapped at night using the sail to attract condensation. The boat had a 20 hp motor, there was a captain, but nobody could navigate properly. One day we could taste the freshwater in the sea indicating there was land nearby; the captain pointed his gun at us thinking we were going crazy, but we tested the depth of the water and it proved we were close. We eventually arrived at Brazil where I remained for a year before heading for Venezuela. I remember Brazil well, and it was hard for me to understand people when they talked, but I survived and worked as a fisherman in Venezuela. Then I returned to La Gomera in 1975 and worked for 5 years with my son on a tuna fishing boat. We used to sing a song in Venezuela which goes: 'Work and don't rest, because when you rest you start to think, and when you think you get unhappy.

The period that Pablo spoke of known generally as *La Miseria* saw many *phantom barcos* (ghost boats): illegal boats journeying across the Atlantic. Rodriguez-Martin (1988) writes about other such journeys during this period of clandestine emigration, when the Spanish government required special papers for the expensive journey across the Atlantic. Pablo's account illustrates his awareness of the exploitation of the factory workers and includes the common theme of poverty and hard work of the earlier days.

A schoolteacher, who grew up in VGR and now works in Tenerife but returns annually, gave a detailed spoken account of what he regarded as the recent history of the area:

Originally the land at Vueltas was wild, just bushes and rocks, it was difficult to cultivate. Much of it was then turned over to growing tomatoes and afterwards, bananas. The first fishermen were seasonal from Tenerife, and they stayed for a period, leaving with their salted fish. The first fishermen to settle lived in rough caves and houses of stone. They just took the land that had no owner. Eventually Casanova arrived, a businessman, he was clever and saw the land that remained and asked who owned it. He then claimed it for himself. Eventually he owned most of the land from the main beach to Vueltas. Casanova opened a shop and started other businesses such as a carpenter's yard; he would exchange fish for his products from mainland Spain and England. He sold shop products to his employees on credit, and when it came to paying them wages claimed that they had already purchased food to the value of their wages, so they went without cash.

People used camels as well as donkeys to carry things, and there was a small packing station at Vueltas for tomatoes and bananas. The *caciques* used the local women for sex and there were many illegitimate children born in the community. In the 1800s there was a lot of emigration to Cuba, which meant money for families on their return, which was then invested into the land. They prepared the terrain, sometimes with imported fruit such as mangos, papaya, aguacate, pineapple, coffee and cotton. This relationship with Cuba was a big advance and many men from La Gomera helped fight for Cuban independence. It was always easy to hitch a lift to Cuba. Venezuelan emigration was also very important, especially after the civil war when it was not possible to go to Cuba. However, men were prohibited to leave Spain as she needed a workforce, but they were so poor that they had to escape: my own uncle fled in a boat and arrived on Martinique in the Caribbean.

The first fishermen exchanged fish for other food. In those days, the 1940s, the floodplain was not protected from the river by a wall and there was a massive flood in 1941: a huge rainstorm destroyed the coastal zone. After this a wall was built in the 1950s, it followed the river channel, and was financed by government money and later by cash from Venezuelan returnees who also helped to prepare the terrain around the beach zone. The first proper house built on the beach was Casa Maria's; they had a saloon and on Sundays people would dance, it was the only time that husband and wife went out, excepting fiestas. The musical equipment was a record player from Venezuela brought out by Maria's father. There was also a small wine and rum bar and in Vueltas the port bar for sailors and fishermen. In those days the women collected water in clay bowls from the local fountain, right up until the 1960s; some would wash in the sea. There were only petrol lamps and some electric generators for street lighting in the upper valley. In 1950 there was a fountain for water, pumped to the wealthier homes.

I think the biggest changes are in the opportunities for education for the youth; there used to be only a couple of people able to go to University, now many people may go, especially women, who previously were confined to the home, even the rich *cacique* women. In the 1950s the labour laws improved life for the workers and protected them from abuse by employers. Before this they were paid whatever amount the bosses felt like and there was no social security: they worked all hours given, from dawn to dusk.

There are differences between the separate *pueblos*, the people from the upper valley go home after work on construction or plantations and work on their own land with potatoes, goats and so on. They're more conservative in behaviour and vote CDS accordingly; they have a fear of the socialists taking their land. But the Vueltas folk go to the bars after work, they socialise and have more ideas, they're more liberal in their views and many more vote socialist.

Tourism is having a big effect on the customs of the people – before the women would sunbathe in bathing suits separately from the men. They didn't wear make-up or smoke cigarettes although the older ones smoked pipes, chewed tobacco or took snuff. There used to be a cinema in Calera, but we didn't get radios until the 1970s; people entertained themselves with cards and dominoes and a little drink. People were closer then.

Maria, a shop assistant and the daughter of a fisherman, was in her mid-twenties in 1995 and wrote a personal history:

When I was born my mother had six children, I was the seventh and two more followed. We lived in a small house with three rooms plus a bathroom and a kitchen; there were two other rooms in a separate building that my mother used for her work as a baker. We had a foreign neighbour, a German who built a house to live in. The relations between the neighbours in those days were closer than they are now: I remember they used to exchange things, like food such as fish and veg-etables, depending on what they could produce. Children played in the streets and there were almost no toys: we invented games, making our own playthings such as cars out of sardine tins, or bows and arrows out of palm wood.

I went to school in Borbolan and then I saw some tourists in the street in winter. I began to learn English at school at about 11 years of age and I liked the idea of being able to communicate with the tourists but the local people didn't like us to talk to them. The tourists were strange people *'gente rara'*, not like us, they had other ideas, they took drugs and went naked; we were fearful of them.

In those days the girls weren't able to go out in public with a boy if he wasn't the boyfriend and there were never any relationships between local girls and boy tourists. Some time later when I was 16 I went out with my girlfriends to the bars and flirted with the tourist boys – we always did this furtively because it was seen as bad – to be seen together would imply that we were having sexual relations; the same idea applied to any couple in the village. I liked to have contact with the tourists because they bring new and interesting things: ideas, music, dress, different ways of thinking: not just sex as the villagers believed.

I met Peter, who was a German tourist, through my friend in the bar. I went out with him in secret, as my family didn't want me to see him. One day there was a big argument in my house between my parents and myself, so I left to live with Peter in Berlin. The way of thinking of my family was that tourists had no real serious emotions: they were always splitting up as couples on their holidays and changing partners; some of the women even came looking for Gomeran men. The local people couldn't understand this behaviour and thought that the tourists were uncaring. I went to Berlin and my father was very angry, he didn't talk to me for a year. My mother was also very hurt and angry and would cry when we spoke on the phone, but I wasn't really very worried and at the time I didn't care much about the pain I caused. It was important for me to learn German in Berlin and I went to school so that I could understand the people and especially my boyfriend with whom I'd been talking in a mixture of Spanish and English. I also had some support out there from my brother's girlfriend who was German.

After six months I returned to La Gomera and Peter followed to live with me. It was very difficult to return and live with my German boyfriend, a real struggle to continue a relationship with a foreigner. It still wasn't accepted that foreigners could come to La Gomera, make business and find a local woman so quickly *'de la noche a la manana'* [from one night to the next morning]. It was a thing of distrust and envy: I even lost my best girlfriend. But my family helped me with everything and when they came to know Peter well they could see that he was normal. Now my parents have much affection for him and treat him as part of the family. Both sides have learnt about one another, my parents can see that to be foreign is not necessarily to be bad.

Vueltas has changed a lot in recent years. It has grown tremendously because of the growth of tourism. Most of the apartments were built by local families, on top of their homes or more unusually on inherited or purchased land. Having apartments in your own home has led to closer contact with the tourists, something that young people don't like because of the lack of privacy at home. Sometimes tourists enter our home looking for somewhere to stay: they walk in without knocking at the door. But the old people don't mind so much, they see it as a way of making money, surviving. For the poorer people with rooms to rent in their homes they have a good relationship with the tourists, friendly contact. The tourists must fit in with our way of life, they walk past our room every day, they smell the food cooking and see us on the stairs; they like this. But the richer apartment owners see it as just business: I know of some tourists who were thrown out of their room before their time was up and were very unhappy about it.

Together with the apartments, the tourism has also led to a growth in businesses such as restaurants and supermarkets that are mostly owned by local people in Vueltas, as opposed to the beach area where the Germans seem to own most of the shops now. The Germans came at the right time to make business that didn't exist before, such as the postcard and photograph processing shops. They can pay more money for the rent; for instance I wanted to open a shop at the beach but couldn't afford the rent and it finally went to a German. Maybe this is why the Gomeros lack the initiative to start on a new type of business: they have a fear of risking money and stick to safe things like building a home that will always be needed. Today the Gomeros are always complaining that there are too many businesses in the hands of the Germans but they never do much themselves to rectify this: they lack imagination and don't compete. But there are a few young ones who are trying to do something different like opening a beauty parlour and a gymnasium. Maybe this heralds a new beginning.

All this change and growth has transformed the mentality of the Gomero. The people have learnt to accept the tourism as inevitable and learnt to live with it. Tourism now is business and not like previously when people just seemed to pass through with little contact with the people. The new contact has brought some positive things to the local people, their minds have been opened, they have accepted new ways of thinking and living and now there is more liberty and less taboos. For example, if a couple whose relationship is not working want to separate they can do so nowadays without this being seen as bad. Also people can live together without being married. Both these examples are direct results of the tourism because people have seen with their own eyes how foreigners behave, and it isn't simply part of general social change and modernisation. Another thing is that now the women have work and are independent. They can go out with men who are not their boyfriends, just as companions.

The relationship between the Gomeros and the foreign residents is quite friendly but it is not too close, sometimes it can be cold. In fact, many Gomeros don't like the Germans, they think that the Germans have fixed ideas *'cabeza cuadrado'* [squareheads] they're cold and they just think about work and money, they're always working: 'money, money, money! Gomeros work to live and they have fun, they love to celebrate and have fiestas. When do the Germans have a fiesta?'

In 1991 Maria was one of a very small number of local women who had had a serious relationship with a tourist and the reaction of her parents and friends illustrates the latent hostility towards such liaisons. However, as we can see, things are changing and the tolerance level of local people is rising, although cultural differences, for example attitudes to the family and work, remain areas of contention. One factor which is touched upon, the Germans' access to money and their knowledge of business and entrepreneurial ideas, leads us to realise the relative advantage which they sometimes have in terms of financial resources and intellectual capital, such as a cosmopolitan education, business knowledge and linguistic expertise. All these advantages give them potential access to business opportunities on the island.

These accounts give a view of events from personal experience and highlight areas that remain obscure or unrecorded by historians. These include the illegal emigration, the establishment of Vueltas and its development, local myths, historical figures, the opinions of the community and its relationship with other communities, changing gender roles and the local perception of foreigners.[16] The accounts bring to the foreground the individuals who have played a part in the history of the community, the agents of change. They give insights into personal and public issues that have led to decisions and commonly held attitudes within Vueltas. We get witness accounts of the dramatic transition that has occurred in VGR. It has turned from a society rigidly divided between a wealthy bourgeoisie class and an impoverished proletariat (who, up until the 1940s, were largely primary industry workers bartering their goods) into one where opportunities, especially education, enable people from poor backgrounds to acquire a material and intellectual wealth previously unobtainable.

Another division has developed in VGR: between those who knew or were close to the extreme poverty up to the mid-20th century and those of later generations who have enjoyed the recent wealth and opportunities. Both look on the earlier days with a certain fondness but the older generation are well aware of the importance of material wealth and the good fortune some can enjoy and they conserve their hard earned money. Much of this new wealth has come from the tourist industry. In these accounts some interesting points arise, including the cyclical aspect of the tourism activity, the relativity of wealth in historical sense, the more widespread distribution of income and the profound affect that tourism has had on some people's lives. These issues will be examined in depth in the following chapters, starting with the next chapter that focuses on the types of tourists visiting the island and their motivation for doing so.

Notes

1. Fernandez-Lopez, of the Garajonay National Park, gives the visitor figures in the periodical *La Isla*.
2. My landlady told me how much safer it now was to walk along the path and her neighbour pointed out that she would place new plants outside to brighten the pathway, which indeed has happened.
3. Throughout this book, where relevant, I have used the 1991 exchange rate of £1– 180 pesetas (pts). This was the approximate average during the first and longest period of fieldwork. The value is given in pesetas where a currency conversion is not especially helpful. The following shop prices from 1991 give an indication

of the cost of living in VGR: (in pence/kilo potatoes 55 p, mackerel 250 p, white fish 500 p, oranges 75 p, carrots 108 p: (in pence/litre) milk 50 p, beer 110 p, fruit drink 165 p, a locally baked bread roll costs 10 p.

4. The people of VGR invariably mentioned this event and pointed out the 'rock of secrets' some hundred metres offshore: at one time a woman burst into song recounting the story whilst we were in a shop, having been told of my interest.
5. See Denevan (1989) on the work of James Parsons, and Fernandez-Armesto (1982) on the history of the islands.
6. I am indebted to the work done by Armas (1990) and Mesa-Moreno (1982) in VGR. This has provided me with valuable information and insights into the community, acknowledged in the body of the text.
7. Whenever I heard the term *cacique* used, I felt an impression that there was a strong divide between 'them', the *caciques*, and 'us', the workers.
8. In his book examining rural and urban life in Spain in the 1950s, Kenny (1961) interprets *caciquismo* as 'squirearchy' and tracing the term as deriving from Cuba, he emphasises the cohesiveness of the *caciques* and their unyielding self-interest. Similarly, in a paper examining *caciquismo* in Catalonia at the beginning of the 20th century, Romero-Maura writes: '*Caciques* were said by some to be wealthy men who abused their wealth, and by others to be politically powerful men abusing their political strength' (Romero-Maura, 1977: 53).
9. This led to problems with the island of Gran Canaria which wished to form a separate province composed of Lanzarote, Fuertaventura and itself, a division which eventually came into being in 1852 and which remains today. There have always been people promoting the notion of complete political independence for the islands but they have never received strong support, although there remains a party promoting independence, the Union of the Canaries People (UPC), and some radical separatist movements such as the Movement for Self-determination and Independence (MPAIAC).
10. See Burriel (1982) for a demographic history of the islands.
11. This explanation seems to be fabricated, as the surname is uncommon: no one else gave me such an assured explanation, even though the name, meaning 'returns', is suitable for a port.
12. This is a very similar story to the development of the fishing settlement of San Miguel in Tenerife, studied by Pascual-Fernandez (1982), that originated when one fisherman settled there in a cave in 1890. It also matches the experiences of the Portuguese fishers who were forced through poverty to squat on coastal lands (see Cole, 1991).
13. Boissevain has noticed the same nostalgiac feelings amongst the Maltese people that he worked with: 'People often remarked to us that Naxxar had changed. It used to be a "friendlier" place. By that they meant that in the past people used to have more contact with each other' (Boissevain, 1991: 94).
14. In 2002, he owned some 16 apartments.
15. His notion of there being three distinct types accords with the findings of the scientist Vos Lusches in 1896 who proposed that the Guanches fell into three types: (1) tall (Tenerife), (2) medium height and long-faced (Gran Canaria, El Hierro) and (3) short with a thin face and fine nose (La Gomera). This is one of many descriptions of the original inhabitants, which now tend to reach broad agreement that they were composed equally of Cro-Magnon and Proto-Mediterranean people originating from Europe, travelling via Africa (see Hernandez Hernandez ,1986).

16. Any personal account will be subject to a myriad of influences, not the least being the age, sex and experience of the narrator, and in ethnographical work, the ethnographer's ability to interpret the meaning and subtleties of dialogue (see Geertz (1973)). Clifford (1986), in assessing ethnographic allegory, has written: 'Both informant and researcher are readers and re-writers of a cultural invention.' (p. 116). My examples show how cultural history can be maintained by the indigenous populous and knowledgeable observers, as well as interpreted by the anthropologist; we gain an insight into the basic diversity and flexibility, as well as potential for imaginative reproduction, that forms history. A variety of opinions have arisen between the main informants, an elderly agricultural labourer, a retired fisherman, his father, a middle-aged teacher and a young shop assistant. These accounts will all be subject to the criticism that they have been translated by myself and reflect my interests in that the informants responded to my questions, although most of the comments were unsolicited and throughout my fieldwork experience much of my note-keeping was clandestine. Nevertheless, I attempt in this section to present a fair record of actual dialogue, as recorded with my informants' cooperation, and present what the people themselves saw as 'history'. Furthermore, they must be seen as personal opinions that do not even claim to be objective or unbiased narratives.

Chapter 3

The Tourists: Types and Motivation

Examining Tourists

In terms of economic resources, tourists have replaced fishing and agriculture as the primary income generator in VGR. This chapter examines the growth of tourism, the type of tourists, their motivations and experiences, foreign settlers and future developments; and it suggests the vast influence that tourism is having on the local people and the environment. It also places the ethnographic data into theoretical perspective dealing with concepts that are currently occupying inquiries into the anthropology of tourism.

Tourism is an important theme throughout this book: whether implicit or explicit its influences have been felt in most of the areas of social life examined. The intention has been to highlight the complexity of tourism and the breadth of scope of its ability to affect the lives of people through their relationships with it. The main focus is on the fishing settlement of Vueltas with the recognition that tourism is an important factor in the lives of the inhabitants. This chapter shifts the orientation from an acknowledgement of tourism to a concentrated examination of it, looking at its development into the major economic determinant in the region and seeing this as one facet of its many dimensions. A central argument is that the historically dominant type of tourists witnessed in VGR (the backpacking 'alternative' tourist) is very influential and that they can have more impact on a host community than the 'timid' package-tour tourists that Graburn (1989: 35) describes as 'likely to have the greatest impact'. The issue of 'influence' is approached by looking at the concepts of choice and role, in the sense that local people have more opportunities and a wider range of possibilities because of their communication and involvement with tourists.

The Growth of Tourism

Towards the end of the 1960s, the first tourists began to arrive in VGR. It was on the fringe of the tourism development being experienced by

Tenerife and Gran Canaria. They were travellers with an explorative tendency, reflecting to a greater degree the general movement of tourists on the islands towards the southerly, sun-drenched parts. The topographical features of La Gomera and the poor transport network filtered out the less adventurous tourist, whilst the gradual development of a style of room-renting and self-catering helped to attract the more independent alternative tourists.

With the installation of the ferry connecting Los Cristianos in south Tenerife with La Gomera in 1975 came a gradual increase in tourism. The tourists themselves were in the main North European, usually highly educated and middle-class, often with an inclination towards the liberal professions. They were mostly backpackers, individualists and travellers. With the increased talk about La Gomera amongst returnees back in their hometowns, so came an increase in visitors, especially from Germany where an advertising campaign in the form of a television programme and literature also promoted the island. During the 1980s, it became a predominantly German destination, a winter resort, with very few people arriving in the summer months. Eventually, together with the development of winter tourism, so there grew summer tourism consisting mainly of people from Tenerife, many having relatives on La Gomera.

In VGR the backpacking 'alternative' tourists still dominate the scene during the winter, although some North European tour agencies have increased the flow of charter tourists who stay in the larger apartment blocks owned by consortiums of local businessmen and professionals from the islands. During the summer, the *veranistas* (Spanish summer holiday-makers) arrive, mostly from Tenerife. The number of visitors from North Europe predominantly during the winter has increased simultaneously with summer tourism.

Figures from ICONA, the organisation that controls the national parks of Spain, show that in 1990 there were 75,000 arrivals on La Gomera of tourists staying for longer than one day. It is reasonable to assume that the majority of these would visit VGR for a while. Statistics from the *Guardia Civil* (Civil Guard or National Police) show that between October 1988 and August 1989, a total of 42,357 tourists were recorded as having stayed in registered apartments: of this figure 55% were German, 26% were Spanish and the remaining 19% were from other countries. These figures fail to take into account the clandestine apartments. By 1999 there were 600,000 visitors to the island (including day-trippers) and in VGR, by 2002, there were 3500 (officially recognised) beds available for rent compared to a total of just over 5000 for the whole island (Editorial Event, 2001).

The Variety of Visitors

Typologies seek to classify tourists according to a particular phenomenon, usually motivation or behaviour. A simple typology divides them into two categories:

(1) *package tourists* – these usually demand western amenities, are associated with rapid growth rates and often lead to the restructuring of the local economy; and
(2) *independent tourists* – these usually fit in better with the local environment and social structure, are associated with relatively slow growth rates and often lead to local ownership.

A more detailed typology by V. Smith (1989c) relates tourists to volume and their adaptation to the local situation along a continuum as follows:

(1) explorer – limited in numbers and accept fully the local norms.
(2) elite – rarely seen and adapts fully,
(3) off-beat – uncommon but seen, adapts well,
(4) unusual – occasional and adapts somewhat,
(5) incipient mass – steady flow and seeks western amenities,
(6) mass – continuous flow and expects western amenities,
(7) charter – massive arrivals and demands western amenities.

Cohen (1972; see also 1979a) produced a continuum of tourist types based on combinations of seeking novelty and desiring familiarity:

(1) the organised mass tourist – low on adventurousness, maintaining own 'environmental bubble' during the trip, often package tourist,
(2) the individual mass tourist – as in (1) but more flexible,
(3) the explorer – independently organised trip, off the beaten track, seeks comfortable accommodation and reliable transport, environmental bubble there as safety net and
(4) the drifter – seeks to get away from home and familiarity. No fixed itinerary, willing to live with local people and immerse in local culture.

The clear majority of non-Spanish tourists visiting La Gomera in the early 1990s were 'independent' tourists and would fit into Cohen's explorer class. These have been described as 'alternative' (see also Macleod 1997, 1998).

We shall look at the types of tourists that visit VGR to gain insights into the sort of tourism that is occurring and the type of people that communicate and interact with the local inhabitants. Tourism has been described as unique because the consumers travel to the destination of production to satisfy their needs (see de Kadt, 1979: X): the product is sold to foreign consumers on the vendor's doorstep. In this respect the type of tourist visiting the destination is of the utmost importance in relation to their expectations and their influence on the host community. A look at the variety of tourists visiting Vueltas reveals the nature of this activity.

The predominant type of tourist visiting VGR is 'alternative', a term occasionally used by themselves. It is useful to consider the division of alternative tourism which Cohen (1987) makes, seeing it as (1) a counter-cultural rejection of modern mass consumerism and (2) concerned tourism. In VGR the counter-cultural tourists include those travellers who stay for a long period of time, for example at the Sannyasin Centre (a religious retreat), live rough in caves or on the beach or in rented accommodation. Some were interested in artistic pursuits, making things to sell, one man fashioned things out of wire, another man painted portraits and one woman made jewelry to sell in the bars. They were non-conventional in their choice of work. Others were interested in personal freedom, which might involve consuming drugs and regularly drinking to excess, playing music on the beach and relaxing. In 1991 there was a fashion for playing drums and some made them out of the bulbous tuber of the Giant Lobelia plant covered with goatskin. Conventional Germans often referred to these counter-cultural individuals as 'freaks'.

Cohen's second sub-group – 'concerned tourists' – embraces the 'green' ecotourists who have an interest in the natural environment. Many tourists wanted to walk around the island, visit the forest, swim in the clean water on an unspoilt beach and eat the fresh produce. German handbooks advertise the island as 'green' and it is famous for the rugged walks on offer. Others expressed concern for the village environment and the new road-building programmes. Many exhibited an interest in the indigenous people and their culture. A majority of the tourists was keen on walking around the island, hoped to see dolphins and enjoyed their interaction with local people. Often they were vegetarians and some had careers directly involved with the natural environment including a biologist, a town planner specialising in greening urban areas and a university researcher looking into environmental change.

In addition to Cohen's two subgroups, we should add a third, the 'backpacking hedonist'. This embraces those who are more conventional but looking for relaxation and pleasure on their own terms. A number of tourists knew of the island's reputation as a place to meet single people, others came because they believed it to be somewhere that drugs were easily obtained and they could indulge at liberty. Some tourists from Berlin told of the island's nickname 'Sodom and Gomera', referring to the presumed licentiousness of the tourists; others said it was called 'Love

Island'. For many it was a place to go for the winter sun, meet other people and indulge whilst being free to choose where to stay and what to do.

Clearly these sub-groups are not mutually exclusive and it cannot be presumed that the visitors to the island could simply be slotted into one group or another. However, they give a broad outline to the variety of tourists defined as 'alternative' and allow us to comprehend their qualities and diversity more easily. Furthermore, this analysis helps us make comparisons with tourism elsewhere.[1] Examples of different tourists are given here and the tourism is placed into a seasonal context, one that has followed a cycle during the late 1980s to the mid 1990s at least, but which is in the process of changing.

Seasons and tourists

Autumn

From September to mid-December the tourists in VGR were predominantly German. They tended to be aged between 20 and 45, and were usually well educated. They were largely backpackers and often did not reserve a room in advance, therefore relying on the private household apartment market. If they look slightly scruffy or too colourful, this type of tourist is often described as a 'hippy' by the local people: a term that has survived since the early days of tourism in the 1970s. Thus, the more casual student look or non-conventional wear of some of these tourists helped to perpetuate the view of them as hippies, drifters, or people on the outside of the mainstream, as were the first travellers to the island. They appear to the local people as a sort of exotic 'other' with backpacks (see Plates 9 and 10).

Backpacking tourists in the valley included people who worked as teachers, lawyers, social workers, psychologists, environmentalists, computer operators and journalists and there were many students in higher education. These occupations give an indication of the general profile of the tourists: with few exceptions they were educated to a level beyond secondary school. The Germans themselves joked that most people who go to La Gomera from Germany are social workers, teachers or psychologists. They often expressed a serious desire to learn the local language, many saying that it is important to know the language of the local population. They are demonstrating their wish to communicate with and understand the people and their way of life. It was possible to tell that the bush telegraph or informal networks had operated in university towns such as Münster and Erlangen, because of the number of tourists from these areas. Many large towns in West Germany were represented, although there were very few visitors from East Germany in the early 1990s.

One East German visitor, Wolf, was living in the Sannyasin Centre. He

Plate 10 Tourists passing time in the Cacatua bar in Vueltas, which is run by a German

worked on the organic banana plantation during the mornings, which paid for his food and lodging, and he would paint for much of the remaining time. Wolf would also make drums out of plant tubers and played them on the beach and at parties. He hoped to sell his paintings and the drums when he returned to Germany. He was not interested in a conventional lifestyle and wanted to make his living as an artist eventually. After two months he returned to Germany with a girlfriend he met through working at the Centre.

A typical day for two female German tourists, friends aged in their late twenties and both working for the same company, involved the following routine. They would get out of bed by mid-morning and prepare a large breakfast lasting for over one hour, after which they would arrange for a day at the beach, arriving around midday and remaining until 6.00 p.m. They tended to use the same part of the beach each day, which eventually formed a small 'neighbourhood' of groups of friends with their own delineated spaces: different groups often became friendly after a day of proximity. Time on the beach was spent reading, listening to music on cassettes, swimming, talking and sunbathing, paying attention to the all-over tan. In the evening they would usually prepare their own meal in their self-catering apartment or occasionally visit a restaurant, spending two hours in the process. Normally they would end the day by visiting a bar until the early hours of the morning. These activities formed the basic ritual of their holiday and were supplemented by walks in the hills and a tour of the island in a hire car. They met and befriended many other German tourists in the bars and on the beach, occasionally recognising them from their hometowns. As for local people, they got to know their landlady and her family, the barstaff of their favourite bar, some men who were regulars in the bars and others who invited them to a beach party. This outline of activities shows the potential for meeting other tourists and local people and for relaxation and change that such a vacation offers, with few restrictions on time and spatial movement but discernible constraints on behaviour. The two women made a large number of new German friends but no deep friendships were formed with any local people apart from their host family.

A different set of female German tourists were two social workers, women in their early thirties, on holiday together to enjoy the walking and test their relationship away from the pressures of working life. On alternate days they would go hiking into the hills, armed with their informative book on Gomeran walks, a map and provisions. They hired a car or took a bus, depending on the location of the walk, and would spend the entire day hiking. In the evenings they cooked their own vegetarian food and rarely went out to the bars. The other days were spent quietly resting, reading or lying on the beach – only one of them enjoyed sunbathing.

The construction of large apartment blocks and a single hotel recently in VGR serving agency tourism, such as the German TUI organisation, has led to a gradual introduction of more conventional tourists of a package tour inclination, the type Graburn (1989) refers to as 'timid'. These may be middle-aged couples with families for example, people that like the security of a booked room. They usually take apartments in large complexes and, in general, are not so adventurous in their activities as the independent travellers and backpacking 'alternatives'. They do not attempt to mix with the local people to the extent that the 'alternatives' do and generally keep to a secure schedule, involving coach trips, recommended restaurants and some organised entertainment. Smith (1989c) labels this type of 'timid' tourism as 'incipient mass'.[2] One local man who worked in the Hotel Valle Gran Rey said that most tourists are in bed by 11.00 p.m. and go out on guided tours during the day.

Winter

The autumn season was fairly quiet, with only one-third of the rooms being occupied in Vueltas. However, as winter and the Christmas holidays approach, the volume of tourists started to build up and the rush and scramble for rooms led to an overburdened village full of backpacking young Germans trailing around from one set of apartments to another. Equally, the locals became aggressive in their efforts to entice the tourists into their rooms, knowing that this was high season and they must make as much money as possible in the time available.[3]

By Christmas the village was packed with tourists: virtually all the apartments were booked up and, at one time there was not a spare bed in the valley. The climate, being warm all year round, averaging 25°C, allows for sunbathing and swimming, although the locals regard it as too cold to do so in winter. One noticeable feature of the winter arrivals was the preponderance of independent single mothers with their children: people suggested that the German social security system made it possible for them to receive their benefits whilst being in a foreign country. Many of them said that life was better and cheaper for them in La Gomera than Germany at this time of year. Women often said that they felt safer in VGR than in most other Mediterranean resorts and, because of the youthful orientation of the resort, it was possible to meet other single people. Most apartments have cooking facilities giving greater independence to single mothers and visitors, in general, as they could prepare their own food. The social network amongst tourists and some local people meant that they were able to leave their children with friends and neighbours to go out at night. One woman arrived with her daughter aged six. She had previously lived in Vueltas with her Spanish boyfriend but they had left for Germany and since split up. She returns to Vueltas occasionally for a holiday, has friends in the valley and is able to leave her child with them and enjoy some liberty during the day and in the evenings.

There were a few more British tourists present during the Christmas to New Year weeks, although the Germans remained in the clear majority: some Dutch and Austrians were also around. The British tended to have heard of La Gomera by word of mouth and one had read of the island in a free magazine: these tourists, like their German counterparts, were generally well-educated, single young people. Most of the tourists were usually very aware of environmental issues, often interested in the local ways of life and prepared to think seriously about the problems of tourism itself. In fact, at one time, a German pinned a notice up in a local restaurant asking tourists to petition against the major road construction going on in VGR. This interest was also evident in their support for the environmental action protesting against the proposal to develop the beach area.

Spring

With the passing of the Christmas and New Year celebrations the number of winter tourists gradually declined, experiencing a sudden uplift for the Easter holiday and then tailing off dramatically. This pattern is now well established in VGR, and the people say that after *Semana Santa* (Easter week) everything goes quiet. The German tourists, having had their two or three weeks break, return to the relative cold of North Europe. May was a very quiet month, although there is a gradual change brought about by the agency tourism, with another type of tourist arriving who is able to take a packaged holiday.

Summer

June, like May, is usually a quiet month for tourism, the locals saying that they are able to relax and enjoy themselves. The village takes on a quite different aspect, with people loosening up from the pressures of work and talking to each other without being pushed for time. The shops are empty of customers and the port is equally quiet, with only a few fishermen chatting amongst themselves. For the visitor this seems quite a transformation but the locals point out that it was always as quiet as this before the tourists began to arrive.

The next event on the tourism calendar is the arrival in August of the Spanish visitors, known as *veranistas*, the majority from Tenerife with some from the Peninsula. The local people said that the Spanish tourists were far worse than the Germans because they left the apartments in a terrible state and created a lot of noise: one of the reasons for this was their tendency to fry fish in the kitchen thereby covering the place with oil. The Spanish usually brought food for the holiday in their cars, making a saving on meals by not buying locally or going out to restaurants and living as a family in an apartment.[4] This type of tourism may be described as 'family vacationing' and would fit into the categories of individual mass tourist (Cohen, 1972) and incipient mass (Smith, 1989c). As a rule, they have pre-arranged accommodation with family and friends and make regular annual visits. The Gomeros had no qualms about criticising their fellow Canary Islanders, some of whom were their relatives. A few said that they would prefer to have less money and no summer tourists because of all the problems they cause. The Spanish tourists themselves were out to enjoy the summer break and would travel as nuclear families, one set of parents and their children, occasionally extended to include grandparents and other relatives (see Plate 11).

One such family group included Javier, the son of a local man. He grew up in VGR and is now a teacher living in Tenerife. He married a woman from Tenerife whom he met whilst she was staying on La Gomera: she now works as a civil servant. In 1991 they had two daughters: one studying to be a lawyer, the other at school. This family of four rented one apartment from a friend at a slight discount for a month. They liked La Gomera for its

Plate 11 *Veranistas* at La Playa, Calera beach

natural beauty, beaches, climate and tranquillity but were aware of the restrictions and boredom of life there as permanent villagers. They spent most of their day on the beach in a family group, eating their meals in their large apartment; occasionally they went for a picnic or a fishing trip and they visited their friends and relatives frequently.

The sister of Javier is also a native islander and she would also holiday in VGR in the summer with her family. Her husband is a lawyer from the Peninsula and (in 1991) they had two sons studying law and a daughter who wanted to be a dentist. The father owns some apartments in a local complex and they use these as holiday chalets. The children of these two families, all cousins, would socialise and together with some other vacationing relatives of their own age travel around and go out in a large group, joining up with local youngsters they had got to know over the years. This particular group was highly educated, the children of the professional classes and the careers to which they aspired included law, medicine, pharmacy, teaching and dentistry. It is noticeable that many followed the professional paths of their parents, especially the lawyers.

Spanish tourists, whilst appreciating the beauty of the island, were not so keen on the serious walking expeditions as were the Germans, preferring to travel by car to a spot and picnic. The pattern of social life was less oriented towards single people and many felt the restrictions of family life involving long periods with relatives in the evening. For the Spanish summer visitors the dominant activity group is the nuclear family, as opposed to the German tourists for whom it is close friends, with two or three individuals socialising together. This has profound effects on their respective activities and behaviour. Role play within the family will necessarily conform (to an extent) to that usually experienced at home, whereas the individual German friends on holiday will be more at liberty to experiment and change.

Those working in service outlets said that most of the bars and restaurants do not do so well out of the Spanish tourists as with the Germans, because the Spanish were more inclined to cook and eat as a family group in their apartments as if at home. The younger single Spanish tourists did go out to the bars and discos in the evenings, usually in groups based on kinship networks, following a fairly set pattern: for instance meeting up at 11.30 p.m. in a bar, drinking there until 1.00 a.m. and then going to the discotheque until 4.00 a.m.

Towards the end of August the Spanish tourists returned to their homes and, by September, the village and port became quiet again with a few diehards still hanging around, talking and fishing at the port, enjoying their last days of relative freedom. There is a definite cycle in the tourism calendar, with winter and Easter enjoying the peak of activity: this pattern is broadly similar to that experienced by the fishermen, with the seasonal intensity of fishing in the winter months. It means that in Vueltas the winter months bring hard work for all, whilst the early summer is a comparative rest period (cf. Puijk, 1996).

People in Vueltas talked about 'getting back to normal' after the tourists have left.[5] However, the cyclic trends in Vueltas have been changing. In the 1990s, with the development of new orientations in the nature of tourism, German package tourists began arriving during the spring and summer months. As well as this, the fishing industry was gradually losing its force; consequently, the whole year may eventually become one of continual activity for apartment owners. In stark contrast to this scenario, however, with changing trends in the types of tourists arriving, the small apartment market may eventually dwindle in the future, giving less custom to the local families and more to the agencies: the seasonal cycle of activity is undergoing major alterations.

Many local people commented on the surprising amount of German tourists in 1991 during the summer months. This was mainly related to the recent increase in package deals advertised in Germany to capture the summer vacation market and was helped by the unpopularity of some Mediterranean resorts due to the Gulf War. Thus, at some points during the year, noticeably in the summer, the larger apartment complexes possessing up to 100 apartments were full up, whilst in contrast, the private household apartments remained relatively empty. The agency-oriented apartment complexes (which numbered six in 1991) are complexes containing from 10 to 300 separate apartments, none of which are in Vueltas but have been built near the seafront towards Puntilla and by Calera beach. They are usually owned by groups of businessmen, in the main from the Canary Islands, and they tend to rent rooms out to travel companies in block bookings at a discount, usually through a middleman. Consequently, tourists in Germany can now book an apartment in VGR through a travel agent in their hometown and purchase a package holiday before leaving.

The character of the resort has been undergoing change, moving from the dominance of independent alternative tourists to one where they are almost equalled in numbers by the package or 'incipient mass' tourists: middle-aged couples in white and pastel casual clothing replacing the younger colourful and long-haired visitors. The local people are aware of the threat that the agency-oriented apartments represent to their source of income, taking away their customers for rooms, shop products and restaurants. The agency tourists also may inadvertently drive away the backpacking alternative crowd, who can see the gradual transformation of the quiet village into 'just another holiday resort'. However, by 2002, there seemed to be an increase in all types of tourists, including the 'hippies' who lived on a secluded beach as well as the backpacking alternatives and the package agency tourists. The vast majority of tourists are German, as ever, and the summer months have seen an influx of Spanish tourists as before. One cause of concern to local people was Spain and Germany's currency conversion to the Euro, which has meant the Germans are spending less in the shops and the Spanish are more cautious.

This section has described the different types of tourist staying at a resort and their potential impact. In the next sections we take this further and examine the attitudes of the visitors and the indigenous population, exploring issues including motivation, gender roles and stereotyping.

Tourists: Motivation and Experiences

Motivation

Why do tourists visit certain places? The academic approaches to motivation among tourists has been framed by Dann (1981) who lists seven elements:

(1) Travel is a response to what is lacking yet desired.
(2) Destination pull, in response to motivational push.
(3) Motivation as fantasy – behaviour not culturally sanctioned at home.
(4) Motivational typologies: (a) behavioural, such as sun worshipping or

wanderlust; and (b) typologies focusing on dimensions of the tourist role.

(5) Motivation as classified purpose.

(6) Motivation and tourist experiences – includes the authenticity debate.

(7) Motivation as auto-definition and meaning.

The concept of motivation among travellers has been summarised by Cooper *et al.* (1999). They embrace these dimensions as follows.

(1) The idea that travel is initially need-related and that this manifests itself in terms of wants and the strength of motivation or 'push', as the energiser of action.

(2) Motivation is grounded in sociological and the psychological aspects of acquired norms, attitudes, culture, perceptions etc., leading to person-specific forms of motivation and subsequently affect the type of travel undertaken.

(3) The image of a destination created through various communication channels will influence motivation and subsequently affect the type of travel undertaken.

Other writers (McIntosh *et al.*, 1995), utilise four categories of motivation that provide a readily applicable means of describing tourists:

(1) *Physical motivators*: those related to refreshment of body and mind, health purposes, sport and pleasure. This group of motivators is linked to activities that will reduce tension.

(2) *Cultural motivators*: those identified by the desire to see and know more about other cultures, to find out about the natives of a country, their lifestyle, music, art, folklore, dance, etc.

(3) *Interpersonal motivators*: this group includes a desire to meet new people, visit friends or relatives and to seek new and different experiences. Travel is an escape from routine relationships with friends or neighbours or the home environment or it is used for spiritual reasons.

(4) *Status and prestige motivators*: these include a desire for continuation of education (i.e. personal development, ego enhancement and sensual indulgence). Such motivators are concerned with the desire for recognition and attention from others in order to boost the personal ego. This category also includes personal development in relation to the pursuit of hobbies and education.

In his analysis of tourism as a phenomenon, MacCannell (1976) writes of the modern tourist's search for 'reality and authenticity' in other historical periods and cultures as well as in what are perceived as simpler and purer lifestyles. He was disagreeing with Boorstin (1964) who argued that modern tourists are shallow individuals seeking only entertainment and are easily satisfied by inauthentic 'pseudo-events' as presented by the tourist industry.

This search for authenticity may be part of the motivating force behind the visitor to La Gomera. But in contrast, they may also be escaping the 'reality' of life in an urban metropolis, with its authentic pressures. The essential problem is one of philosophical definitions tied to personal experience: 'authentic' and 'reality' become terms subject to personal relativity (cf. Pearce & Moscardo, 1986). That which is authentic to one person may appear inauthentic to another. The holiday experience is a prime example of a versatile event in that (a) it may allow people to experience their own personal 'reality' away from the 'roles' that they play in their working lives and at home; and (b) it may seem an unreal experience, an escape from the authentic humdrum of everyday life. Furthermore, the definition of authentic and its contested meanings are at the root of these paradoxes. Wang investigates the idea of authenticity and in a detailed analysis concludes:

> While objectivists, constructivists and postmodernists argue about whether and how toured objects are experienced as real, this paper suggests that even toured objects are totally inauthentic, seeking otherwise is still possible, because tourists can quest for an alternative, namely existential authenticity to be actuated by tourist experiences. (Wang, 1999: 365)

The constructivist view that for tourists there exists a 'symbolic' authenticity – i.e. the projection of stereotyped images held within the tourist-sending societies – is an appropriate description of the experience of some tourists in VGR. Similarly, Wang's 'intra-personal authenticity: self-making' sub-group of 'existential authenticity' – whereby the tourist experience includes self-identity in the sense of shedding their 'work and everyday' roles acquired at home and pursuing self-realisation on holiday – is also recognisable among tourists in VGR, as some of the following examples illustrate.

One student said that her experience of VGR made her feel as if she was still in Gemany because of the number of Germans around: 'The nightlife is just like being in a Spanish theme bar back home'. This illustrates the relativity of the holiday experience, the importance of contrast, both physical and mental in giving the sense of change, the non-ordinary experience (cf Graburn, 1989). This tourist was clearly frustrated, the contrast not being big enough for her to experience the 'non-ordinary': there was a lack of authenticity in the place for her because of the numerous Germans. Despite being in Spain, this tourist was surrounded by people from her own country, an experience that was not exotic enough for her: it lacked the 'reality' of a foreign country that she had anticipated

However the mass charter tourists would have a different 'gaze' (way of seeing and interpreting the environment [Urry, 1990]) to that of the alternative tourists. They would expect to see certain features such as a beach, hotels, museums, specific restaurants and parts of the island, all of which have been described to them by the companies selling them the holiday. It would, by definition, be a more restrictive gaze than that of the alternative tourist, concentrating on established landmarks and designated tourist sights, and would be more influenced by the metropolitan lifestyle, with expectations of living in hotel comfort whilst avoiding the problems of the local population. This is, of course, a generalisation that refers to the packaging of a tour and not the individual tourists themselves who, although influenced by the professionals guiding them, will have their own idiosyncratic views. As a consequence of their expectations, mass tourists will have different motivations for vacationing: motivations both encouraged and shaped by the tourist industry and more likely to be geared towards rest and relaxation – 'getting away from it all' – in a comfortable and safe environment. This is quite unlike the desire for 'authentic reality' that MacCannell believes drives the modern tourist.

Many alternative tourists exhibited a similar discernible motivation to that which once sent the wealthy youth of a previous era on their 'Grand Tours': a search for experience and education, as well as status amongst their peers (see Turner & Ash, 1975). The majority of tourists encountered had a great interest in the island, especially its natural features, complementing their interest in the local people. It was certainly a prestige symbol to speak the local language and most were happy to try out their Spanish, openly flaunting their dictionaries.

In 1991 some Germans said that La Gomera was the new 'in place to be', having taken over from Formentera in the Balearic Islands. It was also known amongst Berliners as a meeting place for single people. Yet this was not blatant – the whole place was suffused with an atmosphere of casual social interaction. Other tourists were there to escape from the pressures of life in Germany. They often spoke of the constrained and regulated life back home and the feeling of freedom that could be found in La Gomera because of the vacation, the island's unspoilt beauty and good weather, and also the apparently relaxed way of life of the local inhabitants. In this sense many tourists said they experienced an escape from the physical constraints, as well as the cultural constraints of time and moral expectations in Germany.

The theme of escape has been explored by Lett (1983) in his examination of the ludic and liminoid in relation to charter yacht tourists. The normal regulations of social behaviour are transgressed: they apparently indulge in non-ordinary activity finding themselves in a type of sociocultural vacuum. However, another way of understanding this is to see the tourists as actors without clearly defined roles: more at liberty to pursue their personal desires. It may be argued that they take on the role of tourists, determined to consume the good life on their own terms, deliberately flouting social norms. The concept of role play is useful in analysing tourist behaviour and shows them not so much in a vacuum or a state of liminality but more in a situation where they can step out of a constraining uniform, relax and sometimes put on a disguise. For many tourists in VGR, the holiday experience became one during which they were able to re-evaluate their lives, facing up to their repressed emotions: some decided to end important personal relationships back home or change their careers. In this respect the vacation may be less of a 'sacred journey', as Graburn (1989) has postulated, and more of a journey of self-discovery – akin to Wang's 'existential authenticity' in the form of self-realisation.

All the 'motivators' as listed by McIntosh *et al.* (1995) seem to be present among the tourists visiting La Gomera, and it is likely that for many individuals there are multiple motivations for travelling. It is also likely, possibly unavoidable, that these tourists are motivated by the norms of their home environment, as well as communicated messages (Cooper *et al.*, 1999).

German women and Gomeran men

One of the striking differences between the German tourists and their Gomeran hosts became apparent in their respective attitudes towards nudity. The German tourists, in general, are quite unself-conscious about nudity and regard it as an acceptable state in appropriate public settings, such as the beach, and they casually sunbathe and swim naked at the secluded 'Playa del Ingles'. The Gomerans, however, in common with many Spanish Catholics, believe it to be shameful to expose certain parts of the body in public. This attitude can be directly related to their feelings regarding the innate shamefulness of women. Such bodily display is associated with sinfulness and women are labelled as *putas* (whores) if they exhibit their bodies in a visibly provocative way. Similarly, men are expected not to go naked and the fishermen ridicule their friends with accusations of being homosexual even if one of them wears scanty or colourful shorts. There is a generation gap in opinion however, with younger women challenging conventions, wearing less clothing or very occasionally sunbathing topless.

In general, there has been a gradual relaxation of attitudes towards nakedness over time. Early in the 1980s nude bathing was severely

Plate 12 Watching the waves at Playa del Ingles

frowned upon and tourists were arrested for exposing themselves on the beach. However, as the local people realised the financial rewards of a nude beach, they turned a blind eye and let the nude bathers continue with their activities in the seclusion of the isolated beach (see Plate 12). With this acceptance came a gradual tolerance, and together with the influence of the mass media the attitude amongst the local people has changed so that topless bathing on the family beaches is accepted.[6]

However, the conservative attitude towards women who flaunt their sexuality as manifested in minimal dress codes on the beach is observable in the local reaction towards tourists. Young men often pursue the female tourists, regarding them as sexually available, and local women are wary of this threat to their own relationships with their partners.[7] Indeed, at least one married man from Vueltas has left his wife and children to live with a German tourist back in her own country. The local women become critical and wary of the local men who chase the tourist women, believing that they will not give up their habits upon marriage and, as a consequence, curtail the opportunities such men have with them. In this way some men may become alienated by their promiscuity with foreign women, reducing their chances in their home territory and consequently restricting their choice of partners to the tourists only.[8]

Most German women come from a very different cultural background from that of women born in La Gomera. They have contrasting notions of acceptable behaviour between the sexes: one of relative sexual liberation, female self-confidence and independence, with access to contraception and sex education. As a result of this, they usually have a different attitude towards sexual behaviour than Gomeran women: the German women also tend to be more formally educated and older than the single women in the village. There is a huge variation between the sexual behaviour and experience of the German women and the Gomeran women. The older Gomeros have grown up in a society where men and women would bathe at separate ends of the beach up to the 1960s, whilst a guard would impose a fine on any man found spying on the women. Together with their lack of inhibitions regarding nudity and the relative freedom of the vacation experience, the German women consequently present the local men with an image of women that is hard to match with their own personal and social experience.

Many local people had regarded German women who freely exposed their bodies and indulged in extra-marital sex as whores (*putas*). This attitude remains in VGR and corresponds to the findings of Zinovieff (1990) amongst the Greeks in relation to female tourists. Duysens (1989: 121) writes of the local nickname for the discotheque as *putatheque* because of the excesses of the German girls: warnings were given by the local men not to get involved with the German girls because of the dangers of sexually transmitted diseases. There were many jokes made at the expense of the German girls: one example was when a fisherman said that a floating platform designed to attract fish would be more profitable as a brothel with three *touristas* on it.

Although many female tourists were happy to meet local men, they tended to stay within groups from their homeland often ridiculing the blunt advances of local men.[9] Relations between men and women amongst the local people are such that the men are expected to make the advances to initiate communication. It is often assumed when a man and a woman are seen together that where there is no obvious alternative, sexual relations are the objective. Men are regarded as predators and are assigned that role in the game of sexual encounters and they unself-consciously behave in such a manner. The local women expect a man to make a sexual advance if they are alone together: the onus, therefore, is upon the man to live up to social expectations as well as pursuing his own desires.

As a consequence of the different social expectations between the Gomeros and the Germans, there are a lot of misunderstandings when the local men and tourist women interact. Many of the German women seemed interested in the local people and their lifestyles and liked the idea of making some friends, being accustomed to platonic relationships with the opposite sex in Germany. But they usually resented the blunt advances made by the local men. The following examples illustrate the problem:

A German woman (aged 21) sat alone in a restaurant and was befriended by a local man. She was interested in him as a friend and went on a trip with him to another town. She recounted her experience:

> There was no physical contact between us at all, and after a few days I grew bored of his continual company and said that I would like to be alone. Some days later as I sat outside the discotheque he turned up drunk and tried to sit next to me, putting his arm around me, I told him to stop and that I only wanted to be a friend. He then called me a *puta de mierda* [whore of shit], and continued to shout at me. After this I felt angry and said, 'Hit me if that is what you want', which he did; I then stood up, inches taller than him, and pushed him to the floor.

This incident, she later added, upset her deeply and she could not understand the man's actions.

An Austrian woman of 18 was visiting a girlfriend in VGR who was living with a local man: she would join the pair of them plus the brother of the local man for social occasions. They would go out regularly as a foursome and she occasionally accompanied the brother for drinks together, regarding him as a friend. She recalled:

> On the last day of the holiday I left the bar with the brother accompanying me to return to the part of the village where we both lived. As we were about to part he attempted to kiss me, but I declined saying that I liked him but was not interested in anything physical. He then got angry, hit me and shouted *Vete*! [Go away!].

She related how the man shouted at her as if she were his dog. She was so scared that she asked for protection on her way from her house to the taxi rank for fear of meeting this man again.

Such incidents are very common and highlight the misunderstanding, frustration and difference in expectations between the people involved. This happens in many countries where men and women misinterpret one another's intentions and, in this instance, it was the aggression of the male party that upset the females. The women wanted friendship and the men wanted sex, again a common situation. The important factor is that relationships between unrelated men and women in VGR are generally sexually based. Local men interpret female interest as sexual invitation and become frustrated when denied physical satisfaction. They pursue roles assigned to men by their society and cannot rapidly adapt these roles to new interpretations made by German women. Occasionally the men achieve their goals, as the following episode describes:

Two German women, in their late twenties, had accepted an offer to go for a drive into the mountains with two local men they had met the previous day. One of the women said:

> The men were quite friendly so we thought it would be good to go for a drink in the mountains. They teased our friend Klaus who stayed behind. He was just a friend and not a lover of ours. They said that he is not a real man if he doesn't sleep with us, calling him a '*maricon*' [homosexual]. After we drank at the bar they drove us to the forest and we smoked marijuana that they provided. My friend went off with one of the men – presumably to have sex. I stayed in the car with the other man who wanted to have sex with me, but I was not interested. He got extremely angry, saying that they had paid for the drink and 'chocolate' (drugs) so why not? Eventually he gave up, but I felt very scared and angry. I think my friend behaved foolishly and she regretted it the next day, especially not having used a condom – so she went to the doctor for a 'morning-after' contraception pill – but he had no idea what she meant. It was a terrible time for both of us.

In general, it is local men and foreign women who are involved in these interactions of a sexual kind. The local women do not enjoy the same degree of liberty that the men do. Emotional relationships between the local women and foreign men are extremely rare, although they do occur.

Cultural stereotypes

One of the areas where attitudes are important and misunderstandings develop is that concerning the image of the other culture, an area where specific features and characteristics are emphasised and repeatedly used to describe members of different communities, especially national communities. Stereotypification is an area of generalisation: there are commonly held beliefs that come through persistently in conversation. First, the attitudes of the local people towards tourists should be examined.

'Strangers are not really conceived of as individuals but as strangers of a particular type' (Nash, 1989: 44). In an essay suggesting that tourism is imperialistic, Nash points out the results of exposure to many people in a short period of time, as opposed to only one or two new faces. This directs us towards one reason why the mass tourist has less impact on the personal lives of the host than the backpacker: the lack of communication between people on an individual level.

Large groups become stereotyped and a language barrier exaggerates this problem. It was clear from talking to local people that, when the first few tourists arrived, the people were able to get to know them well and appreciate them as individuals. Various foreign settlers also enabled the locals to fraternise with people from other cultures as neighbours and friends. Many tourists take rooms regularly every year, becoming firm friends with their hosts and often sending letters from Germany. There is, therefore, ample opportunity for the local people to meet the tourists on a relatively equal footing. The language barrier remains the main problem, but with a few Spanish and German words acquired by both sides, together with a little English, some form of communication is possible. Many tourists make real efforts both to learn Spanish and talk to the local people in their own language. Yet stereotyping still persists on both sides: Germans are sometimes referred to as *cabezas cuadrados* (square heads) by the local people – regarded as inflexible and narrow-minded.

Some local apartment owners told me that they would not let English tourists rent rooms because they thought they were hooligans, an image perpetrated by the media coverage of football hooligans. People often gave me examples of the disrespectful behaviour shown by English tourists in Tenerife. Such stereotyping has been remarked upon by Pi-Sunyer (1989: 189) working in Catalonia, who stressed the importance of valuing common humanity over stereotypes and noted that many residents were strongly influenced by images and stereotypes in their attitudes regarding tourists. Similarly, in his brief study of Los Cristianos, Tenerife, Moore (1976: 26) noted the differing images that the Swedes and the locals had of each other: the Swedes viewing the locals as 'backward, almost animal', and the locals describing the Swedes as 'morally depraved'. Such sentiments have been voiced in Vueltas, between the Germans and the Gomeros.

Specific examples serve to give a realistic insight into this complex problem. As with many national stereotypes, the purveyors of such beliefs via the mass media are partly to blame. It is, therefore, relevant to look at the sort of things that the promotional material for the island mentions. The photography and writing concentrate mainly on the beauty of the landscape and sea and, in one such leaflet designed by a German, photographs of the valleys, basaltic columns on the coast, dolphins, forest, shoreline and old-fashioned buildings all surround a simplified map of the island. There are also pictures of local people that show them in traditional costume, dancing the *Tajaraste* at the fiestas; others portray old men playing the tambors and one young girl is shown holding a goat. These pictures serve to give an image of a traditional and exotic folk, still firmly embedded in an agricultural way of life, an image that panders to the desires of tourists to visit an authentically exotic and rural society. One phrase, in particular captures the flavour of the brochure: 'The nearly continuous fog of this region provides a ghostly atmosphere, most probably one of the roots of many a mystic tradition among Gomeran people.'

This type of evocative fantasising and sales material often forms the first impression that the visitor will have of the island and helps perpetuate the image of a wild, unspoilt paradise where the noble savage may yet be found. A travel article by Tony Rocca in *The Sunday Times* (November 1992) romanticises the inhabitants and their history:

> But La Gomera is different. Its very inaccessibility has allowed it to preserve a character that is truly special, with Guanche Indian blood-lines that still show on the faces of its 18,000 inhabitants despite Columbus.

In this article, the Guanche is referred to as an *Indian* – a description never used in texts or by the local people – an image that serves to accentuate the 'otherness' of the culture. There is also mention of Columbus, again appealing to the knowledge of history that the consumers are likely to possess, glamorising the island's place in such a context. Columbus used the island as a base for his expeditions across the Atlantic because of the natural water supply and other facilities. He is now marketed aggressively in the sales literature for the island, as well as at the port of San Sebastian, where there remain a number of buildings in which he once stayed. One tourist brochure entitled simply 'La Gomera', produced by the Ministry of Tourism, carries the words *Isla Columbina* (Columbus Island) on its back page, with a picture showing some tall ships crossing the Atlantic on route to the Caribbean. Inside the brochure, we read the (poor) translation to English:

> Within its important history one must mention Christopher Columbus' stay before going to America in the year 1492. His house, the church of Nuestra Senora de la Asuncion, the hermitage of San Sebastian, the Torre del Conde and finally the Casa de la Advana, the house of customs, from whose well was taken the water with which the discovery of America was baptised, still reminds us today of his stay on our island. [sic] ('La Gomera', Tourist Brochure 1990)

In its manifestation as a cultural commodity, 'history' is used to sell the island and La Gomera finds itself firmly written into the global history of the West with its crucial part in the discovery and consequent colonisation of the Americas. History is packaged for the tourists. Columbus is a signifier, a shallow representation of history, a two-dimensional commodity. The images on the postcard and in the brochure are directed towards the customer, with the customer's desires in mind.[10]

Modern tourism occasionally becomes a narcissistic contemplation of one's own culture rather than the observation of others. Many German tourists desire to escape from the constraints of their homeland. Some are now disenchanted with La Gomera and will move on to seek their unspoilt dream environment elsewhere. When these Germans see the modernisation or urbanisation of the island, they see their own dreams being destroyed. They have failed to reach the place created by the brochures and their personal desires. Their idealisation of an authentic, un-spoilt destination is proved erroneous. As the 'constructivist' approach (Wang, 1999) would suggest, their 'authentic' island had been constructed at home.

Nevertheless, tourists often said that they had experienced a strong sense of energy emanating from the island and returned there to be liberated from their urban ties. Some believed that the local people's lifestyle was more free and easy than their own: they made continual references to the cold, authoritarian and structured lifestyle of Germany and the invigorating unconstrained life in La Gomera. A typical example was an art student who wanted to live on La Gomera in the hills with the local people, working as a sculptress and selling her products: 'But the people would have to accept me as I am', she asserted. The vacation may become a type of 'sacred journey' as Graburn (1989) has suggested, in terms of a personal quest, but it can also become the beginning of a delusion. The following comments from tourists illustrate the diversity of opinions and reactions to local people that they have had:

> 'The women seem self-confident and proud, like the flamenco dancers.' (40 year-old female musician)

> 'The local boys are really very shy, scared of women.' (25 year-old woman)

> 'People here don't think.' (35 year-old female social worker)

> 'Society here is very macho.' (40 year-old Scotsman)

These brief statements combine simplistic stereotyping with personal experience and are all generalisations. They are some of the more memorable statements that tourists have made and were uttered without provocation: they were unsolicited remarks in casual conversations. It is clear that each person develops his or her own attitudes and understanding of the place according to personal experiences but when in conversation the use of stereotypes and commonly understood descriptions serves to perpetuate various ideas. Numerous people who have grown up in VGR refer to tourists as '*giris*', a derogatory term and a corruption of *gira* (tour outing), whilst they will probably know many tourists personally and will be aware of their diversity.

One group of interest in this discussion of stereotyping is the *veranistas*: there are few excuses for profound misunderstanding as many of them are related to the Gomeros. The main difference, though, is due to the urban lifestyle of most of the *veranistas*. Many Gomeros think that the people from Tenerife and the Peninsula adopt a superior attitude towards them, the urbanites considering themselves to be richer, more educated and more sophisticated than their country cousins. This is not helped by the fact that Gomerans are the butt of many jokes in Tenerife, rather like the Irish have been in England. There are tapes of Gomero jokes, which the Gomeros find amusing, but they dislike the association with themselves. One such joke is called 'coat-hanger' and concerns an artificial inseminator who visits a Gomeran woman to inseminate her cow. She leads him to the cowshed and upon entering it points out a nail on the door saying 'You can hang your trousers up on that'. This joke contains within it the rural image of the Gomeros with their simple ways, lack of formalised education and possible sexual deviances.

Nevertheless, many visitors have a deep affection for La Gomera. Jose, a *veranista* from mainland Spain who visited the island most summers made an observation in 1996:

> There is too much construction going on here, they should control it, maybe make a law to stop it. Soon VGR will be like Los Cristianos; the new big hotel is the worst, room prices will drop because of this. The people here just don't realise that they have something precious in this valley and beach.
>
> The local people are a very close community, and they are envious of those who get away; they call people who get educated in Tenerife and return in summer *veranos*. A gap develops between those who stay and those who go. I think the people here are primitive; the boys like to fight – once they beat up a group of Italian tourists in the disco because they were chasing Gomeran girls. The smart people get away.

The Gomeros often consider themselves to be under-developed in the industrial and cultural sense, especially when compared to Tenerife. This rural self-image finds itself symbolised in the term *mago* (meaning rural peasant but with folkloric content). It is often the case that tourists from Tenerife and, more especially, from the Peninsula regard La Gomera as a backwater rural stronghold and some local people disliked the condescension meted out to them by the Spanish from urban regions. So the notion of a backward, peripheral region being visited by people from the metropolitan core is reinforced annually.

Gomeran apartment owners said that the Spanish tourists (*veranistas*) are messy, mean with their money and demanding. This serves to show that not only is there a potential for friction between these two sets of people but that the Gomeros are not prejudicial against other nationalities in their employment of criticism. In turn, the people from Tenerife see the Gomeros as a very close community and very proud of themselves as Gomeros, describing them as *muy suyo* (very self-possessed), perhaps too defensive and very critical. Some *veranistas* said that they could not live in VGR because of the severe social restrictions due to the prying eyes and wagging tongues of neighbours, a feeling that is captured well in the phrase 'Small village, big hell'. This experience contrasts starkly with the German tourists' belief that to live in VGR would mean greater freedom. Because the *veranistas* come from a Spanish society, often have relatives in La Gomera and speak the local language, they are far more sensitive to social subtleties and aware of the reality of everyday life for a family in a small community. They are sensitive to the constraints of the community, the codes of conduct and particular roles expected of family members and neighbours.

Foreign Settlers

There are some foreign visitors who have learnt at first hand what life in Vueltas can be like. A number of relationships between tourists and local people have become very serious and led to couples living together or marrying. In Vueltas during 1991 there were six relationships where a young local man was living with a foreign woman that he had met when she was on holiday. Of these men, five were under 30 years of age, and one around 37 years old; four of the couples had children. The women worked in VGR as hotel receptionists, restaurant waitresses or washed clothes and helped in apartment cleaning. Another German woman in her late forties lived in Vueltas and had a relationship with a man in his fifties. These foreign women involved in serious relationships had come to abide by the local practice of discouraging women from going out to bars at night unless accompanied by their husbands; whereas the male partner was at liberty to visit the bars or discotheque. One Austrian woman, who had maintained a serious relationship with a local man for five years having met him in his parents' apartments, could not bear the restriction on her liberty intrinsic in the role of serious girlfriend. She went out alone many times, meeting up with friends in the bars at night and had many disagreements with her boyfriend; she suffered criticism from the locals for her behaviour and eventually left the island. This is an area where roles are being challenged and may be changed or where the unwillingness of others to accept great changes leads to the refusal to accept the role and a consequent disruption of the relationship.

Relationships between foreign men and local women are much less common, although there is one resident German who is now married to a local woman. They met whilst he was working in a village bar where he continues to work and is now part owner. In 1991 he claimed he was the only German married to a Gomeran woman in VGR. Another relationship between a German and local woman had led to the two of them going to live and work in Germany. They met in 1988 in VGR and, after a brief trip together to Germany, she returned and waited for him. He returned later to see if he could settle in VGR but found it difficult, especially making friends with the local men: he eventually decided he could not stay there. The woman spoke of her boredom in the village: a common complaint. One other local woman met her Italian husband whilst he was on vacation in Tenerife: they now work in Vueltas and are well integrated into the community.

These examples show how the type of tourism in VGR, predominantly the backpacking 'alternative', has led to young people of different nationalities meeting and foreigners settling in Vueltas. There will be further influences as a result of this as the young German women challenge local ideas of social behaviour and introduce new norms. The children of such couples now attend the local school and grow up in the village with new ideas gained from their mothers. It is impossible to assess the long-term influence of such developments but this is one of the serious results of tourism, especially the backpacking, outgoing, youth-oriented alternative type.[11] A gradual settlement of foreign partners in Vueltas and VGR overall has been complemented by a greater settlement of foreign couples and individuals who stay permanently in the area, usually having first visited it as tourists.

In 1991 the following foreign settlers lived in Vueltas: a retired German couple, a German and Spanish couple, a Spaniard and his German girlfriend, two Italian couples, an Italian woman and her children, seven Spanish women from the Peninsula (four ran a language school and three worked in a bar) and a German and his Canadian wife. There was also a small group of hippies, numbering around 12, who survived by selling jewelry, leather, clothing, drugs and doing part-time labour such as painting. These hippies mixed with the local youths in the bars and on the beaches. They formed a permanently present but internally changing group of radically alternative lifestyle North Europeans: they had a high profile, playing music with guitars and drums and generally partying at the beach. It is often this image of the hippy traveller that is retained by the visitor to the valley but it is a misleading image of the average alternative tourist.

The influx of foreigners has created a cosmopolitan atmosphere within the small village, bringing new ideas, social behaviour and expectations into the community. The local school now has a number of bilingual children with the parents representing English, Italian and German nationalities: so the integration for some will be much greater. The mixing of the North Europeans with the Gomeros has led to some Gomeros going to work or settling in Germany with their friends. At least three families in Vueltas had a son in his twenties working in Germany and living with a German woman whom he met in VGR. There are also opportunities available through friends that have been made from Germany or through Gomeran friends living in Germany. A growing number of young men have been to Germany or Holland to do labouring jobs for short periods of time, proving that opportunities have opened up for local people through their contact with tourists. For many families their social networks have expanded to include tourist friends and relatives living in Germany.

During the 1990s the growing foreign settler community was becoming increasingly cohesive. As previously mentioned, the number of businesses operated by foreigners has increased and the presence of German tourists is virtually a year-round phenomenon. There is a German language newspaper produced on the island and Germans hold drumming sessions every week in the discotheque (opened in 1994) at Calera beach. An event was staged in Vueltas on the Plaza behind the *ermita,* which brought together the international community and local people in a charity fashion show. This event was called 'Summer Cocktails' and was held in aid of the crisis in Rwanda. It was the first event of its kind, and local people and foreign settlers paraded up and down the catwalk – a specially made stage – to a background of rock music. One of the German organisers of this successful event said that it was a chance to introduce the local people to international issues and that 'it gives us a chance to show the local people that we can do something positive, and stop them from criticising us'. This episode demonstrates the evolvement of the foreign settlers into a coherent community capable of group expression and support. They are beginning to shape an identity for themselves in the public forum and are forcefully bringing global issues including warfare, starvation and environmental destruction into the public eye.

According to one local girl: 'People are more open towards the Germans, not simply critical. They are interested in their ideas, some have even travelled to Germany, some even go out with them.' She had studied to be a teacher and wanted to introduce 'culture' to the youth of VGR: 'I want to open up their world. Now they just want to drink, take drugs and watch videos. They never read.'

These sentiments have been echoed by a number of other young people who have left VGR to study or visited foreign countries, many wanting to create something more for the community than the bars and discotheques offer. Indeed one young woman has organised two outdoor rock concerts with the help of some German settlers, local people and financial support from the local council. She had a friend who lives in Germany who was able to liaise with a group of musicians based in Germany and they agreed to perform in VGR. This gave her a lot of satisfaction, in particular the fact that the local people could experience and enjoy the event. Social life for young people in Vueltas is becoming more cosmopolitan and international, in a word, global. They regularly meet people from different countries with different ideas. They watch more TV programmes controlled by urban, cosmopolitan companies with material that draws them directly into a larger world. Politics and economics have taken an increasingly international dimension involving the EU, tourism and international fishing agreements – the global market affects their daily lives. Meanwhile, their own village is becoming dominated by German businesses and the EU-funded construction of roads, tunnels and an island airport continues apace.

Change and the Future

The specific type of tourist, the backpacking alternative, has had a special relationship with the host community, especially in respect to integration and serious partnerships with local people. Strong friendships develop, ideas are exchanged and marriages can result. Foreign visitors bring in new ideas and may act as role models, as well as introducing new economic choices in terms of trade and custom. The backpackers' youthfulness, relative freedom, outgoing tendencies, openness and interest have increased the most important factor in the equation between hosts and guests: communication. Because of this, they develop many relationships with the local people that have innumerable consequences. All this is in strong contrast to the 'tourism of the timid – often parents of the youthful travellers' (Graburn, 1989: 35). The backpackers are at an age when sexual and social relationships are experimental and have a far greater propensity to mix and form serious relationships with their hosts, a very important factor in the equation of change.

Inevitably, the question of imperialism remains at the back of our minds when considering the influence of tourism, especially in the light of world-system theory, the global network and export economy exploitation. Nash's broad definition of imperialism describes the 'expansion of a society's influences abroad' whether 'imposed or adopted by an alien society' (Nash, 1989: 38). Of course, this would apply to VGR where we have seen the undoubted development of a foreign society's interests: notably Germany. However, this use of the term imperialism is not rigorous enough for this discussion and we need to consider the element of exploitation. There are a number of different groups who are involved in making a profit out of others, i.e. expropriating surplus value, and these include the tourism-based companies: airlines, hotels, booking agencies etc. The tourists themselves have gained from a powerful home economic situation (a stronger currency prior to the Euro, cultural and educational capital advantage) and the local people profit through their selling of commodities such as food, services and accommodation. Thus, there are various degrees of exploitation and different groups are beneficiaries.

However, the crucial point is that the equation is changing rapidly. The pattern of tourism to La Gomera is becoming dominated by package tourism: local people are in danger of losing their income from independent alternative tourists. Interest groups with political backing and indirect financing are gaining the upper hand which is leading to a situation in which only big business is able to succeed in the market and might enjoy full exploitation of the country's resources, both natural and human. This situation might be compared to the 'Development Stage' in the 'Tourist Area Life Cycle' as proposed by Butler (1980). Although there is not necessarily a determined life cycle for VGR, it has reached a point where unplanned, locally dominated development is transforming into one where powerful business and political groupings may dominate and this is of crucial importance to the future of the region. Cooper *et al.* (1999: 115) gives us a useful definition of the 'Development Stage' that is of direct relevance to VGR.

> By the development stage, large numbers of visitors are attracted, at peak periods perhaps, equalling or exceeding the number of local inhabitants. By this stage the organisation of tourism may change as control passes out of local hands and companies from outside the area move in to provide products and facilities. These enterprises may have differing aims and time scales from those of the local community in terms of sustainable development. It is therefore at this stage that problems can occur if local decision-taking structures are weak. Control in the public sector can also be affected as regional and national planning may become necessary in part to ameliorate problems, but also to market to the international tourist-generating areas, as visitors become more dependent upon travel arrangements booked through the trade. This is a critical stage as these facilities, and the changing nature of tourism, can alter the very nature of the resort and quality may decline through problems of over-use and deterioration of facilities.

Undoubtedly, La Gomera has been part of a global world system for centuries and the working people exploited as such but the recent small-scale tourism has enabled the proletariat to participate fully in a service economy and sometimes profit from being in control of their capital resources. Nevertheless, this situation may well disappear in the near future. The next chapters consider the issues of economics, power, resources, identity, family and belief in great detail. They examine the relationship between the local community, tourism and cultural change, placing it in context with globalisation and consider the implications of the types of tourist visiting VGR for these developments.

Notes

1. The alternative tourist is a category in opposition to what are referred to as mass tourists: those who take package holidays booked through agencies. Broadly, on La Gomera, they appear as backpackers, aged between 20 and 45 years, are highly educated students or people working in the liberal professions, concerned about the environment, interested in meeting the local people and possessing a strong desire for personal freedom. See Macleod (1997, 1998) for an analysis of alternative tourists and alternative tourism.
2. Two such tourists that I met told me that they had not spoken once to a local villager and one of them had not even visited a local bar, preferring the restaurant next to the apartment complex.
3. I had been asked to be constantly vigilant for prospective customers by my landlady.
4. This behaviour accords with that noted by Kohn (1988) when describing the summer visitors in Scotland, the 'summer swallows' arriving with plenty of provisions to last the duration of the holiday.
5. Jordan (1980) looked at seasonal variations in Vermont, where local people often feel that the village is not their own during the peak tourist season and, in her work on Scottish Islanders, Kohn (1988) emphasised the seasonality of life, drawing attention to the importance of the annual changes.
6. Duysens noted in a paper on the tourism in Valle Gran Rey: 'In part the transgression of the hosts is not intentional, nevertheless the benefits derived from being an important destination for nudists are sufficient for the public morality to turn a blind eye' (Duysens 1989: 123).
7. Duysens (1989: 123) remarks that in VGR the male tourists are seen as objects of taboo, whereas female tourists become objects of desire. However, this is the androcentric perspective: in contrast, local women often see the German female tourists as a threat, being potential seducers of their men. Black (1996) finds similar responses in Malta.
8. A similar situation has evolved in Greece with the notorious *kamakia*, men who habitually chase female tourists for sexual gratification: in Nafplion they are marginalised by local Greek women, who often regard them as ' ugly and stupid' (Zinovieff 1990: 170). In the same survey Zinovieff showed that out of 46 such men, 21 eventually married foreign women. In Vueltas there has not been a similar public grouping of promiscuous men: individuals, however, acquire reputations that hinder their chances with local women.
9. In contrast to the study on Swedish tourism in Gambia in which Wagner (1977, 1986) recorded the aggressive attitude of the female tourists in their search for a partner as they openly approached local men.
10. Moeran has noted the deliberate intentions behind advertising literature: 'The

language of tourism is, yes the experience of society, but an experience of society that appears to have been created by the media' (Moeran, 1983: 107). In a study of the changing photographic image of the Great Lakes, USA, Albers (1983: 144) writes; 'Tourism and its visual expression, particularly postcards, are apt metaphors of modernity, because they obfuscate a critical historical consciousness by making secular fantasies appear real.' See also Selwyn (1996a) on myth-making and tourism.

11. Zinovieff devotes a chapter in her thesis to foreign wives and suggests that they become 'closed' in their marriages to Greek men, lacking the social and family networks of Greek women: they are regarded as 'unfriendly and deservedly isolated' (Zinovieff, 1990: 217). However, she does mention some couples that are more outgoing and behave in an egalitarian fashion reflecting the 'European' modern marriage. Even though Zinovieff does not focus on the impact of tourism, she acknowledges it (pp. 65, 218): the mixed marriages in the town will have influenced the townsfolk in ways not immediately apparent, by offering alternative ways of behaving, representations of different cultures and new ways of dealing with life.

Part 2

The Influence of Tourism

Chapter 4

Work and Property

Introduction

One of tourism's most salient influences is on the economy of the host country. Many tourism texts open with statistics proving the huge economic impact that tourism has in terms of cash flows, employment, gross domestic product (GDP) and so on.[1] This serves to place the industry in context and give a broad-brush view of its influence on the world stage as well as locally. Of course, the influences of tourism on the economy are inevitably as diverse as are the economies, cultures and the people visiting them. And there will be negative influences as well as positive ones, depending on the position of the observer. Scholars such as de Kadt (1979), Crick (1989) and those referred to by Nash (1996) have rejected the simplistic view of tourism as a totally benign form of development and this research recognises its complexity.

The majority of texts dealing with the economic influence of tourism take an approach privileging statistics (employment numbers and percentages, multiplier models, GDP). This chapter, in contrast, has its emphasis on detailed microanalysis and qualitative data – the sort of information obtainable from long-term involvement in fieldwork and, in anthropological fashion, interconnects the economic with the social and cultural aspects of a community. Consequently, it looks at the transforming economy from a qualitative stance (tracing certain trends) and deals with the relevance of the types of tourist: it also examines the tangible, quantifiable results of tourism on employment and specific modes of livelihood, in particular fishing. The chapter then considers how local attitudes have been influenced by tourism within the broad economic sphere, including gender roles, new types of employment opportunities and the way people relate to their property.

Hence this chapter is related to the study of economic influences of tourism as outlined by de Kadt (1979: 11) in his concentration on employment and increased demand.[2] He also draws attention to the fact that expanding opportunities often attract people from other regions of the country and high-level jobs frequently go to foreign incomers. Locally, he notes, young people and women (especially) appear to benefit from tourism employment leading to their economic independence and a resultant weakening of the traditional authority of the family head (p. 12). These issues are explored in this chapter.

In terms of the financial effect of tourism on work and property, we might frame them in a tripartite form commonly used in economic texts (Walton, 1993: 220):

(1) Direct effect: The initial injection of tourist expenditure creates direct revenue for hotels, shops, restaurants, travel agents, transport operations and other tourist services.
(2) Indirect effect: The recipients of the direct expenditure generate additional revenues to businesses or producers supplying them with necessary inputs, e.g. fuel for various forms of transport, food for restaurants, equipment for hotels, construction of hotels, etc.
(3) Induced effect: The beneficiaries of the direct and indirect effects spend their increased incomes on consumer and investment goods, which induces further consumption within the economy.

Other relevant impacts that become apparent include price inflation (due primarily to an increase in demand), especially common in the property market; the displacement of labour from primary industries to tourism-related service employment; and the redistribution of wealth, with tourism enabling people to gain from entrepreneurial activities such as renting out rooms and apartments. These developments have profound impacts on the sociocultural structure of the community, some of which are addressed in this chapter. Gender roles are changing and men are avoiding fishing as a career, consequently changing the cultural composition of the community.

La Gomera, in common with other islands, has experienced problems with limited resources in terms of physical assets and human labour. As a consequence, it imports certain commodities at high costs as well as using skilled workers from beyond its shores. This increases prices as well as raising fiscal leakage from the home economy. Furthermore, certain resources will experience intense pressure – leading to price inflation and their possible exhaustion, such as land and freshwater. These issues occasionally turn into heated competition and have led to conflict, protest and party political platforms – an example of which, centred on the development of a beach site, is examined in the chapter on power and conflict.

In terms of the types of tourist visiting VGR, it is argued throughout this book that alternative tourists have more sociocultural impact than mass tourists (package tourists), in contrast to the views of Smith (1989c) and Graburn (1989). Taken on an equivalent volume basis (cash spent), it is further argued that alternative tourists are likely to have a greater economic impact on the local population because of their propensity to use indigenous accommodation, shops, cafes and other local services. This gives money directly to the local community, increases the likelihood that it will trickle down into other direct/indirect and induced sectors of the economy, hence strengthening the multiplier effect. Whereas package tourists are more likely to use hotel services, their money going into the hands of the owners who are often located outside the community. A close examination of different areas of work highlights the expanding influence of tourism.

The Transforming Economy

Overview

The tourism development that is occurring on La Gomera is part of a subtle and complicated process that has been taking place over a long period of time beginning with the European invasions of the 14th century. Capitalist society and its technology has influenced the region for many years, notably through plantation agriculture, fish-processing and the cash economy, with a subsequent spread of wealth and power within the community. This pattern continues today. Since the 1960s the richer members have gained from radio communication and electronic technology for water pumps, lighting etc., whilst the poorer majority have often gone without. However, small-scale tourism has allowed some individuals to make gains without heavy investment.

Research has produced a picture of tourism that certainly changes society, but one that neither completely transforms nor ravages the host community, a tourism that has many facets. By using a variety of historical accounts we have seen that change has numerous forms, especially economic and political, and that tourism is part of an ongoing process, adding its own distinctive touch. Change, in general, has come about through political and economic forces in the guise of individual agents and groups initiating economic transformations, including capitalisation, industrialisation, communication improvements and tourism.[3] The section on history emphasised the importance of the world system and globalisation as well as giving a close-up view of events in VGR, bringing into the discussion the inhabitants of the village who were the actors in recent historical events and who have created historical records through their own accounts.

Economic and environmental conditions on the island changed considerably during the 1980s. The improvements in the transport system, the capital accumulation and the crisis in the agricultural and fishing sectors all encouraged a reliance on the service sectors in the south. The upper reaches of the valley (above Calera) have not experienced the transformation so deeply. These differences are also reflected in the population balance between the upper and lower valley: whilst the ratio was 54% to 46% in 1940, it had become 44% to 56% by 1981. The coastal zone (Vueltas, Borbalan, La Puntilla, La Playa) grew at an annual rate of 2.6% in the 1970s compared to the upper valley's growth of 0.9% (Burriel, 1982). The secondary sector began developing after 1975 with the construction of apartments and service-related buildings. Records show that, in 1981, there were little more than 15 people employed full-time in tourist-related work in VGR; however, this does not recognise those who gained from tourism by renting out rooms. Women also found employment and extra work related to domestic service such as cleaning apartments, although this was usually undertaken by members of the family and was not waged employment. This balance changed in the 1990s when employment in the tourism sector in apartment complexes and related services rose considerably.

The road system was not upgraded during the 1970s and 1980s and is believed to have limited the potential increase in tourism. Although there was a ferry service between San Sebastian and VGR, it stopped operating in the late 1980s. Fishing activity grew until 1981 with increasing capitalisation, yet during the 1980s developments in the global fishing economy and over-production resulting in unprofitable catches led to its rapid decline. In the agricultural sector, the census shows that between 1972 and 1982 agricultural properties dropped from 792 to 496 in VGR, whilst those people whose principal occupation was agricultural dropped from 389 to 169: this reflects a marked abandonment of this mode of livelihood.

There was an observable growth in the active working population between 1975 and 1986 of 3.6% per annum. This is largely due to an increase in the number of working women, particularly in the service sector, and also marks the fact that they began to be acknowledged by officialdom. This led to a decrease in female unemployment, with VGR experiencing the lowest level in La Gomera at 13.7%, compared to an average of 37.9%. The growth in the female labour force, with the most active age group being the over-fifties, is a salient feature of social change in VGR, with the female worker complementing the male worker in bringing money into the household. The younger generation has been able to benefit from tourism development in terms of work opportunities and an important market has been established in VGR.[4]

As a result of joining the European Community (EC) in 1986 Spain became eligible for special funds for particular projects: a commission decision on 30 December 1986 led to a preparatory study for an integration and development operation for La Gomera. This, in turn, led to the

Programma Operativo Integrado (Programme for Integration or POI) that intends to aid the 'development' of La Gomera: one of the results of this is the structural grant from the EC, supporting road construction in VGR, which was operational in 1991. The general objectives of development according to the POI are:

(a) the creation of employment,
(b) increase in income and the reduction of the difference in incomes between La Gomera and other islands,
(c) correcting the lack of equilibrium between wealth and industry on the island, and
(d) the control of strategic resources (water, energy and environment) in order to improve the quality of life (POI, 1990: 3 January 2003: Madrid).

This emphasis on equilibrium between different regions reflects the ECs commitment to distributing funding with the intention of ironing out differences between rich and poor areas. An estimated £60 million was earmarked for investment in works that included the building of an airport. La Gomera has entered a period of economic change, partly as a result of its entry into the EC, a factor that is compounding the transformation already under way.

Employment and social stratification

The population of VGR was dependent on natural resources for its wealth well into the 20th century, with agriculture, plantation crops, animal husbandry and fishing providing the mainstays of the economy. Together with the manual workers who formed the bulk of the population, there were also businessmen and landlords who owned the shops, the fruit-packing factories, the fish-salting or canning factories, the land and the plantation crops. This division provided the social hierarchy as well – one inherited from the señorial days, and based on master and servant (see Sawyer, 1971: 405). The people of VGR still talk of the *caciques*, the owners of the means of production, the bourgeoisie, influential people who had a powerful hold over the workers. Wealth was the all-important factor. A man with money could rise above others regardless of his background: wealth frees one from the obligation to serve others. Many of the local people continue to see this as the main factor of social differentiation, some saying that it comes down to a simple division between those who control and those who serve. This seems to be relevant within the confines of the valley, although there are undoubtedly more subtle means of dividing classes of people, most notably with respect to education.

Kenny has divided Spanish society into leaders, controllers and servers (Kenny, 1961: 77) and Gilmore (1980: 52) highlights education and access to political power as the means to social elevation but it should be realised that historically it has often been wealth that, in turn, allows education. This seems to be true within VGR, where, as an example, the Mayor (Bethencourt) managed to gain sufficient education to become a teacher and, as such, has respect from the villagers. Historically, the wealthy *caciques* were the ruling class – the bourgeoisie: they had access to education and regarded themselves as superior to the working-class proletariat. However, with the gradual distribution of wealth and a broader access to education, the gap between the two groups has become smaller. Nevertheless, in everyday face-to-face interactions in VGR, there remains an element of competition for superiority and there is a presumed inherent base-line equality amongst working men, for example the fishermen. The differentiating factor of wealth has been partially eroded through the introduction of new sources of income and this chapter outlines the main developments in opportunities to make money.

With the improvement of communications during the 1970s and 1980s, specifically the car ferry between La Gomera and Los Cristianos in 1975, and new roads reducing the distance from the port of San Sebastian to VGR, the fortunes of the valley changed dramatically. Tourism developed from a trickle to a flow and each year sees a growth in the number of people visiting VGR. The economic results of this have been profound and the construction, accommodation and service industries have boomed. Tourism is now also a major reason for outside investment in the area: the Spanish Government and the EC have ploughed millions of pesetas into construction projects. In brief, resources have become more accessible to the entire population of the valley.

Employment opportunities have created new roles in Vueltas, where the old primary industries, particularly fishing and also plantation work, have been superseded in popularity as employment areas by the service sector.[5] Apartments provide an extra form of income for many families. Current modes of livelihood include the established sectors of fishing, plantation work, construction and carpentry; but these have been joined by shopkeeping, bar and restaurant work, apartment cleaning and management, taxi-driving, painting, police work and health care.

Tourist types and specific impacts

The predominant type of tourism found in VGR during the 1990s has been alternative backpacking. These tourists often sleep in a room adjacent to the host's household and mix with local people in bars and other public places, leading to rich communicative relationships between the two parties. This is in contrast to the mass tourism which Olwig describes as inflicting economic changes in the local population who must adapt to the large scale development built to house, feed and entertain the tourists (Olwig, 1985: 120). Olwig implies that tourism is a brutal force victimising a helpless host and refers to the large-scale development associated with mass tourism that caters for this 'timid' type of tourist. In this scenario the tourists inhabit a physical environment designed to cater for their particular desires and are often served by local people who are operating in a professional role: they may as well be going to a factory or an office to earn wages (see Robinson, 1999; de Kadt, 1979). Both types of tourism have a great impact on the community but the backpacking alternative tourism has a far more diverse and deeper influence than mass tourism in terms of human sociocultural and occasionally economic impact because this type of tourist is likely to penetrate the sociocultural environment more profoundly. This view challenges the model produced by Smith (1989c) and the views of Graburn (1989) in which mass tourists are seen as having the greater impact upon a culture simply through their sheer volume.

Tourism has direct and indirect results – intentional and incidental changes – and this study contains specific examples whilst indicating the variety and scope of the relationship between the local people and tourists. Perhaps the most apparent result of the tourism in VGR is a visual one: the physical structure of the village has changed dramatically with local people initiating the construction of apartments to take advantage of the growth in tourism (see Plates 1–6 in Chapter 2). Where there were once bungalows, there are now three-storey buildings; where once there were small winding roads there are now wide metalled roads, broadened with smart pedestrian walkways. Car-hire shops, two in Vueltas, leave their vehicles outside for all to see: the place has been transformed throughout. Then there are the tourists themselves: at peak season easily doubling the population of Vueltas, walking around the village, their stature and colour distinguishing them from the local people, their language contrasting with the native tongue, their clothes contrasting with local fashion.

Business and Employment in Vueltas

The working environment

Tourism offers employment to all types of worker and has radically altered the opportunities for women in the labour market. A look at the development of local businesses in Vueltas from 1991 to 2002 will give an idea of the extent to which they are dependent upon tourism and the changing pattern of ownership.

In 1991 there were 33 businesses recorded, and of these nine were operated by people from outside La Gomera (27%). It can be said that eight of these were absolutely dependent on tourism: two restaurants, one postcard shop, one T-shirt shop, one meditation centre, one bait-and-tackle shop, and two car-hire businesses. Another 19 are probably dependent for up to three-quarters of their custom is from tourists: six supermarket outlets, eleven bar/restaurants, one cafe, one clothes shop and the discotheque.

It could be envisaged that were the tourists to disappear completely, at least half of these businesses would immediately collapse, with those remaining battling with each other to survive. Other businesses (hardware, florist, bakery, electrical and video and white goods) may not be primarily dependent on tourism but indirectly benefit through the demand generated – the multiplier effect – and the fact that the resident population is actually growing in VGR. The only business activity in Vueltas that is independent of tourism is the banana-packing station, which sells almost all its products to the Peninsula. Of the 13 original bar/restaurants recorded in 1991 in Vueltas, one alone was run by a German and three more were run by people from overseas, i.e. 30% were foreign managed.

By August 1995, seven out of the 13 bars and restaurants (three new ones had replaced three which had closed down) were run by Germans and one other by a mainland Spaniard, making 61% operated by foreigners. There were also six new businesses operating in Vueltas, three of which were run by Germans (health shop, ticket office, marine club), one by a Spaniard (boutique) and two by local Canary Islanders (pleasure-trip boat, super-market).

The two businesses that had closed down were a supermarket and a florist both owned and operated by local families. The trend for tourist-related businesses to be operated by outsiders who have business acumen and resources was becoming clear in Vueltas and the steady growth of German operations apparent. There has been a transformation in terms of the relative diminution of local operations as the foreign settlers consolidate their presence. Given the increasing tourism market, this situation can be expected to continue.

Indeed, by 2002, there were 17 bar/restaurants, of which nine were foreign run (53%). Supermarkets were nine in number (eight run by locals). These two areas of business remain popular for local people who understand them and are aware of the risks. In contrast, other types of outlets have expanded greatly and are run by newcomers to the valley: an internet café, a motor-bike hire shop, a jewelry shop, a butchers, a newsagents, a gymnasium, three boutiques and a tour boat. In total, the number of businesses operating in Vueltas in 2002 was 52, compared to 33 in 1991, with the majority being run by people from beyond the island: 27 were foreign operated (52%) – a significant rise from 27% in 1991.

The most obvious form of business that has not been mentioned is apartment-renting. This is wholly dependent on tourism. In Vueltas there were at least 36 pensions privately owned different families and three blocks of apartments owned by families or consortiums in 1991; this figure had risen to 47 by 2002. The income from these forms an important part of a family's receipts, many of which were at one time dependent on fishing. Some of the fishermen also rely directly on tourists who form the bulk of the custom at the restaurants to which they sell their catch. Those who fish for white fish, prawns and pargo usually sell direct to the restaurants, whilst those who fish for mackerel or tuna sell to the islanders or to the Peninsula via intermediaries. Together with this link to the tourism market, many fishermen also own apartments the rents of which supplement their income. For example, one fisherman who sells directly to the restaurants rents out two large apartments which his daughters clean; they also work in a shop which sells about one-third of its produce to tourists and his sons work in restaurants, paint or work in construction. His entire family is reliant upon the tourist trade for most of its income.

One more form of employment that is very dependent on tourism is the taxi trade. This relies upon tourists going to and from the port of San Sebastian, as well as those travelling around the island. In 1991 the public bus service operated twice daily, 5.00 a.m. and 3.00 p.m., to San Sebastian, offering little competition, whereas car-hire companies take potential passengers and often work out cheaper than using the taxi service. VGR had 12 taxi-drivers operating from Calera: one had worked on the large fishing boats as a crewman before his present employment. By 2002 the buses were offering a service five times a day.

Tourism has brought many employment opportunities to the region: in particular, the service-related industries, retail, catering and transport ones, and the less obvious domestic and cleaning side – the valeting of apartments, which is usually performed by female members of the family. The wives of the owners of the apartments will clean the linen and the room, liaise with the tourists and may be helped by other female members of the family in this work (daughters, mother, sisters or affinal relatives).[6] One example in VGR is a set of nine apartments owned by a carpenter whose wife helps to clean the apartments, as does her mother. His wife's brother, a fisherman, lives in one of the apartments with his spouse who helps clean the apartments and her mother takes in washing from the apartments. A total of four women are involved in cleaning the rooms and their contents and they are all related to the owner. In Vueltas, the men of the household usually maintain the apartments if any furniture or equipment needs repairing, calling in specialists when necessary. A former fisherman, currently a supermarket operator, built an apartment's interior walls and windows, tiled the floors, installed furniture and fixed the plumbing. He occasionally called on the help of a skilled man, his brother-in-law, to plaster the walls and help lay the bricks.

A local man built almost all the apartments and extensions in Vueltas: he has now stopped building to concentrate on other related work. A different local man now runs a building company that undertakes work on the construction of apartments as well as doing public works, such as resurfacing roads. The construction industry has enjoyed boom years with the tourist influx because of the demand for apartments and shops. A result of the increase in visitors is the necessity for a better communications infrastructure, including a reliable network of roads. This has led to the successful acquisition of EC 'Structural Funds' for the municipality of VGR, due to the local council's applications for finance to build large roads running down the central valley and along the length of the fluvial plain. This construction necessarily uses many labourers, most of whom are recruits from the upper valley.

It is undeniable that tourism has brought money into Vueltas. Local people have been able to open businesses, rent out apartments and sell produce to tourists, thereby earning money directly from them. Smith (1989c) points to the economic multiplier effects of tourism with the knock-on benefits for cash flow, a series of traders can benefit from an initial cash injection, as is the case in VGR. In contrast, Crick (1989) seriously questions the acceptability of this in certain circumstances and argues that the inter-sectoral linkages may be weak. He writes that, in the 1960s, tourism was seen as a saviour for the Third World, whereas now with the insecurity, price elasticity, fashion changes, leakages of money and high vertical integration, the negative effects are becoming more apparent.[7] This is most relevant to mass (package) tourism, with its high capital investment and bulk all-inclusive payments whereby the 'timid' mass tourists pay rent to hotel owners, eat in large restaurants, with the profits going to investors, and are generally far less involved with the local economy.[8] There is now a discernible shift in VGR towards this type of incipient mass tourism with its associated social and economic risks and leakages which contrasts with the backpacking alternative tourism in which rent is paid directly to the local hosts and products are purchased in local shops and restaurants. This aspect of alternative tourism is becoming increasingly recognised by scholars and it is being promoted as a sustainable form of tourism (see Murphy, 1994).

An examination of tourism in the 'Third World' in a collection of papers edited by de Kadt (1979) reaches conclusions warning of the risks of tourism and the reliance of host countries upon the goodwill of tourist generating metropolitan centres. There are warnings here for the tourist industry in VGR, which may transform from a small-scale cottage industry into a big-business affair. In taking advantage of the tourist wealth, local people may have become too reliant upon it, with the risk of becoming economically dependent. Furthermore, the changing pattern of tourism may lead to a reduction in demand for private household apartments and goods from locally owned outlets. The sensitivity of tourism to changes in fashion and the global economy is well known and, throughout 1990, the Canary Islands newspapers were reporting a crisis in tourism which was affecting Tenerife and other large islands, which have a highly developed tourist industry accounting for some 60% Gross National Product (GNP). The straightforward financial influences, however, are not the only ones changing the society in Vueltas: there are also profound alterations in working patterns.

Whilst the new jobs in the service and construction industries offer opportunities to the young, they also create a number of serious side effects. Many people now avoid agricultural work on plantations and on the terraces, which means that some areas are left abandoned. A banana plantation owner was obliged to let his plantation lie fallow through lack of employees; another man said that he had many acres of workable land but nobody was willing to work on it. The agricultural labourers themselves say it is hard work for little pay and the young men prefer to work in the bars, paint or do construction work. The same problem is witnessed in the fishing sector where few young men wish to follow their father's profession, preferring to work in the bars, paint or study for other employment. This trend cannot be blamed squarely on the development of tourist-related work but it provides an available work option, allowing a displacement of the workforce.

As an example, a local fisherman has six sons, none of whom fish with him: one is a fully employed crewman of a tuna fishing boat, another two work in bars, two more are painters and one other lives in Germany with his wife. One of his sons said that his father would not take him fishing because 'he didn't want me to grow up and work as a fisherman like him'. The son of a different fisherman worked in a cafe but became officially unemployed; he hoped to get work as a painter or in construction and explained: 'Fishing is a hard life, with too many risks; some months there may be no money at all'. The necessity to work in the primary productive sectors is no longer there and many youngsters find alternative employment because of the tourist trade. Not only have the opportunities expanded allowing a greater choice but the pressures to follow in their father's professional footsteps are also no longer present, giving an individual a freedom from economic constraints to continue the tradition of fishing.

Probably the greatest impact of tourist-related work has been the growth in opportunities for women, especially the work done by women within private apartments which may be reimbursed in a variety of ways: in kind, by reduced rents for relatives or by shared work. This labour also accounts for a large amount of paid work, 'contractual' or not. In Vueltas almost every adult woman with the ability cleaned apartments within her family home or outside of it. The other major area of employment is in the retail sector. Shops such as supermarkets and gift shops were usually staffed by women; in fact, all the shops except for the hardware store employed some female staff, invariably close relatives of the owner. This was not so with the bars and restaurants where men were usually employed as bar-staff and cooks, although one bar/restaurant was run solely by women.

The bars are still seen as the domain of the men and the exceptional bar is one run by a group of women from mainland Spain with strong views on women's rights. Their particular bar is an attraction for many of the foreign settlers and the staff has acted as a support group for many women who need employment or help. One foreign settler was having problems getting reliable painters for her new home, so the women at the bar helped her out by painting the building themselves. In this manner, local women have been given a new example of what women can do: traditional practices are being displaced by new ideas and possibilities.

The major areas of employment in Vueltas during 1991 are now outlined. Fishing, the biggest industry aside from tourism, is given a special section. These examples illustrate the specific influence of tourism on different work practices.

Construction

This ranged from bricklaying (both modern breeze-blocks and stone-walling) to unskilled labouring. Most working days lasted from 8.00 a.m. until 2.00 p.m. with a half-hour break at 10.30 a.m., and then after the afternoon siesta, from 4.00 p.m. until 6.00 p.m. Work was usually obtained from a local contractor or from the local council undertaking public works such as road building. There were some professional builders living in Vueltas, at least five skilled men who learnt from their fathers as well as many unskilled labourers. Men were often taken on and laid off at random, depending on whether there was work to be done. The spate of road building financed by the EC and the government had led to high employ-ment for labourers and stone-wall builders in the preceding year. Stone-wall building is an art in itself and most of the builders came from the upper valley where the old traditional skills had been passed on from their fathers. They break the local rock up with hammers and place the flat sheared surfaces on show, backed by cement, to give an attractive finish. The construction of apartments, civic developments and infrastructure improvements (roads, tunnels) had all been highly influenced by tourism.

Painting

Most painting involved the exterior whitewashing of homes and tourist apartments; paid workers did some of the interior painting: many of the younger men work as painters as no training was necessary. The main problem is the insecurity of the job as much work is seasonal, with people tending to redecorate their apartments in the early summer slack season. Many of the sons of fishermen worked as painters, often combining it with other jobs such as bar work. The painters worked whatever hours suited them or according to the agreement with the employer: it was generally a casual arrangement.

Bar/restaurant work

In Vueltas, in 1991, there were 13 restaurants and bars, and one discotheque attached to a restaurant: these employed barmen, cooks, waiters and waitresses and they were relatives of the owner or friends or otherwise. Most bars had full-time staff and employed part-time staff as well depending on the demand from customers: people were also employed in the kitchens and for cleaning. Of the 13 bar/restaurants, five were owned and operated by people from VGR (only two born in Vueltas), four from elsewhere in La Gomera and four by people from outside the Canary Islands. In total they employed at least 30 full-time staff with an average of 10 part-time staff. Some of the bar/restaurants open from 7.00 a.m. until 2.00 a.m., others may open only in the afternoon from 2.00 p.m. until 1.00 a.m. Again the hours depend upon the season; thus, during the winter season bars will stay open longer, some would remain open until 6.00 a.m. The discotheque often stayed open until 7 a.m. during the peak summer season in August.

The restaurants and bars employed cleaners to wash the floor, furniture and fittings as well as the linen: this had provided employment and earnings for a number of German women that live in VGR who combine it with other sources of income. The service industry is a large employer in Vueltas and a source of income for many on a part-time basis: it attracts people from outside the village and forms a source of different ideas, cultures, and attitudes. For example, the following regions and nations were represented by people working in Vueltas: Gallicia, Spanish Basque region, Italy, France, Malaya, Germany; and further along the road towards Borbalan there were also English, Welsh and Austrians working in restaurants. We can see that many of these tourist-oriented businesses were themselves run by incoming foreigners, a renowned feature of the tourist industry. There were now foreign settlers in VGR, and they had begun to create a permanent community of international composition, mostly dependent on foreign visitors for income.

Shopkeepers

In contrast to the restaurants and bars, local people continue to dominate ownership of the foodstores. In Vueltas there were some 6 'supermercado' outlets: these are food stores that may sell other items such as alcohol, postcards or beachwear – five of them were run by families originating from Vueltas and one recently moved from Calera to Vueltas. These outlets are owned and operated by nuclear families (one set of parents and their children), only one of which inherited the shop from their parents, this being the original corner shop in Vueltas. Of the other shops, two owners were fishermen, one having transferred into shop keeping when young, the other continues a fishing career, whilst his wife and daughter run the shop. Another man ran a bar and the shop, allowing his son to work the till in the shop helped by a friend. The shops open between 8.00 a.m. and 10.00 p.m., usually shutting from 2.00 p.m. to 4.00 p.m. unless it is the peak holiday season. There is strong competition between them, with two shops remaining open late at night trying to outlast one another and prices differing considerably between shops, even between outlets run by the same family. Customers tend to develop a loyalty to particular shops, and one shop assistant said that he tries to befriend his customers: the shop was often the meeting point for many villagers. This friendly relationship promotes guilt amongst the customers when purchasing elsewhere, and the assistant said that he became very annoyed when certain tourists came in to ask him for change for the telephone or to buy a packet of cigarettes, but always shopped for food across the road.

In one of the supermarkets the son of the owner has a German wife and has learnt to speak German himself. This appeals to the German tourists who can talk to him, requesting special varieties of food that he will obtain, and become friends with him. Such an assistant is invaluable in the competition for custom. In fact the younger sons and daughters of the shopkeepers are often encouraged to learn some English or German, which allows them to form a relationship with or just communicate to the tourists who make up a large proportion of their customers. Within the shop loyalty to family is very strong: one girl had criticised some food in the family shop of a girlfriend of hers, after which the friend refused to talk to her again.

Many local customers buy their food on credit with their accounts written down in a book; they pay at the end of the month, and at least one shop includes a surcharge for this facility. This credit system ensures a certain loyalty from the customer and is an example of the type of debt relationship that has played a large part in the economic lives of the local people. In earlier days most purchases were made on credit and settled at the end of the month when the wages came. It is said that in the past some shopkeepers who employed local people on their plantations refused to pay them cash wages, claiming that they had already taken the equivalent of their labouring income on credit from their shop.

Of the other shops in Vueltas in 1991, the clothes and gift shop, the hardware store, the electrical goods shop, the toy and sports shop, the plant shop and the furniture shop, all are owned and operated by local families. There was a T-shirt shop run by a German and his Canadian wife who had been in Vueltas for six years, and a postcard shop, which was rented from a local man by a German photographer during the peak tourist season. There was also a bait-and-tackle shop, newly opened by a German and his Spanish wife: he operated a fishing excursion service taking tourists fishing in an 11 m wooden boat which he owned. The tackle shop served as a booking office as well and quickly became a meeting place for German tourists, providing them with a source of information. This is a good example of how the lack of a tourism infrastructure within VGR (there was no central office of information for tourists in 1991) allowed the Germans to initiate development of tourist facilities and become successful.

The cleaning of apartments

Members of the landlord's family usually cleaned the apartments. The large apartment complexes, often owned by groups of local businessmen, employed local women to clean them and local men to act as caretakers and gardeners.

Plantation labour

There were at least ten households in Vueltas in which the main breadwinner worked on a banana plantation. Most of these households had established themselves on the periphery of the village, as can be seen on Map 3 and, as such, were not part of the original settlement but had moved in relatively recently. The men that worked on the banana plantations usually had an agreement with the owner of the land allowing them to take one-half of the income from the banana crop that was produced, a form of sharecropping. The working hours vary with the season and, in VGR, the bananas can fruit at any time of the year, even though the norm is for one plant to do so only once a year. The labourers spend much time pruning the plants, preparing the environment, cutting down banana bunches, irrigating the soil, spraying with pesticides, spreading fertiliser and other related work. Sometimes the plots have maize or mangoes growing amongst the banana plants, in which case the men will tend these as well. The men may also raise goats either nearby the plantation or on their own land and these would have been fed mainly from the banana plants: at least two households in Vueltas did this.

In the upper valley, where most of the workers (*peons*) lived, many were agriculturally minded and had smallholdings: they provided the majority of labour power on the plantations. All these labourers were working on plantations owned by the wealthier local families. One worker told me he earned 3000 pesetas (£16.67) for an eight-hour day – any extra hours work would merit 500 pesetas (£2.78)/hr. The norm was said to be a 40-hour week, although this man claimed to work for 12 hours a day and sometimes a seven-day week. Another worker spent three days on the plantation and the remainder on his own plot of land in Vueltas. The plantations are privately owned, usually inherited, and the owners belong to a cooperative that collects, processes and exports the bananas. One owner believed that there were some 50 plantation-workers in the whole of the valley (only ten in Vueltas). He paid his workers 3000 pesetas/day, and said his plants produced a crop once a year – it would prove too demanding to get two. Other owners divide the income from the crop with the worker at regular intervals.

The sons of the plantation workers occasionally joined their fathers in their work, although in general they tried to obtain other types of employment. Two were full-time fishermen, working as crew members; others worked in bars, or as labourers or painters. The employment on the plantations was probably the most unpopular type of work in VGR. One man said that he could not get people to work on his land, even though he was offering an annual income of £8000. Others told of banana plots left to ruin for lack of willing labourers. The uncertainty about the future market for bananas in the EC and the high opportunity cost of the land combined to increase the desertion of banana plantations and this encouraged the construction of apartments and service outlets on the land.

Banana-packing-station

There is a large banana-packing station in Vueltas that is run by a cooperative of local plantation owners. In 1991, it employed a number of local people: one lorry-driver, five porters, one loader, two bunch-cutters, one class-sorter, three packagers (all women), two box-loaders, two box-assemblers and one manager – a total of 18 employees. The bananas are packaged for transportation to mainland Spain.

This examination of work activity, in 1991, shows that the majority of newly created work was manual or semi-skilled and does not offer long-term security. However, there was a greater choice of work, and hence, the neglect of plantation work and fishing. This suggests a shift from a semi-proletariat-based society (typical of peripheral regions) to one of free wage-labourers – full proletarians, still subject to exploitation. Other trades and professions that were represented by the population in Vueltas included a medical assistant, carpenters, mechanics, taxi-drivers, a baker, a policeman, an electrician, a woman who baked and sold biscuits and another who kept chickens, selling the eggs.

The business of fishing

There were estimated to be 45 professional fishermen fishing out of Vueltas in 1991: of these, 10 were employed on the *faluas*, large boats specialising in tuna hunting. The other men were either owners or the crew of small boats (up to 11 m in length) that hunted for a variety of fish, including tuna, mackerel and pargo; or they may prefer to catch fish in a wire cage (*nasa*) left on the sea floor for some time. Most fishermen employed a variety of tactics to catch numerous types of fish.

For the self-employed fisherman, his main outgoings in relation to his professional activities will be on boat maintenance, equipment, fuel, clothes, social security and berthing fees. These vary considerably between individuals depending on the state of their equipment and general financial position, for example some have to pay interest on a loan for their assets. In Vueltas, income will be determined by the catch, the ability to sell it and the variability of the market price. The fishermen may sell their catches to middlemen who then sell to the public or factories; they may sell directly to the public; or they may sell to service outlets such as bars, restaurants or shops. There are, therefore, a variety of options for the fishermen, making for a flexible market with a lack of predictability. However, this spread of options does not lead to the minimisation of risk associated with 'portfolio theory' (in which risk is reduced by diverse investment) but, rather, the variety of outlets displays the unsettled nature of the market, with fishermen tending to concentrate on one type of purchaser. Some of the following examples give a practical insight into the type of business that fishing is:

A mackerel fisherman can expect a catch that is usually between 40 and 80 kg/day;[9] the price during the year at which the fisherman could sell to the *furgoneta* (van-driving middle man) dropped from 300 to 250 pesetas per kilo (180 pts = 1 pound sterling) after May 1991. It can, therefore, be calculated that a lone mackerel fisherman can have a gross income of more than £21,000 in a year, assuming he fishes five days a week for 46 weeks.

This is before fuel and tackle costs, maintenance of equipment, social security (£720/yr) and berthing fees (£140/yr) are taken into account, to say nothing of asset replacement, an example of which was when Pedro Jimenez changed his engine during the year, buying a new one valued at £3500. It must be remembered that often the skipper divides the income between the crew equally, sometimes giving one portion of the income to the boat to pay for variable costs, maintenance and replacements. This of course gives an incentive for fishing solo.

A man fishing with a *nasa* will have a similar level of gross income to the mackerel fisherman. The catches fluctuate more with this type of fishing, although the diversity of fish hunted (morena, conger, shrimp, vieja, cabrilla) reduces the risk of a poor catch. This assortment of fish is usually sold directly to the restaurant with which the fisherman will have an unwritten agreement: on days when fishing with the *nasa* is not possible, mackerel may be caught by hook and line. The public can buy the remaining fish after the restaurants have had their fill but because of the lack of a fresh fish shop or obvious sales routine at the port, any fish that remain are usually sold quickly. Assuming that the average catch is worth £111 (based on calculations throughout one 12-month period) and that the fisherman has four successful days per week for 46 weeks per year, the annual gross income will be £20,424 per year. In this example the takings are divided equally between the skipper, the crew and the boat: the *nasa* fisherman needs one crew member to help him haul in the heavy traps. This is before paying for equipment, repairs, paint and other maintenance costs. These calculations are necessarily approximate but they serve to give an idea of the area of income that such a fisherman can expect.

For the crew of the *faluas*, the large tuna-fishing vessels, the lifestyle is quite different. They are not so independent, having to rely on factors such as the decision of the owner of the boat as to whether it is worthwhile for them to go fishing or whether the communication systems and transport available are capable of operating and handling their catch. Furthermore, their reliance on one purchaser who is also the owner of the boat (Ramon) limits their flexibility. And, of course, other indeterminable factors such as the behaviour of the fish and the vagaries of the world market also affect them. As an example, during the summer months Ramon had to limit the amount of bonito (small tuna) he would accept from certain boats because the factories in Spain to which he sends his catch would not accept any more for a period of time. Those first affected were the independent fishermen on the larger (11 m) boats who caught bonito and could sell a maximum of 1000 kg to Ramon three times a week. After these, the *faluas* were only able to sell up to 3000 kg to him and, on one occasion, they gave away surplus fish at the port.

The *faluas* themselves were often limited to three expeditions per week because of the lack of demand for bonito during the summer of 1991. The smaller boats were very restricted and the fishermen would talk of their frustration at not being able to work as much as they wanted. One result of this frustration, coupled with the desire to increase profits by avoiding the middleman Ramon, occurred in September 1991. A delegation of two men from Santiago, the largest fishing village on La Gomera, went to mainland Spain to try and arrange a contract directly with a bulk buyer. This is indicative of the potential and desire for change and survival amongst the fishermen.

The division of the income on the *faluas* was not easy to obtain, many fishermen saying that 40% goes directly to the boat-owner, whilst the remainder is divided equally between the crew, with the captain getting a premium. However, a reliable source gave a slightly different calculation: 25% is given over directly to the boat-owner, whilst the remainder is divided equally amongst the crew and captain: this is after the variable costs, fuel and repairs, have been deducted. The captain and engineer also get a fixed salary paid directly from the owner, giving them a secure income, albeit low, and a member of the crew may get around £11,500 in a year. Clearly there are seasonal variations: the captain of one *falua* said that February was a good month with the crew making £1660 each and the captain also receiving his monthly salary of £200. There were plenty of bonito in the sea, as well as mackerel, and if the market opens up, the fishermen would certainly be able to take advantage of it. The captain was optimistic about the forthcoming Single European Market, believing that it would increase the market possibilities for the fishermen of Vueltas (see Plate 13).

Some of the fishermen were aware of the financial rewards of their work in comparison to other manual workers: one mackerel fisherman pointed out that he could earn more in four days fishing than a labourer could earn in a month (£400). This, however, depends on having four very good catches and being able to sell all the fish; however, the point is clear: there is a potential for a good career as a fisherman, providing the market can be relied upon to absorb the catch at a reasonable price. At one time in 1991 the *furgonetas* bought the mackerel for 250 pts (£1.39)/kilo and sold it at 450 pts and above. The salesmen do not have a written contract to buy fish from the fishermen but rely on verbal agreements. An incident where the most powerful middle-man (known as 'Ramon the fish') bought 40kg of mackerel off one of the fisherman for 250 pts/kg, and sold them for just 300 pts/kg, indicates the potential for undercutting and price wars that can occur. Indeed, the fishermen often vented their frustration at the profit to be made by selling the fish when they saw the middlemen doing well; but

Plate 13 Fishing for bonito in the *falua*, with a view of Valle Gran Rey in the background. Spray is being used to deceive the fish as the men hold the bamboo rods over the water

they have not got around to organising their own vending system. Acheson (1981) points this out as a general feature of fisheries, with fishermen having little time to devote to sales. One fisherman said that he sometimes sold fish at the port in the summer when there were enough tourists to buy the fish directly: these are the Spanish *veranistas* who know the workings of the port and, being speakers of the Spanish language, can inquire easily. Nevertheless, an informally organised sales system dominates the tuna and mackerel market and sometimes the *furgonetas* throw away unsold fish in order not to flood the market, thereby maintaining the price: a waste of resources analogous to the butter mountain syndrome in the EC.

On one occasion, Ramon punished a fisherman for selling his fish directly to a restaurant: he would not purchase any more fish from the fisherman, effectively terminating his relatively secure market. The fisherman's friends tried to persuade him to apologise to Ramon, whom they believed would re-establish the trade, but the proud fisherman refused. This illustrates the power of the middlemen, who use methods learnt from the factories to enforce the fishermen's loyalty. One fisherman summed up the power of Ramon in the phrase '*Compra y manda*' (he buys and he commands). Research with informants and personal observations suggests that Ramon operates a monopoly: he has cornered the market for the sale of tuna through contracts with the factories in mainland Spain. So the smaller independent boats sell him their tuna, as there are no other bulk-buyers and he decides the quantity and price at which to buy them.

Mesa-Moreno (1982) used a Marxist model to interpret the lifestyle of the fishermen of Vueltas whom he perceived as being exploited by the factory that purchased their fish and owned their boats: this is also an appropriate model for today's fishermen employed on the *faluas*. He looked at the development of the production cycle drawing attention to the importance of the fishermen's eventual freedom through ownership of their means of production: the boat. This type of analysis serves as a useful model but is not subtle enough for an examination of the contemporary situation of the self-employed and independent fishermen, who do not sell their labour directly but are still at the mercy of economic forces and wealthy men. Whereas some fishermen are employees and may be exploited by capitalist investors, others are owners and users of their means of production and may even be working with and exploiting the labour of fellow crewmen. All these players in the economic game are now subject to global economic trends, even though there are some who, because of the small scale and versatility of their fishing, are more protected from the decisions of others. Thus the *nasa* fisherman who sells directly to a variety of customers is a self-employed man relying upon the bounty of nature and the local market. The tourist market has produced an increased demand for his products but he is not under its direct control, neither is his labour being exploited. However, the local industry that has supported fishermen and their productive assets has been affected by global market trends beyond its control and this can be seen in the closure of processing plants as well as the demise of a local boat-building business.

The smaller boats that the fishermen use were at one time made in VGR; however, the boat-builder (a member of the Ramos family) had stopped working on boats at his yard in Calera beach and was then operating a supermarket which provided him with a more reliable income. Boats are now bought in Tenerife and, in 1991, a 6 m boat cost around £5500, whilst an engine was some £3500, giving a total of £9000 for the minimum outlay that someone starting from scratch would expect to make. This is not the usual case for beginners though, as many inherit their boats, sell off others or buy them second hand. In VGR there are boats aged 40 years still operating daily, although the majority are around 20 years old. It is not unusual for boats to have been radically altered, i.e. extended in length by chopping them in half and adding a new middle whilst also raising the height. The wood for the body is usually pine, coming from North Europe, whereas the wood for the interior and work surfaces needs to be heavier and harder and may have been laurel from the island itself or, more commonly, hardwood from South America.

Normally, the fishermen make repairs on their own boats, although there is a carpenter who tends to do the big jobs such as the preparation for a new engine: he is Ramon Ramos, the grandson of the boat-builder from whom he learnt his trade. He went to college and qualified as a *Principio de Pesca* (first grade fisherman)[10] and is, therefore, one of the most highly qualified of the fishermen in VGR. However, he now works in a supermarket in Calera as the money and lifestyle suit him better. His uncle owns a small hut near the port and also possesses carpentry skills, often working on the major wooden repairs of other fishermen's boats and he occasionally lends out his equipment for the use of others. He also owns a supermarket, which his wife runs.

The fishermen of VGR have experienced an economic change akin to the one felt by those at the Catalan port examined by Pi-Sunyer (1977: 46) where tourists and summer visitors (the urban middle classes) underwrite the local economy and offer the locals alternative occupations. They have taken advantage of the new source of wealth to the extent of leaving their fishing careers in order to work in the service industry. There is no stigma attached to this in VGR, in contrast to the fishermen of Nazaré in Portugal, studied by Broegger (1990), who were reluctant to leave the sea.

> *Estando en la pesqueria, puede pasar diariamente, que aquelle mas intelligente, comete una tropesia.*
> [From here in the fishery, it seems that every day, those who have more intelligence make stupid mistakes.]

As the globalised economy impacts upon the everyday lives of the fishermen, so does the increasingly centralised but expanding power of European legislation. The previous refrain can be seen as referring to the apparently foolish decisions made by those in power and has particular relevance to the EC bureaucrats. For the fishermen there are an abundance of regulations to which they are obliged to adhere. If they are professional fishermen they must have their licences signed monthly by a marine official. More recently, they have been advised that there must be a minimum of two people per boat, a skipper and a crewman who is a qualified mechanic. Every boat should carry specific safety equipment including lifejackets, life-rings and fire extinguishers. Engines are checked for their size, as are the boats. New boats cannot be registered because of the EC's desire to limit the capacity of the fleet. If someone is found at fault, he will be penalised with a fine. Recreational fishermen are limited to selling 5 kg of fish per person per day.

These regulations rankled heavily with the fishermen and they continually complained about them, together with increasing costs and the limitations on the expansion of fishing. They are not alone in their frustration over this and one marine official in San Sebastian spoke of his anger at the 'impractical and impossible' law that he is bound to try and enforce. He said that it would be impossible for all the boats to have qualified mechanics aboard, as there are not enough to go round. It made him despair when he had to fine a man £400 for committing three minor errors on his boat and he spoke of the impossibility of policing the recreational fishermen who sell their fish, adding: 'It is better for the fishermen to go underground and sell illegally. I don't think their future is good at all, their sons don't want to fish anyway.'

As if to emphasise the problem, the government had proposed to pay fishermen for their boats, at £3500/tonne: this together with the restrictions on new purchases of boats led to one fisherman remarking that 'there is no development for fishing, we are going backwards!'. This situation produces conflict between the fishermen and authorities, with another complaining: 'We grew up here and created Vueltas, and now they demand that we pay money for our boats to remain here, even after we retire. They just want our money.' He argued with the local marine official saying he did not want to pay and insisted on berthing his boat in the location he wanted. The official, a man from the upper valley and not from a fishing background, was clearly agitated by the fishermen and their attitudes and said of them:

> They are illiterate and they think they know it all. Not like the *gente arriba* [people from the upper valley] who don't talk so much, but listen and know, like my grandfather. He's eighty years old and can read and write: he's even interested in geography – better than the *burros* [donkeys] of Vueltas.

Adding to this antipathy, the port harbour fills increasingly with the yachts of travellers and tourists. The fishermen are not allowed to carry tourists in their boats and find the abundant recreational craft a nuisance and potentially dangerous. One fisherman standing on the dockside became furious when a yacht berthed within 1 m of his fishing boat nearly hitting it and shouted at the top of his voice across the port: 'If your boat touches mine I'll kill you!'. Other nearby fishermen commented that the yachtsman was a *'marinero de agua dulce'* (freshwater sailor) and must be crazy. The fishermen have to contend with the diminishment of their profession while the leisure and tourism-oriented craft continue to develop apace.

However, one German had spent over two years in obtaining a permit to carry tourists and was offering fishing trips for tourists by the summer of

1991. By 1996 he had expanded his flotilla to four boats (one yacht, one small fibreglass boat, two 11 m fishing boats). These were used for fishing trips and sailing trips, which also involve sightseeing tours of dolphins and the coastline. He had also established a *'club de mar'* (marine club) adjoining his tackle shop. This acts as a showcase for his excursion business and a social centre for tourists in which films are shown and photographic displays of dolphins, whales and various boat trips advertise the trade and promote the cause of conservation. The tours were a great success with tourists.

More interestingly, a new pleasure boat company started operating from Vueltas in 1995 using three ex-fishermen as the crew. The boat is named *'Siron'* (siren) and is advertised as a 'Dolphin Safari' boat offering a trip to the basaltic columns on the coast, snorkelling and authentic Canary Island cooking. The captain of the crew is Paco, who was the skipper of a *falua* and one of the most knowledgeable and successful fishermen in VGR. His crewmen are also ex-professional fishermen from Vueltas. Paco said that he preferred his new job to the work on the *faluas* because it is *'mas tranquilo'* (quieter). By 1996 another boat, a luxury yacht based at Vueltas, was also offering sea trips for sightseers, and a cruiser arrived weekly from the port of San Sebastian to pick up passengers for a tour.

As for the two *faluas*, in 1995 they were both still operating, albeit with 50% new crew, mostly young men (under 30). The shift into the tourism sector by some older fishermen had opened up vacancies for youngsters who could learn the profession on the boat without being dependent on a close relative to teach them. The smaller boats were also active, although overall the fishing was considered bad in 1994 and 1995 because of a shortage of *bonito* (2 kg tuna) that had migrated beyond their reach. However, there was only one boat fishing regularly for mackerel as the market had diminished and Pedro (regarded as a mackerel expert) was devoting himself to shrimp fishing. In August 1996 the *faluas* were idle because of a lack of young mackerel with which to catch the bonito: the crew were left to their own devices to find temporary employment and some worked as painters and in supermarkets. There was, however, an abundance of pargo and many fishermen, including Pedro were concentrating on catching this fish. Pedro complained: 'Young people aren't interested in fishing, they'd rather be at the disco'. In 1994 he thought that his young sons would be unlikely to fish professionally, although by 1995 one of them was proving to be very keen and able and, by 1996, he was helping with the repairs of boats hauled up on dry dock

Pepe, another fisherman, was also sceptical about the future of fishing in Vueltas, saying:

> You can't teach the young to fish nowadays; they're always out drinking and dancing at night and they can't concentrate in the morning. To be a fisherman you must get up and fish at five in the morning; who wants to do that?

Pepe joked with a friend of his who was having problems with his boat engine, advising him: 'Sell one of your apartments and buy a new engine!' He also complained about the bars in Vueltas that create a noise until two in the morning, making it difficult for the fishermen to get a good night's sleep. These are some of the problems with which tourism presents the fishing community. Miguel, who was still fishing regularly, complained that the recreational yachtsmen were taking up the space in the harbour: 'We've been here for over 50 years, why should we have to pay for this harbour when there is no room for us.'

The fishermen are now firmly part of a global economic and bureaucratic scenario: they are small players in a big game within a transforming political economy that Palsson (1991) sees as responsible for the changing social construction of fishing. They are the first links in the chain of production and Anderson illustrates this when writing about Newfoundland fishermen: 'Weighing the marine biomass merely tells us how much we may take; not who should take it. The former is primarily a marine biological and oceanographic concern; the latter a social economic and political one' (Anderson, 1973: 64). A graphic example of the delicate ecological balance between fishers and fish occurred in Vueltas where a breeding ground for *chocca* (sepia) became over-fished in the 1980s to such an extent that, in 1991, there were none left in the area. This creature is used as bait to catch larger fish, especially pargo, and attracts them to its haunts. The lack of control over fishing means that sepia and other types of fish are less abundant or cannot be caught so easily: one fisherman travels for two hours to catch pargo. On a global scale, the depletion of cod, haddock and herring in the North Atlantic Ocean and the North Sea has led the EU conservation policy to reduce the community's fishing fleet, which is affecting the Canary Islands directly. The *artisanal* fishermen of Vueltas now find themselves part and parcel of a vast community: in terms of world-system theory we can see the metropolitan and industrialised cores directly impacting on the peripheral fishing communities by way of market influence and legal restrictions.[11]

By 2002, there were 53 professional fishermen of which only about 20 were full-time – others survived on incomes from rent or different work such as construction. The two *faluas* were still in operation together with 22 other boats; however, the fishing was said to be poor. Some fishermen believe their grandchildren will see the end of the industry. In contrast, the dolphin tour business was burgeoning, with two daily tours by four boats run by the German (small boats) and two large boats (capacity up to 50) taking people on one cruise a day (six days/week). It may be the case that recreational boats in Vueltas are already producing more annual financial turnover than the professional fishing industry – a major watershed for the community.[12]

This section has given an idea of the types of occupations and, hence, lifestyles that there are in Vueltas. Its original character as a fishing settlement has by no means disappeared despite tremendous development since the late 1970s with a growth in job opportunities and diversification of potential employment. The service industry, including restaurants, bars and retail outlets, is the largest employer in Vueltas nowadays, eclipsing the traditional occupations of fishing and agriculture, so that the village exhibits a diversity of characteristics, physical and social, which have overshadowed its older fishing-based form. Yet the fishermen's lifestyle still remains a powerful influence in the community (see also Macleod, 2002).

Changing Attitudes Towards Work and Property

Gender and the division of labour

In Vueltas there are certain jobs that are done exclusively by men – work on the fishing boats, carpentry, construction, painting, mechanical work, taxi- and coach-driving – whereas only women work as apartment cleaners and nannies. In other areas there is a mix: although agriculture is predominantly a male domain, some women do work on the plantations and in the fields; and both sexes work in the service outlets. The gendered division of labour in the workplace, in many respects, mirrors the divisions within the household. It has been associated with group identity and boundaries by Goddard, who argues that men in Naples dislike women working outside their social sphere with people who are 'unlikely to share their system of values, in other words, a "foreigner"' (Goddard, 1987: 185). There seem to be similar sentiments attached to women in Vueltas, with men discouraging them from moving outside locally perceived boundaries. Waged labour on plantations and in factories had been an accepted means of income for women due to economic pressures but family-based employment is the favoured means for women. Therefore, work traditionally associated with women, including cleaning, cooking and childcare, can be undertaken as a means of employment without criticism. In this manner, the preparation of rooms and dealing with visitors and guests has developed into the renting out of rooms to unknown tourists. Women often have most contact with tourists and their work within the household has consequently increased (see also Bouquet [1987]).

This development is one that is altering the economic structure of the community in Vueltas and the relative balance between the sexes in their potential to earn money for their families and for independent survival. With the decline in the male-dominated industries of agriculture and fishing has come the rise in labour-intensive service-related industries linked to tourism, which employ proportionately more women. Bouquet drew attention to the division of labour by gender in an examination of the partition of status on a Devon farm. Women were associated with the house and she noted the important developments associated with having paying guests in the house: 'The domestic labour of the wife assumes a professional dimension within the same universe in which it is otherwise classified as housework, on behalf of the family' (Bouquet 1986: 34). She states that women are able to use the new outsider as a means of 'internal leverage', i.e. as a means of changing the balance of power. Other writers, including Broegger (1990) and Chapman (1986), have noticed the tendency for women to deal with tourists, giving them opportunities to make money and the chance to become independent – these patterns may be witnessed in Vueltas.

Tourism and new work

We consider that a 'culture' has not disappeared because of tourism but that many lifestyles have changed, with some modes of livelihood becoming either marginalised or no longer economically viable. The complexity of changes, as evinced by historical examples, indicates that the process of transformation is a fundamental feature of the society that we are examining. Tourism is not so much an external force, changing all in its path, as an opportunity for appropriating capital and ideas, which the hosts have utilised for a variety of reasons. Regarding tourism, to date local people have been the main agents of change in Vueltas, not the tourists nor external businessmen. It is the local people who make decisions regarding the building and operation of apartments and shops, they have often governed the intimacy of relationships with tourists and they are ultimately responsible for infrastructural work, initiated by the local council. Inevitably, there are serious differences of opinion, as will be seen in the conflict over the beach development proposal discussed later and political interests regarding large-scale development could be gaining the upper hand.

Amongst the transformations occurring, changes in the job market are very prominent and there is much part-time and uncontracted employment in Vueltas, especially within the construction and service sectors. Thus, someone may have two jobs at the same time or claim unemployment benefit whilst working. In 1991 employers often preferred to employ unofficial workers because it released them from the obligation to pay social security, which may account for 30% of staff costs. For example, a restauranteur who opened a restaurant in VGR claimed he paid £277 per month rent for his premises, which is cheap by local standards. He must also pay for kitchen equipment, as well as electricity, gas, water, refuse collection and tax. There are other variable costs, including consumable items, and, furthermore, he must pay his staff wages, each of whom as full-time employees with contracts also require the payment of social security. As a foreigner he was given more leeway to work in VGR if he agreed to employ a local person, which he did. He said that he barely makes £100 for himself at the end of the week. These financial pressures lead employers to take on part-time uncontracted labour (often relatives), thereby avoiding the need to pay the minimum wage and social security. When people want to cut costs, it is usually the staff that are hit first with wage cuts or a loss of the job. In fact, it is the norm for most traders in VGR to use close relatives; the work arrangements are informal and flexible and the income is retained within the family.[13]

The types of employment outlined earlier are the more conventional areas for the indigenous people of Vueltas: there are also more unusual means of obtaining income in the valley and the types of work done by some of the foreign settlers are listed here:

- artists and craftsmen – making and selling postcards, paintings, earrings, clothes, jewelry, sculpture, T-shirts, drums and so on,
- therapists – offering massage, dance classes, astrology and meditation,
- photographers – selling postcards, literature and giving slide shows,
- snack food sales – homemade and sold on the beach to tourists,
- laundry – clothes or linen from restaurants,
- tradesmen and professionals – including plumbers, builders, architects and teachers,
- clandestine work – the selling of drugs to tourists and locals and
- operating excursions – sailing, fishing, dolphin tours and mountain bike trips for the tourists.

These are some of the ways that foreign settlers have found to make money: they are almost all reliant upon the tourists for their custom. There are a number of businesses that German settlers have started up which are unusual and point to an important element differentiating the Germans from the local people: their cultural capital advantage. These businesses include a postcard shop, a mountain-bike and sports shop, and a 'bait-and-tackle' shop that acts as a boat-trip centre. None of these businesses is outstandingly original in themselves but they are new for VGR. They indicate the entrepreneurial spirit of their owners, people who come from a different background with experience and knowledge of the tourist business and the desires of North Europeans and who promote models that some local people may emulate.[14] This is a tangible example of the transference of ideas due to work-related travel and tourism by German settlers from the core European regions to people whose business experience has been that of a rural peripheral region. In VGR, such new and relatively unusual methods of making money open local people's eyes to more possibilities. They are given a greater choice, although they may be reluctant to take on unusual options because of a lack of money, social pressure, the constraints of the system, personal disinclination or the high element of risk.

Business attitudes and new opportunities

In general, local people do not like to take risks with their money, although the younger generation are more carefree, to the chagrin of their elders. To build and operate apartments was a big enough jump for many. When asked why her husband and father did not start taking out tourists in their boat, the wife of a fisherman answered: 'It would be too risky, and anyway, the boat belongs to the family. We want to keep it for fishing, it wouldn't be right to take out tourists.' This illustrates an attitude towards property that equates it with more than just economic value: there is an emotional, familial link to the boat, similar to that felt for the land. The fisherman's wife agreed that this value applied to boats, they become family heirlooms in a way: many of the fishermen's boats were inherited and they have a pride in them together with a strong attachment because of their heritage. This concept is an important factor in the socioeconomic world of many local inhabitants and contrasts with the calculating rationality of the capitalist business world. Nevertheless, it is apparent that many of the German settlers intended to invest more than financial capital into their work and they often derived greater personal satisfaction out of their activity than the pecuniary benefits afforded. In this way they matched the sentiments of many local people who did not always pursue financial profit as the ultimate goal.

As an example of the desire for a quality oriented lifestyle, in 1991 the German owner of the tourist fishing boat said he was 'more concerned with enjoying life than with making money'. He had invested time in making the fishing expeditions and his products ones of quality. He had pride in his work, and enjoyed it, seeking personal fulfilment by his own standards. He had recently started to take tourists for trips and he told me that business was good and that he needed a helper. This entrepreneur was a real agent of change in Vueltas, starting up a business offering fishing excursions to tourists that eventually turned into a dolphin tour concern, a trade that has arguably become the major earner from the sea. He initiated a trend that will change the lives of the children of the fishermen. He said: 'It is too difficult for locals to obtain a licence to pilot the fishing boat with tourists, and anyway, they'd rather fish for themselves'. As a consequence, he had to get another German to work with him (their licence is recognised in Spain). The use of Germans in the tourist services is common as they can communicate easily with most tourists, their fellow nationals, which few Gomeros are able to do. This leads to some disquiet amongst locals who believe they are losing employment opportunities in their own village.

The people of VGR have learnt how to adapt over the years, often in the hardest of circumstances, and one of the ways in which they survive and learn is to copy others who are successful: such is the manner in which the apartment boom came about. Older men have watched their fathers or friends perform tasks and learnt from them, for example construction workers, carpenters, fishermen and mechanics. This applies to the family-based businesses with skills passed from father to son or mother to daughter, kinship being intimately tied to trade. Historically, the father largely determined which form of livelihood his son would pursue, providing an informal apprenticeship for him. In 1991 many of the older men (50+) in VGR were illiterate and could only learn through watching and helping, thereby acquiring skills through trial and error. Copying can also be more clandestine. A local woman bought an apple sponge from a restaurant run by foreigners in order to try and cook an equivalent one: unfortunately she was unable to reproduce it properly but nevertheless created something which later appeared for sale in a local shop as a form of apple tart. The original cook, a Welsh woman, said: 'Now I wouldn't even tell my assistant waitress my recipes for fear of losing my originality and clientele'.

There has been a history of outsiders coming to the valley with new business ideas since the colonisation, a history that includes the plantation owners and the fish-processing entrepreneurs. There is now a new flow of tourism-based ideas, starting with the apartment business and spreading out into catering, specialist shops, discotheques, excursions, arts and crafts and other services.

> *Entre mas gallinas en el gallinero, mas mierda y menos huevos.*
> [With more chickens in the pen there is more shit and fewer eggs.]

This refrain pithily sums up the problems of an over-crowded market. One of the businesses which developed rapidly due to the local people's willingness to copy successful neighbours was the apartment business. There are only a few times in the year when the apartments in Vueltas are all full: one is the Christmas and New Year period, the other is Easter week; together they form the peak periods of the high season. For the rest of the year, the apartments vary between almost empty to three-quarters full, according to the season. For the current demand, the supply is more than adequate. With the addition of the large apartments owned by the consortiums on the outskirts of Vueltas and at the Calera beach, competition has been introduced. The local people realise that the competition has reached such a level that they are not making the profit on their rooms that they did in the past. One fisherman who owns 16 apartments said that they were profitable during the 1980s; however, in 1991 there were not enough customers to give adequate returns.[15]

It is possible that people have overstretched themselves in the race to profit from tourism, taking out loans without considering the interest payments or building apartments that cannot be maintained. At least one victim has been claimed through high interest payments and others are currently saddled with huge debts. This type of outcome serves to reaffirm the local people's wary attitude towards business ventures. They have a resistance towards risking their hard-won savings or income, often because they might have had to risk their lives and physical health in order to earn that money. They are not used to considering their savings as capital with investment potential but see it as insurance against future hardships.

The desire to survive in a competitive economic environment leads to the guarding of knowledge, as seen with some fishing activities, and to personal secrecy over skills and know-how. There is an element of protectionism amongst the local population or, at least, amongst those able to empower it, thereby defending their interests from outside competition. As a consequence, an outsider wishing to set up a business that competes directly with the locals will find it much more difficult to get a permit from the local authority than someone who is not perceived as a threat: thus, restauranteurs have difficulties, whilst postcard shop owners do not. One Austrian man who sold cakes and drink outside a restaurant overlooking the beach was warned and later denounced by the owner and forced to leave the island due to his lack of a work permit. Taxi-drivers protected their interests by hindering the business of a ferry operating between San Sebastian and Vueltas, they also hassle private drivers who offer lifts to others near the rank. The most efficient form of protecting local interests is by denying other potential competitors an operating licence, which the local council is able to do.

> *Tanto va el ratón al molino, hasta que pierde el rabo en el camino.*
> [The rat will go to the mill, until he loses his tail in the road.]

It is difficult to open a restaurant in VGR as the competition is strong and the local council does not like distributing licences. One foreigner had to wait for over a year to open his and then he found it necessary to go over the head of the local council. Not only have the apartments begun to feel the cold wind of competition but so have the restaurants: one in VGR closed down in 1991 due to an inability to pay the rent. Among the deciding factors of success with such businesses is whether the operators own or rent the property: owners who have few overheads on the buildings are able to shut down for quiet periods of the year for whatever reason. One local man did so in order to concentrate on building his own house and to play in a salsa music group: with no rent to pay on his property he could do so without that financial worry. Someone else who rents a building must find at least £300 per month.

Property

Another feature of the boom in tourism and foreign settlement is the rise in demand for land and buildings. In 1946 in Vueltas a square metre (m^2) of land could be bought for 4 pesetas (2 pence), the same price as in 1922, as these were the prices paid for the land on which the Barroso apartments were built. By 1991 land in Vueltas sold at 50,000 pesetas (£278) /m^2: in terms of a day's pay, six times as much. This gross increase in value is a common phenomenon in tourist resorts as both Olwig (1985) and Crick (1989) show.

A German estate agent, established in the Playa Calera for one year, announced that land at the beach was being sold in 1991 for £334/m^2. A one-bedroom apartment with kitchen, dining-room and bathroom could be bought for £39,000 (45 m^2) or £44,500 (60 m^2). The agent said that there were currently only a couple of plots available for development in VGR in 1991 explaining as follows: 'The local families like to hang onto their land for their own kin'. This is generally true, although some locals admitted that they prefer not to go through the agent because of high commission and they also prefer to sell property to a friend or relative. Broegger who assessed attitudes towards land amongst the Portuguese fishing community, concluded that 'the Nazarenos are not conscious of a perfect real estate market in which the price of housing is the outcome of supply and demand independent of human emotion and considerations' (Broegger, 1990: 84). Similarly, Mckay (1987) emphasises 'belonging to the land' as the major factor to account for the importance of property for Jamaicans. These assessments are certainly relevant to the people of VGR, who have not used a formal property market until very recently but passed land and buildings down through generations: there is definitely a desire to retain family land. The reasons for doing this are manifold, wrapped up in tradition and experiences, and there are certainly notions of security and identity involved. In Vueltas almost all of the houses were inhabited by close relatives of the original owners: they were not numbered but referred to by the Christian name of the occupier, depending on whom the enquirer consults.

El muerto al hoyo, y el vivo al bayó
[The corpse is in the hole and the living get the bread roll.]

The inheritance laws decree that the estate is to be divided equally amongst the beneficiaries. It is quite common for a house to be physically divided between inheriting adult children, each one then extending their share of the partitioned building to cater for their own immediate family. Inheritance regulations occasionally leave many owners to one plot of land, or home: all must sign the deeds for a sale to be legally enforceable. This leads to complications in the sale of property, as many signatories may be living abroad. One advantage that a foreigner gains by purchasing through an experienced agent is the avoidance of potential difficulties with ownership.

Some people prefer to buy a plot of land and build their own home. Costs involved in building a house include purchase of land, permission to build, planning and construction. In 1996 one young local couple estimated that it had cost them £61,000 to build their own three-bedroom house using cheap labour. When purchasing an old house, expenses include legal costs and local tax: both proportionate to the value of the house. There is also an additional premium on the increased value of the property over the period of ownership. Stories abound of the dramatic leap in land and building prices in VGR. The fact is that prices have leapt in the tourist zones and may eventually rival those on other islands where the average price is said to be £800/m^2. One feature of VGR in the early 1990s was the lack of registration of many properties allowing the buyer and seller to come to a private agreement on the sale and registration of the property at an undervaluation. This was a means of avoiding taxation and also transferring large sums of money in the form of cash. With the implementation of EU law and the effective removal of trading barriers in 1993, it was expected that property transfer regulations, amongst other things, would be enforced more strictly.

By 2002 the price of a one-bedroom flat in Calera had risen from £39,000 (1991) to £70,000. First-time buyers from VGR are having difficulties buying suitable properties because of the cost and their small size (inadequate for families). New residential apartments are being built in Vueltas and an estate agent has opened a website. Properties are now marketed commercially to a global audience rather than being passed on through inheritance or by word of mouth within the local community as happened in previous decades.

Dramatic price changes and the changing attitude towards property give a highly visible example of changes that are taking place in the region. They form a barometer of transformation. Overall there have been massive changes in employment opportunities, expectations and earning potential, together with the spread of wealth across classes, ages and gender: these have served to reduce previous differences within the local population. Tourism has resulted in an overall increase in the wealth and a more equitable sharing of that wealth. It has introduced foreign visitors and migrants, transforming the economy from one based on the primary industries of fishing and agriculture to a service economy, challenging traditional attitudes towards work patterns and property ownership and introducing many new opportunities. Nevertheless, there remain inequalities, exploitation and powerful groups of people determined to pursue their own interests. The following chapter looks at how issues of power and conflict have been influenced by tourism, in particular relating to resource allocation and how this has led to the direct involvement of political parties and local government.

Notes

1. See Hitchcock *et al.* (1993), Theobald (1998), Cooper *et al.* (1999), Faulkner *et al.* (2000).
2. 'The most obvious and immediate benefit of tourism is the creation of jobs and the opportunity for people to increase their income and standard of living. Employment generated directly in the tourism sector, in hotels and restaurants, is generally shown to yield earnings at least as high as, and often higher than, those available in other sectors, especially agriculture. Tourism also has secondary spillover effects in other sectors. Through increased demand for food products, souvenirs, and other goods, it generates employment in agriculture, food processing, handicrafts, and light manufacturing. Jobs also will be created in construction and capital goods industries when new hotels and resort complexes are built. Special problems may arise, however, when construction booms end and unemployment results.' (de Kadt, 1979: 11)
3. Some of these influences have been examined by other anthropologists studying Spain including Waldren (1996), Barrett (1974), Aceves (1971), Brandes (1975), Douglass (1976) and Cronin (1970).
4. In her work on the Ama, the female 'pearl divers' of Japan, Martinez (1988: 219) noted that tourism gives employment in various areas. She also pointed out the difficulty of ensuring the continuation of such tourism: this is the real economic problem that VGR is now facing in this period of its history.
5. In a paper on 'indigenous tourism', Byrne Swain has written about the role opportunities which tourism has generated for the Kuna indians of Panama: 'Local tourism can offer roles different from those open in the national economy. Role choices generated by Kuna tourism are now available through self-employment, private business, and cooperative ventures, including a women's sewing cooperative [*productures de Molas*], hotel services employ-

ment, and the Kuna Yala Wildlands Investigation Project (PEMASKY) (Byrne Swain, 1989: 83).

6. Broegger (1990: 20) also notes that it is the women that deal with the tourists in his study of fisherfolk in Portugal.

7. Crick gives a quotation from a declaration by the Tanzanian youth league: 'Investment in tourism is a lopsided one, it serves a sector that is hardly related to the economic structure of the country. It is above all a risky and temporary industry whose viability and continuity depend on the goodwill of the tourist generating countries' (Crick, 1989: 322).

8. The findings of Sinclair and Bote Gomez (1996) support this and they agree that multiplier values tend to be higher for the cheaper categories of accommodation. This is based on a survey in Malaga, Spain, into short-run and long-run GDP multiplier values for expenditure on different types of accommodation and on food, drink and entertainment.

9. These figures (and others relating to catch statistics) represent averages of statistical information recorded on a daily basis for two weeks in 1991, and thereafter on some weekdays throughout the year. The mean weight and price are used in order to reach the gross income figure that represents a guideline.

10. Fishermen say that the official grades of fishermen are: *Patron Literal* (small boat skipper), *Segunda de Pesca* (second grade fisherman), *Principio de Pesca* (first grade fisherman), *Capitano* (captain).

11. A. Davis writes about the consequences of the world market: 'Institutionalisation and professionalisation compel players to adopt the world-views, the rationalities and behaviours of the dominant institutions that control access to livelihoods. In short they compel compliance' (Davis, 1991: 8).

12. An estimate of the tour boats and dolphin expeditions annual gross takings based on 2002 figures gives 635,000 euros; this is marginally more than the gross takings for the fishermen, estimated at 630,000 euros (£420,000). These are calculated as follows: big tour boats, 11 trips/week at 50 weeks/year at 30 people per trip at 30 euros = 495,000. Plus the dolphin trip takings of 4 trips/day at 7 days at 50 weeks at 5 people/trip at 20 euros = 140,000. For the fishing industry, gross takings assuming 20 full-time fishermen experiencing good catches throughout the year, based on 1991 figures of average £21,000 20 = £420,000 1.5 for euro = 630,000 euros but not taking inflation into account to balance optimism. Exchange rate of 1.5 euro = £1 Pound Sterling.

13. In 1991 one of the problems regarding social security was that people found it hard to get full-time jobs in the area and even harder to get contracts arranged. For example, one presentable young woman who speaks fluent English took 18 months to secure work in VGR, even though she had worked in Tenerife for two years and was experienced in the service industry. Having secured a job in 1991, her employers put her on trial for at least 6 months before agreeing to offer her a contract: she has some security as a person can only receive unemployment benefit if she has worked a minimum of 6 months. The benefit is paid for approximately half the period of full employment up to a maximum of 24 months, after which the unemployed person may receive another type of social security according to assessment. Local people believed that the benefit amounted to £305/month, whereas social security payments are often about half the amount of the unemployment benefit. According to a government pamphlet (Ministry of Work and Social Security, 1990), benefit for the first 180 days will be 80% of the basic minimum pay. The difficulty for many young

people in VGR is finding a job with a contract of a minimum of 6 months that will ensure them some security if they lose it. There was consequently a large pool of floating casual labour: men and women who operated within the service and construction industries, making ends meet, some of whom supplement their income by selling drugs.

14. Kenna (1988) draws attention to the fact that most of the new businesses dealing with tourists on a Greek island are operated by 'migrants' with experience of urban Greece, as does Mckay (1987) in relation to Jamaican returnees

15. The prices for apartment rooms vary according to type and season. An average price for a two-bedroom self-catering unit would be £10/night in 1991. Costs to be covered by this include an annual license of £67, power and running water, sanitation and garbage collection. On top of these, there are repairs and renewals, daily maintenance and cleaning to be considered. And finally, gross takings are subject to taxation of at least 5%. Consequently, there is a real need to compete for custom in an increasingly tough market.

Chapter 5
Power and Conflict

Introduction

Conflict enters almost all areas of human social activity, especially where resources are involved. The previous chapter dealing with work and property highlighted growing competition between members of the local population where potential customers for apartments and other services were concerned. This chapter concentrates on the competition and conflict over physical resources and its relationship to formalised political structures and the social networks of informal arrangements that create and support systems of power. Such conflicts over resources may be accentuated on islands:

> In small countries, especially islands, even modest tourist developments may place considerable pressure on physical resources and the environment, with immediate and dramatic consequences for the welfare of the inhabitants. (de Kadt, 1979: 16)

Hall (1994: 3) gives a broad overview of power, directing attention to the importance of values:

> Decisions affecting tourism policy, the nature of government involvement in tourism, the structure of tourist organisations, and the nature of tourism development emerge from a political process. This process involves the values of actors (individuals, interest groups and public and private organisations) in a struggle for power.

Similarly, when considering the basis for conflict, Barke (1999: 251) writes that 'cultural norms and beliefs underlie attitudes to most phenomena, including the environment, land and resources'. We will see that such norms and beliefs are apparent (and diverse) within the indigenous community as well as being more generally manifest in differences between the indigenous community and others such as visiting tourists or political groupings like the EU. Robinson (1999: 9) has considered the opportunities for cultural conflict that exist within the tourism framework when members of different cultures interact and he suggests that there is a 'mesh of variables' that represent '[d]egrees of distance between the value systems, social class, attitudes, and patterns of behaviour which tourism individuals and groups possess, and those held by the host community; all points of potential misunderstanding and conflict'. This is, of course, true but it is also worth bearing in mind that the host community is not a homogeneous unit of like-minded, politically similar people but a collection of individuals with differing interests whose affiliations may vary, intersect or clash on numerous planes. The examples that follow detail the complexity and diversity of the local population (small as it is) as it deals with issues of resources and values, often stimulated by tourism developments, and struggles to achieve a variety of goals.

The chapter opens with a look at the impact of the EU on Vueltas as a way of emphasising the community's involvement in the broader European political network. It then narrows its attention to the local party-political situation and the council, relating this to personalities and eventually to the issue of patronage. Throughout this exploration, the diversity of opinions and objectives becomes clear and the final section focusing on the protest over a proposed beach development brings these conflicts of interest to a peak.

Global Events: The European Union and its Impact on Vueltas

There have been many areas of economic life in VGR that circumvent officialdom, where people deal face to face with each other without the intervention of state apparatus in the form of taxation or legal requisites: these areas include illegal employment and unofficial deals. In some cases people avoid legal requirements and carry on as they have done before bureaucratic procedures altered matters.[1] With the creation of the Single European Market in 1992, there have been changes within the Canary Islands and VGR and (in theory) bureaucratic regulations have become enforced. Access to jobs is easier for foreign nationals and competition is stronger: those with linguistic skills and qualifications having an edge over others. As a consequence, we can assume that local people lose out in such fields as the service industry and professional work where knowledge of foreign languages and qualifications are an advantage.[2] In 1991, a receptionist admitted: 'The village is just not prepared for tourism or the future developments in Europe. There are no central facilities or information centres for tourists.'

Some fishermen believed that the open market would give them better opportunities to sell their fish, therefore increasing work for them, whereas other types of product, such as bananas, which already face stiff competition from the Americas, could lose out. Nobody was sure about what would happen to the banana plantations;[3] however, by 2002 they were still being exported to the European mainland (by the 'Copalaca Eurobanan' organisation). The Canary Islands were given money and advice from the EU on, for example, agriculture: a delegation of experts visited some islands on the 3 September 1991 to examine the potential for developing such cash-productive crops as oilseed, grain, sugar and tobacco.

In a book outlining the implications of a Europe without frontiers, Owen and Dynes (1989) drew attention to the pooling and sharing of resources in the community, which La Gomera is now experiencing. The EU has helped to invest in La Gomera at least £30 million for the scheme Programma Operativa Integrado de la Isla de la Gomera (POI). This was intended to 'develop' the island and integrate it into the rest of the Canary Island community: areas of investment include an airport and the road construction to which VGR has been subjected through Fundos España Desarrollo Europa Restructura (FEDER) funds. In its policy on specific regions and its intention to smooth out disparities in wealth, the EU is keen to promote tourism as a means of improving a poor region's financial position. However, whilst the money from the EU creates employment through work on construction projects, the businesses given the building contracts are the real winners and, due to the scale of ventures such as airport construction, specialist workers are imported. Finally, the entire scheme invites a new type of tourist, those on charter trips with package deals, who can change the whole character of a place favoring big business to the detriment of local landlords and shopkeepers.

One aspect of economic life that is expanding with the increasing influence of the EU is the bureaucracy related to such things as trading standards and fishing regulations. Currently the regulations for marine activity are suffused with directives from the EU and these directives are often impossible to implement to the full in everyday life. We noted how frustrating and unrealistic the regulations were for the fishermen and those charged with overseeing them. The following extract from a report on the Common Fisheries Policy is an example of current movements within the EU to control fishing:

> The Economic and Social Committee stressed the need to conserve fishery resources and proposed that regulatory measures should, along with TAC, and Quotas, include criteria such as the duration and number of fishing days, the number, size and engine power of vessels, and the characteristics of fishing gear, though excessive regulation could prove detrimental to safety on board fishing vessels. (Bulletin 5: 1992)

The fishermen have become very frustrated with bureaucratic rules; they feel that the government is against them when legislation prohibits the expansion of the fishing fleet. They are restricted from purchasing new and larger boats by the EU Common Fisheries Policy, which seeks to limit the number of fishing boats within the Community, partly due to conservation reasons. One fisherman said that he wanted to purchase a larger fibreglass boat but was restricted from doing so by the Marina, the enforcers of marine law. Another pointed out how he was refused an annual fishing permit because he sent in a badly taken photograph of his boat in which his camera had clipped off the two ends, the bow and the stern. Many feel angry because they are charged berthing fees by the authorities for anchoring their boats in their own harbour.

A study by Byron (1986) of a fishing community in the Shetlands undergoing change in the 1970s, due to oil-related development, found many trends comparable to the ones now causing concern in VGR. These were a proliferation of bureaucratic rules, EU policies on stock conservation, the restriction of fleet capacities and a general apprehension about the future. Such an apprehension is present among the fishermen of VGR and furthermore, they resent the gradual development of the harbour into a recreational zone with its consequent restrictions on space for mooring and manoeuvering their vessels as well as charges for berthing. The broad European economic and political transformations impact on the lives of everyone in VGR: as an example the reduction of resources – in terms of the European fish stock – has led the powerful core in Europe to implement blanket measures that cover the periphery, thereby limiting their ability to catch fish. Political power, from its pan-national to regional council manifestations, can be seen to govern the allocation of resources and have immediate consequences for the people of Vueltas. The next section examines this relationship in detail.

Local Politics

Formal structure

The Canary Islands are an 'Autonomous Region' within Spain, subject to Spanish Central Government decisions on certain matters including military activity and international relations. The islands themselves are divided into two provinces: West (Tenerife, Hierro, La Palma, La Gomera) and East (Gran Canaria, Lanzarote, and Fuerteventura), which are controlled by one Canary Islands Government that alternates between the capitals of the two Provinces, Santa Cruz (Tenerife), and La Palma (Gran Canaria). Each island has one central council, *Cabildo*, and local councils, *Ayuntamientos*, in the municipalities. VGR is a municipality and the

Ayuntamiento is seated in Calera. It is made up of the executive in the form of the mayor and his ten councillors, the judiciary, a justice of the peace and the administrative staff, as well as numerous council workers including two local policemen and garbage collectors.

The council and mayor are elected every four years by open elections for those on the electoral roll in the relevant municipality. During the elections, not only are local councillors voted for but also Cabildo members and parliamentary candidates, Diputados. The posts are not mutually exclusive: for example, in 1991 the current mayor of VGR was also a member of the Canary Islands Parliament.

According to Article 25 of law 7/85 (2/4/85), in order to manage its affairs and in the interests of its obligations, the local council is able to promote all classes of activities and hire public services which will help to satisfy the necessities and aspirations of the community. Other 'activities' of the mayor, according to Article 41 of the Royal Decree 2568/ 86 (28/11/ 85), determine that the mayor presides over the corporation, and also includes the following powers:

- control over the local police, who may be armed at his request;
- concession of 'licenses to operate' for factories and commercial enterprises and any other nature of business;
- concession of license to general works, except those ordered by the Government commission; and
- the signing of deeds, documents and official papers.

The mayor holds a very important and powerful position in the municipality, specifically in his capacity to influence and empower the allocation of work and his ability to grant or refuse permission for businesses to operate.

The elections

Three of the national parties were represented at the elections that took place on Sunday 26 May 1991. These were: the CDS (*Centro Democratico y Social*) in coalition with the AGI (*Agrupación Gomera Insular*), the PSOE (*Partido Socialista Obrero Español*) and the PP (*Partido Popular*). The major parties reflect the national parties in their manifestos for the Islands Parliament and may be broadly categorised as follows: CDS, a liberal democrat party: PSOE, a socialist party; and PP, a right-wing, conservative party. Each party had supplied a candidate for mayor with ten potential local councillors supporting him. The parties also supplied a candidate for the Cabildo, and a candidate for the Central Islands Parliament. The voters, therefore, had to make three separate choices.

The seats on the local council are allocated according to the proportion of votes that their party gains. In 1991 the voting gave the CDS–AGI the mayor's seat and seven councillors and the PSOE three councillors.[4] This was the fourth time in succession that the CDS, or Centrists as they are popularly known, had won the election, with the same mayor each time. The composition of the various party candidates for the local council seats was as follows:

CDS – 14 men, including four teachers, a council worker, a construction manager, a maintenance man and an agricultural worker;
PSOE – 12 men, two women, including three teachers, an ex-fisherman, a bricklayer, a shopkeeper, an agricultural worker and a lorry driver; and
PP – 11 men, three women, including a medical assistant, a hotel reception-ist, a painter, a bar manager, a shop assistant, a school cook, a student and an unemployed youth.

The candidates came from all walks of life, although women were not well represented. The prospective mayors were all educated men: two teachers and a medical assistant.

Before the day of the election, there was a month of activity involving the various parties canvassing for votes. Each party held a meeting in the upper part of the Valley and also in the lower part, in the school grounds. Vans and cars circulated the district with loudspeakers exhorting the elec-torate to vote for their candidate, the taped speeches being punctuated by musical jingles. Dinners and fiestas were held for the party faithful: men and women in their best clothes set off dutifully for the meetings. The village, indeed the entire island, was in a state of excitement over the forth-coming elections and, in Vueltas, politics became a popular topic of conversation for weeks. In many cases, it was obvious who would vote for which party and old political enemies studiedly ignored each other. Many local people bemoaned how seriously the villagers took party politics and felt that this was an unfortunate but nevertheless important part of life.

The two main parties in the local battle, the CDS (Liberal Democrats) and the PSOE (Socialists), each issued literature that gave a clear picture of their interests and perception of important issues (support for the PP was almost non-existent). The CDS produced a small pamphlet with photo-graphs of its two candidates, with the interior containing a list of construction projects, headed by the phrase, 'Done in the past four years to guarantee the future'. The list included the following: the Cultural Centre, the access road to VGR, the plaza at Arure, asphalting at a church in Tagaluche and streets in Vueltas: in total there were more than 60 examples of construction. There were no other words on the leaflet. Such citations served to prove the party's ability to function, to access resources, to provide labour and to move towards the future with material modernisation. In contrast, the PSOE issued an equivalently small leaflet with a photograph of the candidate for mayor. Inside a series of paragraphs were headlined: Agriculture, Herding and Fishing; Education, Culture and Sport; Health; Transport and communications; Tourism and Leisure Time; Urbanisation and the Environment; Social Politics and Living; Municipal Management. The PSOE use the red rose as a symbol (as does the UK Labour party) and headed their pamphlet, 'Vote PSOE, a decision for progress'. In another pamphlet, photocopied for the occasion, the PSOE criticised the CDS propaganda saying that the list of construction projects could not be credited directly to the local council and that many were attributable to the Central Government, Cabildo, EU and other such bodies.

The 1991 elections throughout La Gomera produced results solidly supporting the PSOE party in every municipality except VGR, giving them five wins out of six, highlighting the political uniqueness of VGR. One of the reasons for the continual success of the CDS in VGR lies in the economic influence of the local council, especially through job creation due to construction financed by the central government and the EU. If the council can provide jobs, local people will support them. They are also unlikely to cross the council if they know that it may lead to them suffering economically as a consequence. Examples follow relating to the powers of the local council to affect people's livelihoods directly, in particular the patronage that operates within the community, translating the statutory authority into local power relationships between individuals. Another reason for the continuing success of the CDS is due to the mayor (Bethencourt) who has represented the party at all the elections. The same party, with the same leader, remains in power at the time of writing (July 2002). By studying the men leading the parties, we can see these actors in their political roles pursuing goals that unite the network of party followers.

Personalities in politics

An ex-councillor aged 26 declared: 'Here in VGR the election is very much about personalities, it is really about the candidate for mayor'. By 1991 the CDS candidate, Esteben Bethencourt, was well known as an experienced politician and a member of the Canary Islands Government. He is someone who has influence, proven by his ability to bring money into the valley. Many of the construction projects in VGR, such as road building and improvements, were undertaken using money from the EC 'structural funds' (FEDER) which his council had presumably obtained. This construction work meant jobs for the men and money for families, as well as convincing people that VGR would be prepared for more tourism, benefiting from the improved communications infrastructure. Bethencourt began life in poverty in VGR and fished with relatives, his father having died when he was young. He managed to qualify as a teacher and is well known to the people. As such he is a 'son of the village' (*hijo del pueblo*), a fact of which he proudly boasted during political gatherings, pointing out that the other two candidates are not so loyal or local. He also has the support of family and friends in the municipality. Bethencourt is in favour of developing VGR into a bigger resort and actively promotes construction projects.

Clearly the position of mayor confers a lot of power on a person and this can be used to help people get work and open businesses: in short, it can give immense influence to one individual and his close friends. Certain municipal employees were friends or relatives of the mayor: other men who were of a different political persuasion eventually changed their views because business was to come their way through council projects. In some instances, these men would persuade their parents and friends to change voting patterns of a lifetime. It is pertinent to note that people tend to vote as their parents do in VGR: economic pressures have persuaded some to change their party allegiance.

The leading candidate for the PSOE, Jaime Casanova, was also born in the municipality but was based in Tenerife. His family is regarded as *cacique*, local landowners and businessmen who wield power: this factor was believed to go against him, as many socialist voters had an instinctive distrust of such families. Casanova, in his campaigning speeches, broached the *cacique* issue, saying that he had the freedom to choose his own political party and his family background should not detract from his political beliefs. He also brought up the issue of tourism, saying that the environment must be protected against the advances of construction and that equilibrium should be sought. He had been a major player in the campaign against the proposed artificial beach scheme (examined later), writing newspaper articles and canvassing support. He further proved his honourable intentions to the audience by supplying a copy of a letter that he had sent to a newspaper in his youth many years ago, warning of the dangers of tourism. However, the turnout for PSOE meetings was poor: despite sufficient advertising only some 50 people turned up in the lower valley, and even fewer in the traditionally conservative upper valley compared to well over 100 for the CDS meetings.

It is interesting to note that the long-time representative and mayor for the CDS came from a poor family and was, at one time, a fisherman, whereas the candidate for the socialist party (PSOE) is a member of a wealthy family regarded as *caciques*, showing that family origins do not always dictate political persuasion. Indeed, economic impact seems to be the most persuasive factor in changing the attitude of people who come from families with strong political traditions and a number of families in

Vueltas have changed their habit of voting socialist because members have established close working relationships with the mayor.

A local *practicante* (medical assistant) who originated from Tenerife was the leading candidate for the PP (Partido Popular). His fellow candidates were all local people with little or no previous experience whom he had rallied to the cause. His deputy was a politically inexperienced young woman who would be responsible for his work in his absence, which was a likely situation as he was also campaigning for the parliamentary seat. Judging from previous results the success of the PP was highly improbable: in 1987 only two councillors had been elected on the entire island. Their performance in the 1991 local election was also extremely poor and shortly afterwards the practicante left the municipality.

EL POZO DE EL ALTITO TIRA EL AGUA AL BARRANCO I IMPIDELO
[The pool of the Mayor takes water from the river and impedes it.]

This was a graffito written on the outside of a bar in VGR and refers to the mayor who is believed to be diverting the wealth of the valley into his own pocket. The governing party often has an advantage in its historical base to influence the electorate. For example, more money can be spent on the campaign, certainly true in VGR where T-shirts and cigars were handed out at the lavish and well-orchestrated CDS meetings, compared to a can of beer and a rose at the comparatively casual PSOE meetings. Another major factor is the ability to affect people's lives economically and the current mayor had managed to provide employment through the massive receipts of money from the Government and EU, ostensibly to turn VGR into a viable and competitive tourist resort. This cash, much of which was channelled into construction, had allowed him to exercise great political persuasion.

'*Manga*', meaning 'sleeve', is the local phrase for influence or the ability to persuade those in power. This graphically describes how someone may have a slight hold on a politician or another person with power. It can be seen that those who have no *manga* may have trouble in certain areas of their lives, such as opening or operating businesses, gaining permission for construction work and obtaining employment. There is consequently a certain amount of fear amongst local people who do not wish to be considered as opponents of the current mayor. Some people said that they would vote for the PSOE but would pretend that they voted for the CDS by telling lies or switching envelopes. The strength of the networks based on party political allegiances can be seen from the importance that people attach to the voting process. Party supporters knew each other well, favouring one another in the job market: this occurred in local council employment, contract construction work for the government, as well as less directly associated areas such as fishing crews and the granting of licences to operate businesses.

A number of individuals suggested that the voting process itself made it possible to tell for which party someone had voted, even though it is supposed to be a confidential act. According to informants, dark blue envelopes were sent out to villagers containing a list of the current mayor's party candidates. Villagers were then expected to send these in or place them in the box on voting day. At the polling station other envelopes and lists of the other party candidates were provided. The voters queued up and put their envelopes into transparent boxes and there was a curtained booth provided for voters to use in private. It would appear that those voting for the current mayor simply walked in and deposited their dark blue envelope into the transparent box not needing to use the booth. I was told that other envelopes were lighter blue and the difference showed up: one enlightened local person took the PSOE list back to his parents who then placed them in the darker blue envelope to deposit. There were many helpers at the polling station and some would presumably be looking out for people not supporting their favoured mayor. Even if this is an inaccurate account of the procedure, the belief in the corruption serves to indicate the fear and paranoia amongst the people in the village.

Political power and patronage

MENOR COMER CABRAS, Y MAS TERRAZAS
[Less eating goat, and more terraces.]

This statement is another example of political graffiti and refers to the CDS gatherings during which goat-meat is consumed, symbolising the general good life enjoyed by its supporters, whilst at the same time the agricultural terraces become abandoned through lack of investment. It indirectly refers to the patronage given by the dominant political group. The following accounts (summarised from conversations) are examples of how local people perceive political influence operating within their community, showing the way in which people in power may gain or appease supporters:

One man wished to open up a restaurant in a section of a building underneath some flats: he had installed the equipment and was preparing to open up; however, some tenants complained to the local council that there would be an unacceptable level of noise at night. It was believed that, as they were CDS supporters, the council decided in their favour and did not grant the man a license to operate. He proved that there was no technical reason for this in law and that he satisfied the conditions for opening the restaurant. Finally, after many months of struggle, loss of earnings and a hunger strike, he obtained permission from the Cabildo to go ahead and did so after having wasted over a year with an inoperative business.

Another restaurant owner, a well-known socialist and opponent of the mayor, waited for over five years to open his restaurant having been refused a licence for 'petty reasons' in the words of a family member. This was widely interpreted as political maneuvering. Eventually he went over the heads of the local council to the Cabildo (which after the 1991 election was predominantly socialist) and was allowed to open up his restaurant: he then awaited the reaction of the mayor who let the matter pass.

A young woman, totally inexperienced in politics, had been asked to act as a councillor by the PP candidate for mayor because of her interest in improving opportunities for young people. She managed to extricate herself from the candidacy (with some difficulty) and described the serious problems both she and her husband, a lifetime socialist, had experienced with other villagers ignoring them in public, whispering about her and generally being antipathetic towards them both. She was extremely upset by this and came to realise the crucial importance of politics in the valley. She had not experienced this before as she had lived abroad for most of her life with her parents who had been employed as migrant farm-workers. Indeed, she had already managed to gain her job working in a hotel through the socialist friend of her father-in-law who knew one of the hotel's owners. Political connections were also helpful in her claim for insurance after an accident involving a wall collapsing on her car which the council refused to reimburse: a socialist lawyer, another friend of her father-in-law, was able to defend her interests and gain compensation for her. This young woman's good intentions to act positively for the youth of the valley led to her involvement with an unpopular political party (PP). This aroused the anger of all those who had helped her previously, expecting her loyalty to the Socialists and support in exchange for their initial aid. She concluded: 'You must belong to a political party here in Valle Gran Rey, it means friends and a job.'

These examples have been recounted by local people and are public knowledge: they show how politicians and people of influence favour their supporters and hinder their enemies. The type of relationship illustrated here, whereby someone cultivates potential supporters by offering them help, advice or work, has been well documented throughout literature on Mediterranean countries.[5] The concept of patronage itself is a broad one and may generally be described as the act of submission by one individual to another for mutual material benefit (Gellner & Waterbury, 1977).

These examples serve to illustrate the granting of help in terms of favours or the recognition of supporters through defence of their interests. They also demonstrate how individuals can connect with action-sets in the guise of political interest groups and how particular groups can defend their interests against individuals who pose threats to them. Kenny (1961: 135) is very clear on the subject and describes the relationship between patron and client: 'The former acts as a protector, at times as a model to copy, and always as an intermediary in times of need, with persons or situations more powerful than the client'. This description correlates with the examples in terms of the power ratio, although the relationship is not as permanent as Kenny implies.

In Vueltas, there were certainly established relationships between people in authority with political ambitions and others to whom they offered advice or helped in other ways with the expectation of their political support. It would be possible to extend the net of patronage to other social relationships but this is not the objective of this study, which acknowledges the machinations of political behaviour in VGR. One important factor in the developing equation involving economics, politics and tourism is the way patronage relationships affect foreign settlers, with some foreigners being unwilling to accept particular ways of behaving. Foreign settlers expect more assistance from formal legal and political authorities: they are offering new challenges to the operation of traditional political relationships within the valley.[6] In these expectations we see the new actors refusing to accept the role that they are expected to play in the patronage drama. They look for the roles that they knew in their former countries, often places where the close personal network of a community did not have such an influence.

This chapter has given examples of the links between politics and economics on both a small scale and a larger one, i.e. the grants obtained from the EU to develop the tourist potential of the valley. Earlier chapters have shown the broad sweep of political power that has affected the economy, with the Spanish colonisers imposing a monoculture economy of cash crops on the island and, in a different manner, the victorious allies ignoring Spain and indirectly influencing Spain's economy after the Second World War. Politics has continued to influence economic life in Vueltas on a macro-scale, with the EU and globalisation involving a worldwide trading network and tourism; whilst on a micro-scale local patronage systems and party interests affect work patterns. During a conversation between two fishermen after the election activity, one described the local council as 'the new *caciques* '. This observation recognises the increased power that the council has acquired, particularly in regard to the allocation of jobs through huge development grants. In some respects, the old class dichotomy remains the same, with the bosses and workers forming the dominantly recognised social division in the valley; however, this difference based largely on wealth is diminishing, particularly as a result of the tourist industry.

The Socialists were unsuccessful in the 1991 election, gaining only 34% of the votes. This was despite their candidate's involvement in the successful protest against the beach development scheme during November 1990. The entrenched economic interests of the working population and the strong conservative tradition in voting behaviour of the Upper Valley remained unswayed by fears of the valley's ecological destruction. As previously mentioned, the turnout to hear his speeches was poor, his family background a disadvantage. There is no direct causal relationship between concern for the environment and voting behaviour, particularly in VGR where political traditions are deep and hark back to the Spanish Civil War. Nevertheless, patterns are changing and traditions are being broken, with people placing their daily livelihoods before political ideals – short-term goals tend to obscure long-term interests.

Tourism has been a theme on which politicians have concentrated in their speeches. As a major driver of the economy in VGR, it is extremely influential and, as an industry, it has attracted funding from the EU and the Spanish Government. In this manner, the tourism industry is a major issue for professional politicians and frames their approaches to the electorate in relation to future developments and previous projects. The impact of tourism has also been felt in other areas where the issue of power matters. As a wealth creator, tourism has offered opportunities to various sectors of society in VGR and given some the chance to achieve wealth and, with this wealth, a change of status in society i.e. to become someone who is able to be independent, no longer a servant – possibly a boss. As such, it has enabled a redistribution of resources and, consequently, a reallocation of power at the grass-roots level. However, resources and power are inextricably mixed in terms of control (who decides to do what with them) and there are clear divisions of interest within the valley over what type of tourism and, consequently, what type of tourist to pursue in the future. This conflict came to a head late in 1990 and is now described.

Local Conflicts and Global Issues: The Protest

> It is a crazy plan. I have no more words to describe how I feel. (A young woman commenting on a proposed development plan)

The crowds were too big to fit into the packed theatre of the *Casa Cultural* (Cultural Centre) and spilled onto the newly constructed terrace outside. The bright evening sun still had enough strength to bring sweat to the brows of onlookers as the men in suits climbed onto the platform inside the building to inform the people of the valley about the new plan. It would transform the huge natural bay into a tourist pleasure beach through the strategic placing of sea walls and the building of a promenade studded with vending kiosks. The sand would remain all year round instead of being washed away during the winter and the tamed sea would not produce any dangerous waves. It was, they argued, what the tourists wanted and what the municipality needed.

This development proposal was but a relatively insignificant offshoot of a larger plan known as the POI intending to 'develop' and 'integrate' La Gomera with the rest of the Canary Islands, a plan which had first seen the light in 1990. The POI had been attacked in articles in the press. Rodriguez, a spokesman for the 'United Left of the Canary Islands', brought attention to its acceptance by most political parties, with the exception of the following organisations: the political Left (Izquierda Canaria Unida), neighbourhood associations and ecological groups. These organisations had initiated a movement against it: they saw the POI as a deception and a social and environmental barbarity. They described it as

> An investment plan recently approved, which involves almost £60 million, the majority of which goes to infrastructural works, roads, recreational ports, an airport and beach reconstruction, with the intention of opening up La Gomera to mass tourism and predatory destruction. (*La Gaceta de La Canarias*, November 1990)

One spokesman for this group, a lawyer, had at one time opposed plans to develop a beach at Avalos (on La Gomera) that involved destroying many palm trees. He believed that the development was for speculative purposes and legally dubious, indicating that some politicians had a vested interest in it through friends and family. He later wrote that corruption is institutionalised in La Gomera, stating '*Caciquismo* dominates everything' and said that those who oppose certain powerful men must emigrate: he himself had received violent threats.

In September 1990 the cultural and ecological organisation based in La Gomera named 'Guarapo' (after the indigenous palm tree drink) produced its first pamphlet that criticised the POI and highlighted the island's sanitation problems. It emphasised the lack of investment by the POI in the traditional sectors of employment, the primary industries of La Gomera, with only 4% of funds going into agriculture and nothing for fishing or pastoral activity: whereas almost 80% was allocated for infrastructural work relating to tourism. The POI, which intends to invest the published sum of around £60 million, will receive up to half its money from EC development funds; one such fund, known as FEDER, is already operative in VGR. The massive investment and implementation of POI was taking place with little opposition and the local council of VGR had added a proposal, which was for the 'reconstruction' of its natural beach and coastal zone. This proposal looked like becoming a foregone conclusion, having been accepted by the relevant authorities; but this was not to be the case.

An article written by Jaime Casanova, who was later to become the socialist candidate for mayor in VGR, appeared in the daily newspaper *El Dia*, on 2 November 1990. This article criticised the development projects in VGR, particularly the road that has led to the destruction of vegetation in the valley and drew attention to the type of tourist that visits VGR, someone who is attracted by the natural beauty and wild environment of the island:

> Unless it is intended to scare off the so-called alternative or green tourists, the only truly profitable type for the valley and its inhabitants, nothing that is done at the municipal level makes sense. (Casanova, *El Dia*, 1990)

Not only is the beauty of the valley being destroyed but the micro-climate and its special qualities that draw tourists are also in trouble. Casanova also vented his spleen on the new proposal, labelled '*Proyecto de regeneración de litoral de VGR*' (Project for the regeneration of the coast at VGR). This plan, recently approved by the local council, proposes to construct a series of sea walls perpendicular to the natural beach, creating artificial bays and halting the natural movement of the sand, consequently retaining it for the winter season. It also involved concreting coastal pathways and the construction of bars and kiosks and other tourist-oriented buildings. Furthermore, the two historically important natural pools by Vueltas known as the 'Count' and 'Countess' (regularly used by young children for bathing) will be artificially reconstructed. The estimated total cost was £6 million. Cassanova criticised this project as a manifestation of self-interested political megalomania and he believed that the struggle for public knowledge and debate had to be undertaken immediately:

> We must ask, before it is too late, that there is a debate on television or radio over the wrongs that have been done, and the future of Valle Gran Rey. (*El Dia*, 1990)

On 22 of November 1990, there was a public appearance before the media of the newly created *Coordinacion por la defensa de VGR* (The Committee for the Defence of VGR). Their picture appeared in a full-page article in the periodical *La Gaceta de Canarias*, sub-headed 'The group born through opposition to the plan of coastal reconstruction'. The committee members, all residents of VGR, announced their intention to inform the islanders of the plan, which, in their view, was a highly politically motivated business. They criticised the actual viability of the civil engineering project and showed its ecological destructiveness: the walls could not even withstand the tidal onslaught. The Committee's final blow was levelled at the shortsightedness and lack of insight shown by the planners in their knowledge of tourism:

> The European tourists look for different authentic sensations. If Valle Gran Rey is converted into a tourist attraction similar to other islands, it is likely that the project will be a failure in this respect also.

The issues were at last quite open to the public. On the following day at the Casa Cultural in VGR there was a public meeting to hear about the proposed project from the mayor and two engineers involved in its creation. By 6.00 p.m. the hall was packed with about 500 people from all walks of life. The great majority was local villagers. On the platform the three speakers informed the audience of their plan, whilst members of the audience criticised them in a respectful manner. Eventually, those who were against the plan were allowed to go up on the stage and use a microphone: they arrived to a tumultuous applause. A pamphlet criticising the plan was brandished, copies of which had been circulating in the village for some weeks previously. A professional engineer outlined the weaknesses of the plan for all to see and an ecologist branded it as ill conceived and dangerous. The audience was almost completely in support of the critics and visibly mocked the proposers of the scheme.

Before the open publicity, there had been pamphlets circulating the valley, produced by 'Guarapo' and the 'Coordinadora', outlining the beach proposal and its weaknesses. Points emphasised included the destruction of natural beauty, the heritage of the people, destruction of agricultural land, degradation of the traditional architecture and style of the village and, finally:

> Whilst for tourism there has been an investment of millions, there has been no help for fishing or farming, which are being considered as disappearing sectors. (Guarapo, 1990)

There was a petition organised on La Gomera and Tenerife and it was rumoured that 16,000 signatures were needed for the authorities to change their minds (La Gomera's population is 18,000).[7] The protest spread through networks of friends, relatives, colleagues and casual acquaintances, with the most active group being young men, many of whom ran local businesses. On the evening before the meeting, there was a lengthy debate in a bar in which two fishermen criticised the whole plan as a shambles and ecological disaster in opposition to one of its supporters, a business-minded local professional. Within a couple of months the petition had reached 8000 signatures, with many of them coming from other islands, especially Tenerife: approximately 1000 represented people from VGR. This show of public support plus the increasing criticism of the plan led to the local council backing down and shelving the idea. There was continual coverage in the media, especially the newspapers, and such was the impact of this community action that a Tenerife-based newspaper ran an article that included the following lines:

> We are able to say that at last democracy has arrived in Valle Gran Rey. (*La Gaceta*, December 1990)

After the successful outcome of the petition, another pamphlet was issued in December 1990 by the 'Coordinadora Popular' entitled 'The Voice of Valle Gran Rey'. The leading article, 'History of a Popular Movement', went on to give details of how the movement had led to the momentous meeting in November, only one month after the council had released details of its decision to let the development go ahead. The editorial, in an emotional front piece, announced:

> A committee has been born. The cry, like a silbo,[8] has broken the silence and woken up those who assist indifferently, or perhaps help the bonfire which is consuming the patrimony we have inherited from our elders: the countryside, our customs, our traditional lifestyles, all part and parcel of nature.

The entire episode relating to this proposed beach project raised people's awareness of their environment, the impact of tourism, political man-oeuvering and their own power to influence their future. It demonstrated that individuals could create action groups through personal networks and determine their own future by confronting officialdom and challenging decisions. This is particularly remarkable in an island like La Gomera where the ruling élite has been used to getting its own way and where, in VGR, the political dominance of one party has created a strong tendency to comply with the status quo. During the campaign, fishermen discussed the potential impact of the sea walls on the currents and the fish. Young people spoke emotionally of the ruin of the beautiful beach, of the poor sanitation on the island and the misdirection of money and parents argued with children over the benefits of the project. Many older people believed that the increased investment would be good for the valley: the building programmes already undertaken had certainly given plenty of work to the men and it was felt by some that the beach development would do the same. The whole issue and its outcome have brought to the surface vital concerns for all inhabitants of the valley. The powerful dismissal of the proposed project, a successful campaign that found moral support on other islands, may well prove to herald a fundamental change in attitude towards mass tourism and development in general.

This event has highlighted how deeply interrelated are many facets of life within the valley and, by logical extension, the western world and human society as a whole. Politics, economics, lifestyles and the environment were all among the issues enmeshed in a decision concerning tourism and development. The question of values and identity became serious matters used as rhetorical ammunition in the debate and the importance of history and sentimental attachment became clear.

There have been few opportunities for the villagers to stand up and halt decision-making by rich men and politicians; but with the case of tourism, a flexible industry, it is possible for people to influence plans directly for their own economic future and physical environment. Tourism has now become part of party politics in the municipality: this fact was made quite clear during the election campaigns of the two major parties, the centrists (CDS) and the socialists (PSOE) in May 1991. Both leading spokesmen, the prospective candidates for mayor, stressed their attitude towards tourism. The current centrist mayor had emphasised VGR's luck as a tourist resort and the fact that he had secured money from central government to develop the valley's potential as a resort. Whereas, in contrast, the socialist candidate associated himself with the ecological interests: he talked of finding equilibrium between tourism and the environment. Tourism, therefore, with its association with money, the economy and the future is a major factor in any politician's manifesto.

Seen in a temporal perspective, tourism is the latest in a succession of 'export' industries that have dominated the economy of the Canary Islands (sugar, wine, ochineal, tomatoes, bananas) and brought it into a globalised trading network: the Canaries have remained a peripheral exporting economy within a world system. And, importantly, as has been pointed out by de Kadt (1979), Crick (1989) and others, with tourism the customer visits the producing country to consume the export, which largely accounts for the unique sociocultural influences of this industry.

The protest, debate and consequent polarisation of opinion provides an excellent example of the issues and problems that the inhabitants of VGR must face up to in their daily lives. The conflict of opinions are to be found everywhere and everyone is presented with the consequences of decisions relating to tourism and the environment from the construction of roads to the increase or decrease in tourists. It relates to people's livelihoods, environment, heritage, freedom, identity and, of course, their future. The beach area is a major part of the people's lives: many spend their leisure time there; some rely on it to provide them with marine resources; some enjoy its invigorating healthiness. It is part of the personal and collective memory and an important asset of the whole community. The transformation of the beach not only signals the loss of something valuable, it signifies the loss of the people's power over their environment. Many people had secretly resented the destruction of the natural habitat around the valley, but they had had little opportunity to safely vent their feelings or to make any difference. The meeting in the Casa Cultural allowed them to say a collective 'No' to a specific programme.

This collective voicing of antipathy towards the building construction and ecological destruction was just a small indication of a much larger sense of frustration felt within the community; in this sense it is a micro-conflict encapsulating a macro-issue. In another sense, it is a local conflict representing the global issue of environmental destruction (see Hannertz [1992: 255] on global movements). Similar scenarios to the one described here may be found in numerous tourism centres around the world, to say nothing of the general protests against ecological destruction (cf. Hitchcock *et al.* [1993], on tourism and environmental issues). The conflict of interest between business developers and conservationists represented in VGR is occurring in many other situations and exemplifies the struggle over resource use that will determine the world's future. Furthermore, in VGR, it becomes a struggle between left-wing parties and the right-wing platform – a conflict over power, resources and wealth – a class conflict in which the majority of the working population seek control over an area of their lives which, as yet, has not been definitively dominated. This contest between capitalist business interests and the working population permeates the history of the island and remains in the present-day experience of the islanders.[9]

A community's sense of identity is influenced by its historical experience and its relationship with the natural environment. The people of VGR have long been intimately involved with their environment as farmers and fishermen but with the advent of tourism, among other factors, they are moving away from this dependence and close relationship and developing a new way of interacting with and viewing the sea and land. Moreover, they have a complex sense of identity related to themselves as islanders, members of particular communities on the island and as inhabitants of a place long considered peripheral and relatively powerless. Such perceptions have been challenged by recent events related to tourism, the closer embrace into Europe through the EU, globalisation and the arrival of foreign visitors. These issues are examined in depth in the following chapter.

Notes

1. Broegger (1990) has classified the fishermen of Portugal as 'pre-bureaucratic': I will not make this distinction for VGR but agree on its importance as a characteristic of certain communities and particular exchanges

2. Dalton's observation about the transformation of a pre-capitalist society to capitalism also applies in its generality to the expanding market within Europe: 'Modernisation consists of displacing local dependence with external dependence on markets, and by so doing integrating the village community into the region, the nation, and through foreign trade transactions, the rest of the world' (Dalton, 1971: 28).

3. In 1996 the agricultural official at the Island Council was unsure of the future for bananas but thought it would be bleak.

4. In 1987 the results gave a council consisting of the same CDS mayor, six CDS and four PSOE councilors.

5. See Gellner and Waterbury (1977), Eisenstadt and Ranger (1980), Boissevain (1966, 1974), Pitt-Rivers (1977), Wolf (1966), Gilmore (1987) and Kenny (1968).

6. Scott (2001: 19) writes about gender and sustainability in the Mediterranean and makes a point relevant to La Gomera: 'Substantive patron–client relationships are usually between men, even though the point of connection may be through women (for example, between a woman's male relatives and her husband), and are activated by appeals to local identity and kinship. But alongside these informal networks the EU has in recent years put in place a series of formal networks which appeal to – in fact, seek to create – a sense of common European identity and citizenship.'

7. I found out about the whole issue when asked to sign the petition by a friend in a shop. When I asked her what she felt about it she answered: 'It is a crazy plan, I have no more words to describe how I feel. The council destroys everything that is beautiful.'

8. Silbo is the unique whistling language practised on La Gomera.

9. This development project would seem to be an example of the problems resulting from a lack of serious collaborative planning and partnership between different bodies of people with an interest in its outcome, the various stakeholders. Bramwell and Lane explore this topic and draw attention to the considerable advantages of such collaborations (and the disadvantages). They advocate cross-sectoral intersections between parties, and emphasise: 'The cross-sectoral reference is important: partnerships that seek to create sustainable tourism need to be holistic in outlook' (Bramwell & Lane, 2000: 1). There is a lesson here for the policy-makers involved in the development of La Gomera. See also de Kadt (1990) on alternative tourism, sustainability and lessons from Development Studies: 'Sustainability, with a stress on resource use and renewability, scaling down, and a renewed interest in equity, has become central to alternative development; its sharper analytical approach is relevant to alternative tourism' (de Kadt, 1990: abstract).

Chapter 6

Social Identity

Introduction

Identity is a concept that has numerous definitions: although there has been a tendency with writers of late to shy away from giving an all-embracing description, many would agree with Hall (1996) that it is a strategic and positional entity.[1] One way of approaching identity is to consider it as inherently social, a quality that can best be understood in relation to an oppositional other: 'Identity is the test to which all human beings living in society are constantly subjected It becomes impossible to build up identity without abutting it against the identity of others' (Lanfant, 1995: 7). This is not to say that identity cannot be a private personal experience but to suggest, for the purposes of this work, that it is a socially determined possession, as well as something that can have a deeply personal resonance. This chapter concentrates on social identity but recognises that individuals can have a strong impact: they are able to act as agents on the formation of such an identity. Individuals and groups can be born with an identity, can achieve an identity and can have an identity thrust upon them (Macleod, 1997).

The first part of this chapter deals with the historical development of the community from its roots as a pre-Hispanic Guanche community and assesses how this history impacts on the people's identity in modern times. It looks at the image of the Gomero – an island identity that unites inhabitants and places them in opposition to outsiders, most directly with people from Tenerife. The extension of local variations in identity makes us realise the importance of the local context: people from different parts of the village have certain ascribed characteristics. Identities often build up from a complex broad, micro-scale base, to a simplistic, stereotypical nationalistic apex.

Given the subtle picture of local attitudes and variations relating to social identity, we are better able to appreciate the influence of tourism on the community. Placed in the context of globalisation, especially the mass media, the particular influence of tourists remains strong and areas such as gender roles, eating habits and social activities are all directly involved on a face-to-face level. Similarly, the broader influence of tourism has repercussions in terms of cultural identity for the people who are changing their economic base from fishing to tourism.

Many writers have considered the tourism industry and its inclination towards fabricating the composition of destinations.[2] Lanfant (1995: 8) sees identity as a manufactured and packaged product that is offered to the consumer. This is certainly true of many resorts but La Gomera has been represented on a small scale through a cottage industry of postcards and guidebooks, written by German ex-tourists/settlers and Canary Islanders. Only recently has it appeared in the national press and on travel programmes and it has not yet had an image imposed upon it. Rather than a look at the thrusting of an identity on a place, this chapter focuses on the indigenous grass-root development and achievement of various identities and their consequent engagement with and influence by the tourists. The people of Vueltas are very much the agents of identity creation in this process although they will inevitably have less power over the way they will be represented by others in the future.

Local Identities

Pre-Hispanic influences on identity

An examination of the pre-Hispanic historical identity of the island shows that there are a number of possible origins of the name Gomera, including its derivation from the first settlers in Africa, collectively named after the biblical character Gomer, grandson of Noah. Others say that the name derives from a Spaniard called Gomez or that it may come from the word Goma meaning gum. However, it is generally felt that its origins lie in pre-Hispanic days, like many of the names of villages currently on the island, such as Arure, Chipude and Agullo, and a number of studies cite similarly named places in North Africa where the Berber influence is strong. Indeed, there is evidence, according to Concepcíon (1989), to support the contention that the Guanches are descendants of a Berber group that populated the islands: there are numerous cultural and physical parallels traceable in the physiognomy, language and agriculture of the Guanches.

Some remnants from the pre-Hispanic days form part of the Gomero's unique identity and are often promoted as folkloristic items, both to local people and especially tourists (cf. Hernandez-Hernandez, 1986). *Silbo* (a whistling language) is foremost amongst them: it is a substitute language that mimics the sound of words using different tones to represent letters and phonemes. The silbo's special quality lies in the fact that it can be transmitted over very long distances, up to 6 km and is particularly useful in the steep-sided valleys, where ordinary speech cannot carry and a simple silbo message saves hours of walking. It is still used in the rugged uplands by farmers and pastoralists and it is possible to see herdsmen in the upper valleys whistling messages across ravines or even to hear someone ordering a round of drinks in a bar by whistling his order to the barman. The fishermen use it occasionally, although they tend to limit its use to calling out names. Some people refer to this whistling language as the 'Gomeran language' and say they speak both Spanish and Gomeran.[3] The whistle is made by inserting part of a finger into the mouth and blowing, allowing air to escape in a small gap at the side.

The origins of silbo are unclear, although some say it came from Africa with the first Guanches and developed into its present form over the years. In his book *The Guanche Survivors and Their Descendants*, Concepcíon (1989) illustrates the cover with drawings of Guanches using silbo; however, there is little information about the history of the silbo in the text. An annotated photograph of a Gomero silboing describes it as a 'Guanche language that has survived until present times' (p. 59). Others believe that it developed amongst the Guanches after Spaniards cut out their tongues to stop them speaking their own language. Continuing this theme, some people from Tenerife firmly believe that the silbo started because Franco cut out the tongues of his enemies or those who attempted to escape from the islands. Folk explanations often reveal more about the people generating them than about the actual subject and it is most likely that silbo developed along with the Guanche culture to ease communication across the huge ravines on La Gomera. The survival of a number of Guanche words which represent basic phrases such as *Fiyoo* (What do you want to say) and *Ejey* (yes) indicate its pre-Hispanic origins. Until recently, the language had never been recorded in writing and had only been taught within the family; however, one man who teaches silbo at the local school has created a rough translation into the alphabet. The Gomeros are the only known people to have developed a whistling language capable of reproducing a spoken language's variety of meaning (see Trujillo [1978] for an informed and technical account of silbo).

Music played on *chacaras* and *tambors* (large castanets and hand-drums) accompanied by singing and dancing, known generally as *baile de tambor*, is also said to derive from the original pre-Hispanic inhabitants. Most villages have musicians capable of playing in this style and there is a group known as *Los Magos de Chipude* who are specialists, with recordings of their music. The music is played at fiestas and accompanied by a dance that employs subtle footwork, with two rows of people, usually divided by gender, moving sideways. The dance, known as the *Tajaraste* is still popular

Plate 14 The procession of the Virgin del Carmen on the way to board the fishing boat, led by musicians playing the pre-Hispanic *baile de tambor* with *tambors* and *chacaras*. The statue is carried by men from Vueltas

and men and women of all ages enjoy participating in it. It is also performed during the religious procession on a saint's day when the dancers precede the figurine as it is carried around the parish (see Plates 14 and 15).[4]

A number of ancient crafts (*artesanía*) are still practiced, with people selling locally produced items. These include *Ceramica*, pottery made without a wheel (centres for this are Vallehermoso and Chipude), *Cestaría* which uses palm leaves and bamboo to weave baskets and hats, and the making of wooden musical instruments and household objects. Knowledge of Guanche food and drink preparation continues to be passed on and includes the specialist items such as *guarapo*, the fresh sap of the palm trees drunk within a day of tapping (a highly skilled process), and *miel de palma* (palm honey), a treacle created from the raw *guarapo*. A particularly strong drink known as '*gomeron*' is made from *miel de palma* mixed with *parra* a powerful alcoholic spirit distilled from the fruit of the 'mother vine' (a phrase describing part of the plant). As well as being available throughout the island, these items all form part of the goods that are on sale for the tourists. Perhaps the most ubiquitous foodstuff which has survived since pre-Hispanic times is *gofio* (a flour made out of crushed and roasted

Plate 15 As the Virgin del Carmen returns from the boat to the *ermita*, people dance the *tajaraste* in front of the musicians who precede the statue and the priest

barley / wheat) which may be eaten with milk, wine, water, as well as being a complementary staple carbohydrate in soup or with meat and vegetables. The Guanches reportedly used stone mills to grind barley, wheat and beans into meal that they then roasted in a clay oven.

Another continuing tradition is the pastoral lifestyle: the Guanches raised goats, sheep, pigs and dogs, using the goats and sheep for milk and cheese and all the animals for meat. Pastoralism was the primary mode of livelihood of these people, surviving throughout the Spanish colonisation and continuing for the more isolated communities despite the dominance of Spanish society and their plantations. Today there are still men who pasture animals, mostly goats, on the steep ravines and some use long poles for vaulting gullies in the style once favoured by Guanches. One pre-Hispanic pastoral practice that remains involves the coating of goats' teats with *tabaiba* milk, a plant product that becomes rubbery and stops the kids from suckling during daytime.

The Guanches lived in caves, extensions of natural crevices excavated out of a soft stratum of rock. This means of abode was still quite common during the late 19th century as recorded by historians who noted the rural populations on some islands living in caves which were once inhabited by

Guanches or houses built out of stone and clay. There was a home in Santiago, La Gomera, located in an ancient cave overlooking the harbour: being supplied with electricity and water, it remained occupied in 1991 but has since been converted into a restaurant. Further into the valley at Santiago, there are huge caves, set half way up the mountainside, in which separate rooms and levels had been cut providing domestic quarters for the Guanche residents. It is interesting to note that the first settlers of Vueltas lived in caves at the beginning of the 20th century.

Islanders regard many of the ancient arts and crafts as folkloristic and there are certain individuals that are specialists in the practice of these skills. One such person is an expert instrument-maker and *silbador* (whistler) from Chipude, who carries an identity card on him stating his qualification as an artisanal expert. He occasionally appears on a television programme for the Canary Islands, promoting the special attributes of La Gomera, and is well known throughout the island: he often appears at fiestas with his friends playing the *baile de tambor*. He operates a taxi, works on his land in the mountains and also makes instruments to order and he is a recognisable force in the continuing traditional culture of the island and its unique identity.

These examples all illustrate how the arts, crafts and skills of the past continue to have use today, not always in a self-consciously ritualistic way but often as an integral part of daily life. At the same time, they are becoming regarded as folkloristic items, a heritage worthy of preservation and presentation and, importantly, as cultural commodities: this latter quality can be seen in the tourist brochure images portraying men whistling, women making pottery and the tambor players performing. There is now a Visitors' Centre in the Garajonay National Park that displays the skills of local craftsmen. It also sells their products and has a model of a traditional Gomeran house that is visited by coach-loads of tourists on day trips from Tenerife. Money from tourism and development funds has helped in the promotion of traditional arts and crafts on the island.

Some of the things that go to make up the cultural traditions, arts and crafts of the Guanches, and which Gomeros believe to be an important part of their contemporary identity, have been described. People invariably cited the 'folkloristic' themes when asked what it meant to be a Gomero, particularly their dancing and whistling, as well as stressing the people's friendliness in contrast to the coldness of urbanites from Tenerife or mainland Spain. A young woman questioned on whether there was such a thing as a specific Gomeran identity replied with the stock themes including silbo, fiestas and friendliness and referred to a comprehensive book about the Canary Islanders. Asked if there was a Gomero mentality, she responded more thoughtfully:

> Yes, I think there is a Gomero mentality but it's different, depending on the person. I mean the old people, when they talk about the new developments such as the new ferry, they think it will bring bad things, robbers, rubbish, problems – but young people like it, they see it as a means of getting out, going to Tenerife by car. Most people of my age like the growth, more open, more contact with the outside. But I think that the new ferry will be shit – more cars and problems.

It was suggested that this might be a fairly common generational difference in attitude, and she replied:

> That's true but there is a Gomero mentality. I just can't put it into words. Well, OK, it's a form of thinking – very individual [*desconfiado*], they don't trust anyone – people they don't know. Sometimes I think that my parents are like Guanches, they just want everything to remain the same, yes, monotony is what they want – no changes, they are happy to live like that but I can't. They're reserved, and they're clever [*listos*], it's a tactic: it affects their relationship with foreigners, even now, today. The Gomeros have been more isolated than the people of Tenerife, and they're very different from the Germans. For example, with the education of children – it's very important to have direct contact between parents and children here. The family here is very important and very united – but the Germans don't have family, or no contact anyway.'

This extract of an interview highlights the differences and similarities between the younger and older generations, both valuing the family, with the elders being more distrustful of strangers. It also demonstrates the use of the Guanches as a comparable cultural example in everyday speech. Furthermore, it draws on the recent introduction of foreigners into the daily lives of the local people, giving them a strong sense of difference and, consequently, emphasising their own group identity.

The Gomero

The people of Vueltas held many attitudes, some contradictory, concerning themselves as a group but there was certainly a great pride in being a Gomero (a native of La Gomera). Those from Tenerife say that the Gomero is *muy suyo* (self-possessed and proud) and close to his or her family. On many occasions, it was pointed out by Gomeros how good they were at their work: tuna-fishing, banana cultivation, goat-rearing and cheese-making. The people of VGR were well aware of the valley's outstanding physical characteristics: this was emphasised by the mayor in his political speeches continually exhorting the people to take pride in their heritage. At the same time, however, the weight of history bears down upon the people, with the tremendous emigration of the past and the continual movement in search of work for sons and daughters, especially the highly educated ones. They usually go to Tenerife, a much larger island (population 600,000) possessing a university, international airport, urban centres and highly developed tourism, oil and agricultural industries. An academic once half-jokingly said that the purpose of La Gomera was to supply labour to Tenerife. One local expression sums this up poignantly:

> *Tierra ruin no se la lleva el barranco*
> [Bad soil is not carried away by the flood.]

Thus, the people who remain in VGR have a perception of themselves, in some sense, as failures (the bad soil), the ones that did not get carried away overseas. The annual return of the successful, rich, worldly emigrants reinforces this perception. Many people spoke proudly of their wealthy and successful relatives in Venezuela or their professional relatives in Tenerife. The summer visitors from Tenerife, the *veranistas*, with their urban ideas and material goods also reinforced the popular contrast between the urban sophisticate and his poor country cousin. Indeed, La Gomera is commonly portrayed as the poor little sister of her larger neighbour. VGR is often regarded by the islanders themselves as the more wild and backward part of La Gomera, due to its physical isolation and its settlement by migrants from other islands. It is on the periphery of an island, itself on the periphery of a group of islands, themselves on the periphery of Spain. Within VGR, there are also sociospatial divisions, with some inhabitants believing Vueltas to be the least savoury part of the valley. The division between the people of the land above, *Gente de arriba*, and those of the coast, *Gente de bajo*, is strong because of their lifestyles and historical differences. The fishermen were once landless settlers and the people of the uplands say that the men of the sea are *bruto* (coarse).[5] Some people still regard Vueltas as a 'new town' where the immigrants settled. Yet Vueltas, a peripheral settlement in many senses, has become one of the most dynamic localities on La Gomera, in a growth region receiving millions of pounds from Europe. VGR has become the centre of the tourist industry, one of the primary sites of economic focus for the whole island.

   There are particular descriptions used by the islanders referring to the inhabitants of various parts of the island. Those from VGR are described as *charlangueros* (like to chat and socialise); those from Santiago, the other fishing centre as *surros* (fighters); those from Chipude, the ancient stronghold of Guanche culture, as *atreversos* (daring, brave); and the people from

San Sebastian as *pareceros* (concerned with appearances, vain). The people from San Sebastian, the capital, generally regard the people of VGR as *magos* (meaning yokels or unsophisticated peasants).[6] Nevertheless, many make light of this and in 1991, there was a bar named 'El Mago' in Vueltas owned by a man known locally as 'Mago': he was from Chipude where the *magos* are said to be most abundant. The concept of the *mago* is a durable one, synonymous with rural peasantry, and certainly folkloric. It holds a powerful symbolic meaning and is an area of ambivalence in the minds of the Gomeros in the sense that they are at once proud of and embarrassed by the description.[7] The strong link with the countryside and the various arts, crafts and skills associated with the *mago* (especially silbo whistling and folk dancing) form a major part in the image many Gomeros have of themselves and it is also promoted by literature, including tourist brochures.

The following descriptions demonstrate the contextual relativity of identity. One individual may be described in numerous ways: as Spanish, a Canary Islander, a Gomero, a man from VGR (*charlanguero*), a man from Vueltas (fisherman), a man from one part of Vueltas (Italia) or from one particular family. Clearly it depends on what context and with whom the individual is engaging. Thus, the role situation will determine the stereotypical characteristics with which the actor is typecast.[8] The real issues here involve the differentiation of personal and social identity. Individuals have a multifaceted identity that allows a person to use different facets in different social contexts or be seen in a particular social role: it is a complex thing, not a rigid and fixed quality but fluid and dynamic (see Macleod, 1997). We will now look at a source of social identity, the mode of livelihood (fishing) with its personal and cultural ramifications.

The fisherman

For the fisherman, the port is the arena for work and for social activity. It is a place where he performs a variety of roles relating to his positions as fisherman with work to be done and as a man in the community, fellow villager and friend. Major maintenance on the boat will occupy possibly one month in the year, plus occasional periods for minor work. There will always be someone working on his boat and there will invariably be another fisherman chatting to him, passing the time of day, offering advice or waiting. Exchanges are very casual with men often not acknowledging each other or joking and teasing. Arguments are frequent and shouting common, yet rude exchanges are rarely taken to heart and the men brush off any apparent verbal assaults. Some specific examples will give a sketch of the daily routine for the fisherman.

Night fishing for mackerel usually commences around 2.00 a.m., lasting until 8.00 a.m. Depending on the requirements of the salesman, it may last until 11.00 a.m. After this, the fisherman will stay in the port area talking and drinking coffee or wine or he may go home; he usually remains awake until after the midday meal, when he takes a long siesta until 8.00 p.m. After this sleep he will go to the port to meet friends, often taking a *cortido* (strong cup of coffee) and follow this with alcohol in a relaxed manner until 11.30 p.m. Finally he will return home and rest until it is time to go fishing, usually within three hours.

For the *nasa* (wire cage) fisherman, getting up to go fishing at 5.30 a.m. is the normal routine. Fishing involves hauling up traps full of fish with the help of a crewmate, returning to port between 10.30 and 11.30 a.m. After half an hour spent selling the products to restaurants and the public, followed by a drink in the bar, he returns to his home. He takes a rest in the afternoon after the midday meal until 6.00 p.m. and then goes down to the port to walk around, chat to friends, drink some beer and play cards or dominoes. This continues until around 11.00 p.m. when it is time for bed.

The *falua* (20 m boat) fishermen are usually at the boat by 5.30 a.m. They then prepare the bait and set off fishing, returning between 3.00 and 8.00 p.m. depending on the type of fishing trip, weather conditions, amount caught and other factors. Usually the men head straight to the bar after changing into clean clothes and terminate drinking before 10.30 p.m. if they are to go out the next day.

Other fishermen have different routines: pargo fishermen work during daylight hours, as do the calamari fishermen. There are no rigid routines but there are definitely strong patterns. These examples demonstrate that there will almost always be someone actively fishing during the daylight hours and during the early hours of the morning; equally, there will be fishermen relaxing at all times of the day. This is important because it means that there will always be men around the port area, providing plenty of opportunities for social interaction. The bars remain open throughout the day from the early morning, 6.00 a.m. until 1.00 a.m. as with Bar Puerto where the fishermen may be seen at every hour, drinking, playing dominoes and cards or watching television. This continual bar life contrasts strongly with the more restricted lifestyle of the agricultural workers in the upper valley where the men do not usually use the bar until midday.

The socialising, interaction, exchange of ideas and movement of people gives the port an active and interesting character. Fishermen often know other fishermen from different ports and other islands: there are some crews from Tenerife who are based in Vueltas once a year and many Vueltas fishermen stop off at Santiago to offload fish during the week. At the harbour in Vueltas, they meet and get to know the yachtsmen, the tourists, in fact anyone who cares to pass by and talk. This gives them an extrovert outlook, which contrasts with the secretive side of their profession. They have a lot of opportunities, therefore, to interact with tourists in their roles as apartment owners where they cultivate friendships, in the bar socialising and around the port relaxing or working. They get to know the regular visitors to the port and the different yachts that reappear. Often a fisherman would point out a particular yacht which they thought was bringing drugs in from Morocco and the subject of drug trafficking was a common conversation topic, with the fishermen joking amongst themselves about selling fish and buying drugs. They were also critical of many tourists who appeared to them as dishevelled or improperly attired – especially the modern hippies. One fisherman inquired: 'Why do these dirty smelly hippies come here to La Gomera? Can they live like that in Germany or England?' The fishermen often expressed disgust at the hippies, who were a small but high-profile group living on the beaches and in caves: they preferred sensible youngsters who got educated and worked in sensible jobs. Nevertheless, many fishermen had good friendships with regular visitors to the island, especially the Spanish *veranistas*, and were happy to offer advice on marine matters, sometimes teaching them how to fish at the harbour side.

Fishing: a man's world

It is commonly believed that the fishing profession is a man's world and this is certainly true of Vueltas where there are no female professionals. On rare occasions the German wife of the son of a local fisherman accompanied her husband out on a mackerel-fishing trip, the spectacle of this blonde woman being rowed out to a fishing boat strongly contrasting with the usual all-male scenario. The wives of the younger fishermen sometimes help their husbands to clean their boats but usually they will turn up to the quay simply to collect their husbands, help weigh the fish or pass over information or food. The boat area is definitely the male domain and the older women almost never enter it (see Plate 16). They may walk along the sea wall or around the concrete harbour area but they rarely talk together with a group of fishermen at their boats. This contrasts with the Portuguese community of Nazaré where women go fishing in a small boat close to shore (Broegger, 1990); and it differs even further from Vila Cha on the north coast of Portugal, where women work on the boats with the men (see Cole, 1991). The incident of the German woman helping her husband is an example of a radically different attitude towards fishing which many female tourists and settlers have in comparison to local women. German women have not grown up in Vueltas with the opinion that fishing is only for men and they are uninhibited in their desire to experiment with and experience fishing. They do not feel the social pressures as strongly as the

Plate 16 The port and work area, with fishermen looking out for new arrivals. Note the different colouring on the central boat, showing the upper (*morte*) and lower (*vivir*) areas either side of the floatation line: also visible are the fine lines (*canas*) just below the deck level

local women do and prove that it is possible for women to do many things usually regarded as the province of men. The German woman in the boat with her husband challenges the local female stereotypes (knowingly or not), offering a new, albeit relatively unusual, choice of behaviour.

The boatyard is a zone where the men can relax, joke, be crude and indulge in horseplay: the men urinate in the shadow of their boats and tease each other obscenely without fear of embarrassing a woman. In fact, one of the main pastimes is teasing a slightly retarded young man, Jose, who works with a lorry-driver at the port. The men gain tremendous enjoyment from agitating their victim until he loses his self-control and starts to throw things or shout at them, and so they hoodwink him and gang up to deceive him. For example, one may simulate sex with him and pretend to kiss him or perhaps grab his genitals and exclaim on their size, insinuating his manliness in ironic mockery. At other times, a number of individuals will furtively throw stones at him without his seeing them, until, agitated, he picks up a huge stone and threatens one of them or even throws it at a small boat: they usually manage to placate him before serious damage is done.

It is worth noting that many people in VGR tease young children in a similar manner, causing them to cry and lose their temper, frustrating them and mocking their weakness. This serves in a way to prepare them for the frustrations of adulthood, teaching them self-discipline and control (cf. Friedl, 1962). Thus, Jose's fundamental childishness, despite his mature years (early twenties), is exposed, as is his lack of masculinity, accentuated by his forced sexual submission. The dominance of Jose may also serve to bolster the dominant attacker, perhaps someone who feels inadequate for a variety of reasons.

In this behaviour, the general anxieties of the men can be seen working their way out into the open: the retarded scapegoat becomes a sounding board for their fears and, at the same time, a means of reaffirming their mutually held beliefs. Thus, areas of anxiety relating to masculinity, such as sexuality, self-control, independence and maturity are explored by the teasing of this man. Other general problems relating to the fishermen's work are also explored, particularly the bureaucratic pressures and, at one time, they threatened to send Jose to the port of Santiago to see the official there because his papers (fishing license, which of course he does not have) were not in order. This is an indirect form of social criticism, and again reaffirms or challenges role play. After the action is all over, the damage is repaired and the victim is consoled. Jose himself has a terrific sense of humour and gains satisfaction from mocking others, including the Guardia Civil.

Nicknames and teasing are common in the social interaction between the fishermen – one is known as *hablando solo* (speaking to himself) due to his habit of muttering alone in his boat, others are known as *niño* (child), *Canario* (canary) or simply derivations of their Christian names, such as Manolin or Manolito for Manuel, Tonio or Tonito for Antonio etc. Sometimes physical habits are mocked: one fisherman tends to hold the arm of his friends when explaining something and his friends say that he holds his wife's breast when talking to her. Another very poor man whose name is Ramon is teased by being introduced as the wealthy fish salesman 'Pescado Ramon'. There are endless opportunities for humour that relieves the tedium for many and allows them to exercise their wit.

Friendships seem to be most common between members of the same boat crew and between men of the same age group. This at least roughly determines the company that the men will keep in their free time, drinking and talking. There are some rivalries of course but these go on unspoken, with very few serious public conflicts as the rivals usually avoid one another. Because of the general sense of individuality, with the continual verbal confrontation and competition, it is difficult to differentiate the stronger bonds from the weaker ones; however, the overall pattern of spatial proximity betrays a certain emotional connection between people.

There are groups of people who gather together, whether it is to play cards in the bar or to talk at the port and it is of relevance that the groups usually have similar political leanings, possibly over-emphasised when the local and general elections were taking place. This political cohesiveness is understandable given the important part it plays in economic affairs, for example the political discrimination of one boat captain in picking his crew, and certain bars, known for their political sympathies, attracting a similar minded clientele. During the elections, there was a marked cooling down of relationships between opposing supporters amongst the fishermen.

The fishermen say that there are no unwritten or formal hierarchies amongst themselves; however, respect is given to the older and more knowledgeable men for their wisdom and experience. Although the captains of boats certainly assume positions of authority in their capacity as chiefs on the boat, there is an egalitarian quality to their behaviour ashore when mixing with the crew where they join the men to drink and play cards in the bar. This scenario is similar to that described by Byron (1986: 147) about the Shetlands where the skipper retains his '[q]uiet and assertive pride in self, in family, in crew, but without setting himself as in any way extraordinarily powerful or socially superior'. It also finds an echo in Chapman's (1986: 89) study of fishermen in Brittany, in which he writes about the 'undifferentiated status of the crew, despite the fact that they are actually the employees of the skipper'.

Even though the boat in Chapman's example is bigger than those in VGR and the relationship between the captain and the crew is one of employer and employees, the essential sentiments ring true, with the conscientious effort made by all in public to emphasise the brotherliness of the organisa-tion. Acheson (1981) draws attention to the egalitarianism common among fishers and relates it to shared responsibilities, reduction in risk through a sharing of the catch and the sense of the crew being co-adventurers not wage-earners: all of these characteristics are found in VGR. However, a different picture was painted by Mesa-Moreno who stated that there was a hierarchy amongst fishing families in VGR that materialised when a fisherman wished to marry another fisherman's daughter (Mesa-Moreno, 1982: 106).

Gender roles

The bar: theatre of masculinity

Many of the men in Vueltas spend a lot of their time in the bars, which are open most of the day. One in particular, Bar Puerto, the oldest and nearest to the port, is very popular with the local men and is open from the early morning, 6.00 a.m., until 1.00 a.m. the following day. It is especially popular with the fishermen and they are joined by other local men, plantation workers, builders, painters etc. During the afternoon there is always a group of men, some five to ten, playing dominoes and cards together; most men spend some time each day in one of the bars. The exceptions were those that worked in the supermarkets with long opening hours and some of the older men who preferred to save their money or could not afford to go out and drink regularly. During the early evening in the bar, many men would drink a *cortido*, a strong coffee with milk and sugar: later they would drink alcohol, the most popular choices being beer, wine (usually red), whisky and rum. Drinks are usually paid for after the session is over, when the drinkers wish to leave: this relies upon honesty, which is expected of the villagers.[9]

The wives of the men do not usually accompany them to the bar and very rarely, if ever, go out drinking alone or even with female friends. They may appear on a prearranged date or they may accompany their men-folk for a meal (e.g. on a Sunday) but usually they are absent. Younger single women occasionally go into certain bars with friends, both men and women, but this tends to be at weekends, Saturday night being a favourite night out for the villagers. Here, as in many other areas of social life, there is a divide between the generations, with younger women frequenting the bars more often than those over 40 years of age. There was one woman, a divorcee, who accompanied her adult daughter to the bars in the evenings: she was privately criticised by other women for this, insinuating that she had loose morals. Some of the bars have TV sets continually playing, showing either networked channels or videos, so the men need not leave the bar to see their favourite programmes or watch the news. The bar is, in effect, a social centre, a meeting point for the men, a place where women rarely join the activity. In this sense it becomes a theatre of masculinity, where stereotypical male behaviour is the norm: aggressive posturing, competition, sexual bluntness and lightheartedness are tolerated.[10]

The use of the metaphor 'theatre' serves to highlight the social situation in which people involved in dialogue and actions are conscious of being observed. Their conversation, therefore, is not private but can become part of a public discussion and is, consequently, a socially shared event, a display of their public identities. In this context, activities tend to conform to socially acceptable or expected norms and conversations may develop into a public examination of a man's character. The men in this case are acting according to a socially prescribed code of conduct and may on occasion be called to account for their performance in front of the audience. Thus, the men become actors playing a socially assigned role in public. Of

course, the role varies with time and place, as does the actors' interpretation of it; however, the tendency to conform to general perceptions of
acceptable behaviour is evident.[11]

Such perceptions of masculinity will include independence, which is
demonstrated in the ability of a man to pay his way, buy rounds of drink
and pay his debts. Self-control is also recognised in a man's ability to drink
regularly and keep up with the intake of his friends whilst maintaining
control of his physical and emotional actions. Men may shout and argue
very aggressively but they never lose control over their aggression: in fact,
being able to forcefully display the potential for violence is another
masculine trait that is respected. An example witnessed in a bar was a discussion that developed into an aggressive and heated argument between
two fishermen who had shared a catch. They had been fishing for mackerel,
the owner of the boat being joined by his friend (an experienced fisherman).
This 'employee' had been having difficulties fishing and was, therefore, in
a potentially vulnerable position, being partially reliant on his friend for an
income. The reason for the heated argument related to the fact that the boat-
owner wished to give the 'employee' some extra cash for the share of the
catch. He was waving a large wad of notes in the other man's face, whilst
the latter strenuously denied his need for more cash and started swearing,
which further increased the owner's gesticulations with his fistful of notes.
Eventually the 'employee' finished his drink, slammed the empty glass on
the bar and walked out – a defiant gesture, illustrating his independence,
aggression and pride. Other drinkers had noticed this dramatic scene,
drawing their own conclusions and commenting to one another on its
climax.

This disagreement may well have been settled quickly in private
between the two in the boat. But in the bar, with an audience, it became an
issue of individual independence and pride, *'respeto'*, the potential
recipient of the money not wishing to seem dependent on the other, or in
need of charity indicating shame, *'verguenza'*. This example also illustrates
the flexible social hierarchy in Vueltas, which local inhabitants insist is
determined by who can boss whom: men like to prove that nobody owns or
controls them.[12]

El borracho y la puta va solo [The drunk and the whore walk alone]

Mention of the masculine public bar social life leads us to the subject of
drunkenness. In VGR the drunk is regarded as a fool, someone who cannot
control himself and someone who should be avoided. Local drunkards are
infamous and mocked both in public and private: people tend to avoid
them when in a bar and a drunkard may clear a small bar of its clientele. At
one time, a drunk entered the bar and a fisherman commented:

He hassles people when he's drunk. Normally people drinking are *tranquilo* [calm], although in the bar next door the youths have fights with the Germans. But here, if my friend is drunk or seems to be aggressive I will leave him to it, we all will, as we do not want to be dragged into his problems.

In a small, close-knit, face-to-face community, where one often relies on one's neighbours, the drunkard is someone who will let others down. There are examples in VGR of such men who have lost work through drink; they have broken one of the most important social codes, that of self-control, the foundation upon which respect is built. A local saying emphasises the situation: 'The drunk and the whore walk alone'. One of the strongest forms of social sanctions used in VGR is that of isolation; in this manner, those who contravene expected norms of behaviour are ignored. This can happen on a simple interpersonal level between one-time friends; or, in a more general way, when economic survival is threatened, as well as psychological stability. This is the method employed with the drunkard and there are examples of men whose careers have crashed because of attributable factors, the main one being alcohol. Other people lose confidence in them and so look elsewhere for a job to be done. Masculinity in VGR is, in a large part, demonstrated by self-control and, in relation to alcohol, proved by the ability to drink it and retain control.

An examination of gender role play and construction reveals an area of transformation in Vueltas that has been influenced by communication with tourists, especially through emotional and sexual relationships. It is generally acknowledged that local girls may have had sexual intercourse before marriage; however, most people stressed that this would be with their potential spouse (cf. Goddard, 1987: 176). In Vueltas, daughters were usually strictly confined to the homes at night by their parents until 18 years of age, although they inevitably could commune with friends if they so desired. Control cannot be exerted over them when they go off to other places to study or work but expectations to be chaste were implicit. In general, sexual knowledge was poor due to a lack of education at school and the unwillingness of parents to talk. One 22-year-old student said that when she experienced her first menstruation period she was totally unprepared for it and did not know what was happening to her. She believed this lack of knowledge to be common and said that there were many unwanted pregnancies amongst girls under 16 because of their ignorance of human biology and contraception.

Local gender role construction portrays men as sexual predators and women say that villagers believe that a man who does not make an advance towards a woman if the situation allows it is not a real man. A similar attitude is reported by Brandes (1992) amongst the people of rural Andalusía. In VGR, women tease a man if he allows his wife to be seen talking alone with another man: people criticise and ask questions or start rumours. This form of social control, prescribing roles for men to play in their relations with women, limits the freedom of men and women to form adult friendships: social pressure from all sides sees to this. The German wife of a local man admitted: 'I enjoy seeing other men as friends to talk with but pressure put on my husband has led me to stop such meetings'. This difference in attitudes may eventually lead to a redefinition of mixed gender relationships amongst the people of VGR. With such examples of gender behaviour, the local men and women are shown new possibilities for social interaction that can lead to real change.[13]

Some local women suggested that the reason for the sexual implication in any friendship between a man and a woman stems from the lifestyles of the men: being fishermen they left their wives alone for a long time and needed to be sure that they were not seeing other men. Historical accounts by Burriel (1982) show the high illegitimate birth rate in earlier centuries and there seems to be a traditional fear of sexual infidelity. As well as criticising the men's sexual philandering, many women complained that the men were lacking in care, incapable of being gentle towards them: 'Men do not treat women well' was a very common criticism from younger women. This again contrasts with many of the German male tourists' approach towards women, which is less aggressive and much more of a meeting of equals.

In Vueltas the married women (when not at work) spent most of their time in the house, working, cleaning and cooking, occasionally venturing out to the shops or to see friends and relatives. One wife who nursed her invalid husband claimed that she had not been to the port to socialise for five years (it was only one minute's walk away). Many younger married women talked of their isolation in the home: they rarely went out with their husbands, some only once a year. The men could go down the bar alone at liberty but the women could not, as they would be criticised: they were required in the home to look after the children. Married women, when they did venture out, avoided looking at other men in the eye; they would not wish to be seen to invite the attention of other men or be suspected of having an affair. There is a sexual shame attached to women.[14]

People generally agree that the man is regarded as the breadwinner who wants a clean house and a prepared meal. However, women bringing in good wages are undermining the postition of the man as the main earner in the household. This is largely a consequence of the expansion of the tourist industry. In the opinion of most women, men were generally incapable of looking after themselves and the majority could not cook or clean. Yet young men cook seafood in a paella pan and the captain of a fishing boat prepared an excellent meal for his crew whilst at sea. These are examples that show that the stereotypes are not good guides as to the capabilities of either sex but indicate generally perceived norms and suggest that roles are contextually determined. In Vueltas, there are clear ideas on the gender roles within the home, at work and in personal relations but these are being challenged at a growing rate – especially by the growing number of women in full employment.[15]

One young man from Vallehermoso (in the north of the island) thought that the young men of VGR were *loco* (mad): this was because of their general beer drinking, smoking, motorbike-riding, macho behaviour. He, like many other men on the island, represents a contrast to the stereotypical Mediterranean male: this must be emphasised, as the variety of masculine attitudes and behaviour is far more diverse than some accounts would have it. Many of the local men were quiet, sensitive, artistic and intellectual – and certainly too sophisticated to indulge in violent displays of bravado. Even so, macho behaviour predominates amongst the young men of Vueltas. Some of the young women who leave La Gomera to be educated in Tenerife return and say that they feel themselves to be totally different from the people who remained behind. They think that the young men of VGR are immature and silly, with their interests centred on drinking, football, sex and motorbikes. In this we can see a major transition within the characteristics of the two sexes. These women have outstripped many local men in educational achievements and intellectual aspirations: they form part of an educated élite when returning to the village in the summer vacation and often distance themselves from their peers who remained behind. In one generation, the switch has been huge due to educational opportunities and the highly educated women begin to have more in common with their student equivalents from other parts of Spain among the tourists than with their village friends. The mass media and education, both global influences, are impinging on local gender roles in an increasingly noticeable way among the younger generation.

Global Influences

The Canary Islander has his feet in Africa, his head in Europe and his heart in South America.

There are numerous influences on identity and self-perception within the society of Vueltas and yet another complexity to add to the picture is one covering the Canary Islands in general. Their history has given them contact with three different continents: Europe through colonisation, culture and their current status as an autonomous region of Spain; Africa through physical proximity and the original inhabitants ('Guanches') who arrived from Africa over 1000 years ago; and South America through continual contact via the Atlantic trade route and migration as well as a shared cultural history as a Spanish colony. These regions each have their particular influences on the people. The local refrain summarises the islanders' complicated cultural identity. Many people return to La Gomera after living and working in Venezuela, Cuba and other Latin American countries and the most popular music at the fiestas is Latin American salsa. Soap operas on the TV are from Latin America, and colloquialisms from there have entered the vocabulary, including '*GuaGua*' for bus, whilst the Gomeran accent is said to resemble Venezuelan closely. Witchcraft is another aspect of local culture that has been influenced by Latin America. The society has, therefore, been open to a variety of cultural influences through its geographically nodal position, subjected to globalisation and creolisation over the centuries: a process that continues apace to this day with the arrival of tourists from the metropolitan centres of northern Europe.

Strangers

At the same time as being subject to cultural influences from three different continents during its history, the island population of La Gomera, and particularly VGR, has been at times very isolated. Up until 1975 there was no regular connection between the south of Tenerife and La Gomera. The conditions of the roads meant that the journey from San Sebastian to VGR was an arduous process: some 2½ hours by car around the island in an anti-clockwise direction, traversing ravines and turning more than 300 sharp bends. This consequently had a restrictive effect on the number and type of visitor to VGR. Communication between municipalities was limited and the inhabitants of adjacent municipalities regarded each other as *extranjeros* (strangers), a word that is applied to both foreigners and strangers alike. One man living in Vueltas had spent his youth and working life in the north of the island but came to Vueltas, where he had some friends, to end his days. He is popular with the locals, impoverished and often a figure of fun; however, even though they all know him well, he is regarded as an *extranjero*. Another example, a couple, the wife from the north of the island the husband from Tenerife, described how they were regarded as strangers even though they had lived and worked in VGR for some ten years.

By popular consent, the criterion for being regarded as a *hijo del pueblo* (son of the village) and not an *extranjero* is to be born and brought up in the village. A quarrel between a local young man and another man who had been born in Venezuela but lived in VGR for many years, induced the local man to shout '*Naci aqui!*' (I was born here!), thus isolating his enemy: his security in his sense of being a son of the village was obvious to all onlookers. This sense of belonging, and confidence in the *pueblo*, was reiterated during the political campaigns when the current mayor, speaking on behalf of his fellow councillors representing the centrist party, pointed out that they were all '*hijos del pueblo*' as well as neighbours. Whereas, he emphasised, in contrast the candidates for mayor in the other two parties were either from another island or currently living on one.

Belonging can be both a relative and an absolute quality. To have been born and brought up in the village, i.e. to be a true son of the village, is the most absolute indicator of belonging and, after this, there follows a sliding scale of belonging.[16] The pride that inhabitants have in being born in the community shows that there is an ultimate referent, which they are happy to utilise when the degree of belonging is in question. 'Class is not so important as being a son of the pueblo' (Kenny, 1961: 84): this sentiment is valid for VGR as far as public proclamations give evidence.

With the tourist influx of the 1980s, the local people were inundated with strangers from other countries. The sheer number of the foreigners, together with the quick turnover, militated against getting to know them well and so characterisations became generalised. The tourists from Germany are sometimes referred to as *cabeza cuadrados* (square heads), the English are regarded as 'hooligans' and the Spanish are seen as 'mean, noisy and untidy'. With the appearance of these *extranjeros*, so came an increased awareness of difference and, in this way, the people of VGR were experiencing the boundaries of their group. In these circumstances, the different groups give broad-brushed descriptions of each other and may adopt defensive attitudes. This is an example of the agent interpreting the 'unknown' through his/her own system of logic, his/her own set of 'meanings'. The use of stereotypes allows the user to rapidly categorise something fully and diminishes the need to explain; in other words, it is a convenient short cut, most commonly employed where a lengthy analysis would not be appropriate. Stereotyping also creates a notional 'other' and confirms group boundaries, reflecting cultural preoccupations and values (cf. McDonald [1993] on stereotyping). An example of defensive group stereotyping can be found in the attitudes regarding friendships between locals and tourists. In VGR, local girls are warned against getting involved with foreign boys: they are criticised by others and regarded as *loca* (mad) if they socialise with them. Contrastingly, the local boys chase the foreign girls and will often try to strike up a conversation or make a comment to them. If a group of local boys are passed by a foreign girl, it is inevitable that one of them will shout out '*Hola chica!*'. A foreign girl is generally seen as fair game.[17]

For the foreign settlers who live and work in the village, there can be specific problems. One German who worked in a shop told of how some local people did not like to buy things from him because he was a foreigner, and in their opinion, he was taking away their business: this may be seen as a form of economic protectionism. He believed that he had no real friends in the village apart from the brothers of his girlfriend. He was the unique example of a German with a local girlfriend – there was one other German who was actually married to a local woman, who claimed that they are the only such couple on the island. Another German working in VGR told of how the local men often became abusive towards him, especially if he himself was drunk. A couple, both Spaniards, claimed the local children tease foreign children at school, using the phrase *'heder extranjeros'* (smelly foreigners). Nevertheless, there is no doubt that the children of foreign settlers do play and mix with the local children in and out of school. But these incidents show that local people sometimes isolate foreign settlers through teasing and economic ostracism.[18]

On the other side of the coin, the foreign settlers themselves have some negative and stereotypical opinions regarding the local people. A popular criticism was that 'they have no culture': this was explained by one settler as the lack of professionalism and qualified tradesmen, together with the lack of amenities such as theatres. In this sense the word 'culture' relates to 'high culture', perhaps represented by museums, opera houses, theatres, libraries and an élite professional class. Even so, this criticism is somewhat unjustified: there is a library in VGR and there have been theatrical performances at the recently built *Casa Cultural* (Cultural Centre).[19] The lack of awareness by the foreign settlers of the cultural richness of the local people, manifested through traditional dance, music, crafts, oral history, skills and language, is evidence of the chasm of misunderstanding between them.

A further common observation made by settlers was that the local people could not be trusted when they said something: 'They simply do not tell the truth'. Some settlers believed that the local men had no respect for women, some of whom had been subjected to verbal abuse by local men (who were usually social misfits in their own community). However, many were appreciative of the indigenous population's skill in surviving in a harsh environment and admired their group cohesion. Even though the settlers mixed with local people during working hours, they rarely seemed to sustain social relationships with them outside of them. There is even a *barrio* (neighbourhood) in the upper valley that is occupied predominantly by Germans, which they describe in good humour as a ghetto. One major barrier to integration is language and many settlers could not speak Spanish sufficiently well to appreciate the local people, leading to a general mutual misunderstanding. Those who made the effort inevitably began to mix more with them, exchanging gossip and jokes and some made good friends. An examination of the experiences of a few foreign settlers recorded in 1991, given here, gives a clearer picture of the sort of situations that have occurred and the types of interactions that have developed.

Juan, a Spaniard from mainland Spain, met his German wife whilst travelling in Greece, and now lives in Vueltas. He worked as a waiter and realised the advantages of running his own restaurant, so he rented a property and purchased the necessary equipment. Unfortunately, he experienced serious problems gaining a license to operate due to complaints from his neighbours but managed to solve this problem after much protest by appealing to a higher authority than the local council. The pressure of work and disagreements over his wife's social activity led them to split up and their two children now live with his wife in a separate apartment. She has worked as a restaurant helper, a language teacher, a cake saleswoman and is now employed by a travel company.

Juan has found it hard to make good friends with the local people; he has been restricted by his working hours and feels that he has different interests from them being a well-travelled arts graduate. He thinks that most foreign couples experience similar problems. Although his children go to school locally, their closest friendships are with the children of other foreign couples. Juan is bored by restaurant work, he cannot cook so waits on tables, he is thinking about starting another venture as a tourist guide around the island, a form of ecotourism, but he needs contacts in Germany. He owes a lot of money on his business and also has personal difficulties with his family; furthermore, he feels trapped by being in the same locality with the same people all the time. The family has been in VGR for six years and Juan thinks that the new developments are ruining the place, saying that even the new Casa Cultural is a waste of space. He has had problems with the people living above his restaurant but they are over now. Only one person is still abusive towards him: this person asked for a fight and threatened to kill him. Juan called the police, despite which the man continued to shout at him, saying that he would 'kill him like a dog'.

Another Spaniard, Fernando, and his Spanish wife have lived with their four children in Vueltas for over ten years: he is a medical assistant and she teaches secretarial skills. Fernando is in favour of development for VGR and is scathing about the local people's lack of culture. He comes from Tenerife and wanted to introduce a Red Cross facility in the community but was opposed by the powerful *caciques*. He likes tourism because it brings in new ideas as well as money. Due to his qualifications and dynamic personality, Fernando believes that he has been a threat to the established élite in the valley and says that they have tried to isolate him. He has bought into a development project for a large building containing apartments and shops and will be the representative for the PP (Partido Popular) during the local elections, when he wants to capture the youth vote. However, he has had opposition for all his projects and is embittered: 'The people are deceptive, they don't tell the truth; they don't trust clean, honest outsiders'. Fernando feels that there is a feudal situation in VGR, with a *cacique* – slave mentality, saying that the *caciques* manipulate the people: foreigners are feared and loathed – even his children are teased. He thought that most foreigners have problems in VGR, with the general belief that 'those not born in the village are enemies'. In his view there was no moral law in VGR but only *'derecho social'* (socially determined rights) – brother fights brother; for example, in VGR one girl left her family aged three and returned as an adult to claim her inheritance but her brothers refused to hand it over. Fernando says: 'The people can only accept others who are as bad or worse than them, like the drug dealers'. After the elections in which his party did disastrously, Fernando and his family left VGR.

A British couple were running a cafe in Borbolan just outside Vueltas, they were 18 months into it and had experienced a lot of problems during the first six months, with complaints from the ex-owner and their neighbours. They believed that they were charged higher prices for stock than local people and were generally distrustful of them. At one time, Paul had a serious argument with the deputy mayor and it was rumoured that he had actually punched the mayor: this rumour apparently brought him respect amongst the locals. His wife, Samantha, recalled that a local man had been extremely insulting to her, so she swore at him and slapped him in the face, after which he showed her deference. Despite teething problems, their cafe was initially a success. This was due largely through their ability to converse with the German tourists in English (neither of them speak Spanish), their amiable personalities and their English breakfasts (which were unique in the valley where breakfast usually consists of little more than coffee and a bread roll). They believe that the local people were envious of their success and tried to copy Samantha's recipes. Paul said: 'The locals twist the truth, you can't trust them'. Even though they do good business the profit is low, partly because staff costs are prohibitively high. They employed one local woman because she spoke Spanish, which gave them an advantage in obtaining a license to operate in 1990 and helped with the workload. As the second year of their venture progressed problems escalated with an inspection requiring them to replace storage equipment and the construction of a road outside the front door which put off the customers: the pressure became too much and one day Paul left the island. He returned some days later and remained for a while but the couple soon departed for good.

Peggy, a woman brought up in the USA, ran a private lending library for many years in Calera, stocked with books written in English and German. She had arrived with her husband and children over 30 years ago. She knew the community very well, spoke Spanish fluently and was possibly the first person to rent out apartments in Calera. However, she was dismissive of the benefits of tourism, pointing out the increase in drug and alcohol usage, the permissive sexual activity, nudity on the beaches and the increased materialism and competition amongst the local people. Her library was an information centre for many tourists who dropped in and enquired about rooms or timetables as well as receiving friendly advice in English. Peggy had a religious mission and she was a major component in a foreign community network in which English speakers can gain access to others as well as work and resources.

One such couple able to use Peggy's knowledge of the community and network of friends were Jim and Janet from England. Janet has a sister living in VGR and after visiting on a holiday decided to stay for a longer period of time, up to a year. Jim is a plumber by trade and was able to find plenty of work in the valley through his English-speaking contacts. They rented an old cottage in the upper valley and were able to survive doing odd jobs for six months. Unfortunately, they had problems with their Swiss neighbour which led Jim to damage some property, after which their Gomero neighbours described his actions as *feo* (ugly) and, in his own words, 'blanked' (ignored) him. They enjoyed their experience in the valley but felt that many of the foreign settlers could not be trusted, and eventually they returned to England.

These examples give the impression of foreign settlers encountering problems with local people and with other foreign settlers. The reality of settling down and earning a living in a foreign country is quite different from the experience of visiting a country as a tourist. Some have had serious misunderstandings with local people, involving denunciations to the local council or the threat of violence. Their lack of experience of the social etiquette and codes of conduct of the local community has led to them accidentally insult people or to do things that are socially unacceptable. Compounding this is the fact that they are foreigners, arriving into a very tightly knit indigenous community, introducing new and sometimes radical ideas and often being successful in business. Local people, who do not always have the knowledge or skills to achieve their goals, are often envious of successful foreign settlers. Furthermore, the region has had a long historical experience of difficulties with outsiders: invading forces, regular attacks by pirates, a civil war and exploitative foreign bosses. But more recently, bad experiences with tourists, who may have damaged or stolen property, absconded without paying bills, sold drugs or behaved in a manner regarded as morally depraved, make them wary of '*extranjeros*'.

Perhaps it is inevitable that people highlight negative aspects of their experiences as foreign settlers as they are more memorable and make good conversation. Nevertheless, a general impression is gained that there are invisible boundaries between local people and foreign settlers, boundaries of intimacy and trust that very few have crossed. For example, even though one German had entered into a long-term relationship with the daughter of a fisherman, fished with her father and been accepted as part of the family, he still had major problems associating with other men in the village. He said that they would not befriend him and enjoyed provoking him to anger, which he interpreted as their way of testing his *facha* (social mask), something that they do to most male foreign settlers.

Despite the attrition of some foreign settlers, others continue to arrive, attracted by resident friends or their experiences as tourists. We can see from the previous example that foreigners introduce ideas and skills to the local community, whether they are professional skills, new religions, first aid or different culinary knowledge, they all have the potential to enrich and influence the local people, to give them new choices and opportunities. This is especially so with the German entrepreneurs who have introduced dolphin tour businesses, postcard shops, a film theatre, boutiques, restaurants and a mountain-bike shop. The foreign-settler community is expanding with the increased growth in tourism businesses and ease of access to employment due to the EU open market. Nevertheless, they tend to socialise amongst themselves, forming an ethnic minority in the valley.

Mass media and education

Examples given of the traditional arts, the crafts and music of Gomeran culture provide an impression of the potential diversity of experience and opportunities for self-expression and perception on La Gomera. There are innumerable other examples of things which influence identity and self-perception and one of the most salient in Vueltas is that of the popularised mass media, especially music, television and film. The young people of Vueltas have, since the 1980s, grown up surrounded by the images and products of the industrialised West and they are able to participate in the ubiquitous popular culture available to most people in Western Europe, part of the process often referred to as globalisation. They have, therefore, a wide range of potential roles to play and their behaviour has been given the chance to adapt because of opportunities introduced by tourism. The proliferation of bars and the accessibility of money – direct results of tourism – have facilitated the cultivation of a youth culture, consuming music, fashion, clothing, alcohol and drugs: this has also led to situations of stress and conflict.[20]

In Calera, the Casa Cultural houses a lecture theatre (where the heated debate over the beach development took place), various games-rooms for children, a television and hi-fi room and a non-lending library. The Centre was built in the late 1980s and the library acquired some 4000 books, including works by the anthropologists Lévi-Strauss and Malinowski: these reflect the interests of those who make the central allocation decisions for the municipalities. It shows a serious concern for the more intellectual side of culture and the contrast between this 'Casa Cultural' and the 'Visitors' Centre' in the National Park serves to illustrate the division as perceived by the authorities. The Casa Cultural reflects the desire to modernise the community and promote formal education and the arts of the industrialised West, whereas the Visitors' Centre represents a perception of the past and stands as a monument to local history in the form of a sentimental folk heritage. The Casa Cultural is almost a 'shrine' to mass media and education: with its electronic equipment and books – vital elements of the western information society – it purveys the 'knowledge' and interests of an industrialised state, one increasingly dominated by the metropolitan values of consumerism, scientific enquiry, progress and rationalism. Nevertheless, in 1991, the Cultural Centre was not very popular with the teenage youth of VGR: perhaps it reminds them of school.

Another source of identity is religion: this is taught in schools and encouraged in many homes. Roman Catholicism, through the creation of parish boundaries, determines a corporate identity, which is emphasised during the fiesta rituals when the procession marks out the boundary of the parish.[21]

Religion also plays a part in the personal identity of most of the islanders.[22] One fisherman said that he had respect for only two things, 'God and death', and his friends agreed with him. Women almost exclusively attend mass; nevertheless, the men claim that they themselves are religious and many had helped to pay for and even build the chapel in Vueltas. They also attend the funeral masses. Tourism does not seem to have influenced attitudes towards religion directly but it may have provided further distractions for the youth of Vueltas, leading them away from religious activities. At one time, a reading from the Bible was given in German by a local man on Palm Sunday: this was for the benefit of the foreign settlers and the few tourists that attended, as well as giving the reader social prestige. The degree of personal association with Catholicism varies across the generations and between the sexes, with the older generation, especially the women, adhering to the traditions. Many young people admitted that they were suspicious of the motives of some of the congregation and that they had no confidence in the priest for confessional purposes. Religious belief is an area that is indirectly influenced by tourism due to its general provision of wealth and distractions and the arrival of people with contrasting opinions on religion.

One extreme example of the arrival of new ideas can be seen in the establishment of a settlement near Vueltas of followers of Bhagwan Shri Rajneesh, who describe themselves as 'Sannyasins'.[23] These followers, predominantly German, have also established a centre in Vueltas which offers therapy and services of varying kinds to the public, usually advocating meditation. Some of the members mix with villagers and they hold parties to which a few local youths turn up. The Centre has become more tolerated over time and some middle-aged local women visit for physical exercise sessions. Local people are thus introduced to a different 'religion' that gives them an opportunity for choice, even though they may not be looking for an alternative. The point is that tourism has introduced people with radically different ideas into the community who might influence their hosts in many ways, changing their beliefs or strengthening them, or simply making them more aware of themselves as a specific type of religious community.

Tourism and social boundaries

As mentioned earlier, the sense of being a *hijo del pueblo* is still very powerful and is used to unite the local people, either by their own volition or through the rhetoric of politicians, churchmen and others hoping to gain from this group identity. The experience of meeting tourists has led to a greater awareness amongst the islanders of themselves as a separate group.[24] In this way the visiting tourists and foreign settlers have enhanced the Gomeros' awareness of their own personal ethnic distinctiveness.

There is, together with this sense of difference, a discernible trend in VGR to look back at pre-tourist days with nostalgic sentiment. In the face of the sudden and continual arrival of unfamiliar people, some people resort to thinking of the times when the village was not a tourist attraction, the times when there were very few *extranjeros* around. Many of the local people said that with the rapid changes in VGR due to the tourism, the village community had lost something important, even though there were material gains. People stated that there was too much competition and business activity, leading to a lack of time for socialising. This type of sentiment was not only expressed by the older generations: many people under 30 years of age admitted having feelings of loss. One woman aged 23 said: 'We've lost something, the fiestas are not the same, they are too commercialised now, and the beaches are overcrowded'. She also recalled the peacefulness of the days of her childhood, the genuine spontaneity and simplicity of the fiestas. A man of 25 remembered how he would make toys with his friends when young, including wooden spinning tops and surfboards, lamenting: 'Now they just buy everything in the shops'. He complained that there was no real spirit of excitement during the annual festival of San Juan when bonfires are lit around the valley and added, 'We used to collect rubbish for up to two months before the fiesta, now nobody cares'. In 1996, a man in his early twenties who works in Tenerife recalled:

> The last ten years have brought tremendous changes, the youths aged around 14 years would work during the vacations in the plantations and with the fishermen, almost everyone, me included. Now they want the tourist lifestyle, working in discos and bars. Some don't even bother to work at all: they're spoilt. Tourism's a risk – too much dependence, and old customs are abandoned. Look at Guada in the upper valley, all the terraces have been abandoned, and lots of buildings: at least the foreigners look after the old buildings.

These young people were aware of the abrupt changes in the village and in their lives. However, they had been brought up with television and other means of modern mass communications, softening the blows of a tourist invasion. Almost all the people questioned on the matter said that they preferred the earlier days, even though many fully realised the benefits of change, the work opportunities and the general increase in wealth. There seems to be a historical watershed that occurred in the mid-1980s and is directly related to tourism. This has affected the identity of the inhabitants, with many making a conscious historical division between the pre-tourist days up to the early 1980s and the period afterwards

Tourism has challenged behavioural patterns in Vueltas by offering new role options for men and women and this is exposing weaknesses and uncertainties within the moral and behavioural norms of local social life. We can see that there is a greater variety and complexity of attitudes and perceptions amongst local people than may, at first, be realised and that tourism has exposed some of these differences as well as offering a greater diversity of choice. By using the concepts of actor and role, we discover how individuals differ and can change their potential behaviour and this is one way that the tourists have influenced local people by giving them new roles to perform which impact on their family, beliefs and values. Some of these issues are explored in the following chapter.

Notes

1. For example Abram and Waldren (1997), Bhaba (1994), Macdonald (1993) and Lanfant (1995).
2. See Selwyn (1996a) on myth-making, Dann (1996) on tourist brochures, Abram *et al.* (1997) on tourism and identity, Lanfant *et al.* (1995) on international tourism and identity and McCrone *et al.* (1995) on heritage and identity.

3. My teacher would translate the Spanish words into 'Gomeran' using the alphabet and then whistle the words.

4. Galvan-Tudela (1987) is a detailed account of popular fiestas in the Canary Islands.

5. It is worth noting that Cole (1991) records similar divisions between fishers and agriculturalists in Portugal where the fishing community originated from poor landless children of local peasants. Acheson (1981) draws attention to this division as a common occurrence, with fishing communities often at odds with agricultural ones.

6. Rural people are supposed to dislike this description and some girls from San Sebastian pleaded with me not to tell the people of VGR that they had said this.

7. This ambivalence correlates with the attitude towards shepherds within Greece, Scotland and Corsica, where they are regarded as embodying admirable qualities representing the genuine native but they are also seen as backward and unsophisticated (see Mckecknie [1993], and Parman [1990]).

8. Zinovieff notes that: '[i]dentity is negotiable, and exists not in itself, but in relationships and exchange . . . '. Whilst agreeing with the contextuality and negotiable nature of identity, I would argue that identity does exist in itself, as any introspection reveals – otherwise the dictum 'know thyself' is irrelevant: there is a relationship between the conscious mind and its object of concentration.

9. Gilmore has written about the rounds system in Andalusía, concluding the following: 'Thus the underlying ethical principle of casual friendship is one of immediate and balanced reciprocity by which everyone breaks even in the long run' (Gilmore, 1980: 190). I agree in principle with Gilmore; however, his conclusion is in error: if reciprocity is immediate and balanced, then everyone would break-even immediately and not worry about the long run. Reciprocity in Vueltas was not (in my observation) 'immediate': although groups of drinkers certainly expected everyone to eventually pay their way in the rounds system and occasionally fishermen would tease someone over not paying for their drinks. The friendships were, in general, more than casual, due to the length of time that the men had known one another. Reciprocity was not immediate, as there was an underlying assumption of trustworthiness amongst friends who would ultimately repay their debts.

10. The usage of the theatrical metaphor has been remarked upon by Sant Cassia (1991) in his discussion of personhood, agency and identity in the Mediterranean: 'Rather the theatrical element of social life is perceived as an indigenous concept, and the deep awareness of the illusion and self-illusion inherent in a flawed world contributes to the sense of social life as theatre' (p. 1991: 13).

11. This situation of relative flexibility contrasts with those analysed by Goffman (1969) who concentrated on situations that are constrained within 'concrete social establishments' such as the workplace, depicting 'performers' presenting 'parts' to 'audiences' as they consciously work on 'impression management'.

12. This attitude is similar to that amongst the Greek islanders of Nisos, where, according to Kenna (1976: 348), 'To retain his self-respect a man must regard himself as subordinate to no one'. The word 'honour' also comes to mind, and one is reminded of an incident in North Africa cited by Lienhardt (1979: 87) in which a man shot another during an argument over who should pay for the taxi.

13. Ortner (1989: 201)has written on this means of creating change: 'Change takes

place because alternatives become visible, or because actors have or gain the power to bring them into being'.

14. Shame is a theme examined in detail by Campbell (1964) and Pitt-Rivers (1954).

15. In a wide-ranging examination of tourism and gender, Kinnaird *et al.* (1994: 16) note the way that areas of tourism work both reinforces and transforms gendered divisions of labour. They also refer to its impact on family life and values – especially the increase of autonomy for women.

16. The sense of belonging has been examined by Cohen (1982b: 6), who writes of belonging being evoked by '[t]he use of language, the shared knowledge of genealogy or ecology, joking, the solidarity of sect, the aesthetics of subsistence skills'.

17. Bowman (1989) examines the relationship between local Palestinian merchants in Jerusalem and female tourists from Europe and the USA, drawing conclusions about the political power games consciously employed by the men in which they attempt to gain revenge on their socioeconomic masters. This aspect of the relationship is also commented upon by Zinovieff (1990: 168) who focuses on the *Kamakia* in Greece, a group of men who pursue foreign women, implying that they get revenge on the 'supposedly richer societies'. This does not seem to be part of the outlook of the men in VGR, who are simply out for sexual conquests, something difficult to obtain with local women without long-term implications, although occasionally serious relationships with tourists have led to marriage. Loizos (1992) has analysed the relationships between Greek men and female tourists, emphasising the physicality, lack of emotion, and public mockery displayed by the men when telling their friends of their conquests. In the cases from Jerusalem and Greece, it is worthwhile considering the male behaviour – the tales of bravado and conquest told to peers – as public role-playing. It is a display of the 'indifferent' male stud demonstrating his power to his friends and thereby both confirming and perpetuating the socially circulated stereotype of masculinity.

18. Waldren (1989: XI) examined identity in her thesis, specifically the notions of 'insider' and 'outsider', concluding that there is a 'renewed sense of solidarity in a period of socioeconomic change' (abstract). She points to the division between the categories of *Deianenc* and *estranger*, stating that by using these categories the local population are 'expressing symbolic boundaries'.

19. One such performance was from an avant-guarde Cuban company, which gave an explicit representation of a South American myth, semi-naked on stage. This created a panic amongst the audience, many mothers hurrying out with their children, angry at having waited for an hour outside for this, the first play to be seen in VGR. There were one or two aesthetes, however, who were appreciative of the experience and a few older members moved nearer the stage to gain a better view.

20. 'The cultural expansion of the North and West in terms of consumer goods, associated cultures and consumerist values which possess the capacity to challenge and change cultural identities continues to invoke conflicts' (Robinson, 1999: 25).

21. Christian examines communities identifying with religious figures in his study of religion in northern Spain: 'Different religious figures have come to stand for different identities that people of the valley share. The linking of a religious figure to a shared identity seems to have this effect: it elevates or generalises the

basis for identity to the status of a family relation under love, authority, and protection of a divine parent' (Christian 1972: 12).

22. The vast majority of people that I spoke to described themselves as Roman Catholics.

23. See Thompson and Heelas (1986) for an examination of this movement.

24. Cohen, following Barth, has reiterated the importance of the interaction of different groups in helping to create identity: 'It has been cogently argued that it is at the boundaries of ethnic groups that ethnicity becomes meaningful: that is, groups become aware of their ethnic identity when they engage with others' (Cohen, 1982b: 3).

Chapter 7
Family, Belief and Values

Introduction

In this chapter we examine part of the local community that might be regarded as its core: the family, beliefs and values. In so doing, we are considering perhaps the most profound impact that tourism can have in the personal arenas of the private household, the domestic lives, emotional experiences, deeply held beliefs and the moral fabric of the group of people who form the community. Specifically, we look at the composition of the family, the meaning and importance of the house and home and the potential marriage partners of the indigenous population. In addition, we examine their religious and supernatural beliefs, moral values, sets of attitudes embracing envy, competition and criticism, as well as the concepts of respect and shame. All these elements are considered in their own right as traits of the indigenous population in the classic manner of an ethnographic monograph, while the influence of tourism in its various manifestations, usually indirect, is recognised. Finally we look at the more apparent social and cultural ideas influencing the younger generation who have had direct contact with foreign tourists.

The Family in Vueltas

The concept of the family has remained central to anthropological works on Europe when looking at kinship, and it serves a useful purpose as a model from which to start analysis. Campbell (1964) retained the idea of the family as a fundamental part of Sarakatsani life, and Peristiany's (1976) collection of essays looked at the variety and importance of family life. For Mediterraneanists, the family has been a very important aspect of their work and they have remained aware of the variety of forms that it takes in their region of interest. Ethnographic accounts have analysed the kinship relations and created specialist terms for the common structures that they found. Although the nuclear family, in the sense of a married couple and their children, seems to be the most popular formation in Spain, there may be numerous variations around this basic model (cf. Bestard, 1991). This section examines the family unit in its manifold roles and draws attention to its fundamental place at the heart of the community of VGR.

In Vueltas, the most common kinship unit is the 'nuclear family', living in a separate home, with cognatic or alineal affiliation to relatives, bilateral inheritance of equal parts between all sons and daughters, and independent or ambilocal post-marital residence. In many cases very strong links are maintained with the parents of the couple.[1] Occasionally, couples live in the same house or in an adjoining apartment to one set of parents: in such cases, meals may be shared with the grandparents, parents and grandchildren. Such an arrangement may be described as an extended family, although the arrangement is usually a temporary one in which the independent nuclear family is the ideal to be achieved: closely maintained links between generations are emphasised by economic necessity and support. There are strong bonds between the grandparents and the grandchildren, with the grandparents usually babysitting whilst the parents work. In some cases, the grandfather spends far more time with the children than the father. These may be the parents of either spouse, although, in most cases, they were the parents of the bride.[2]

In 1991, there were a few houses in Vueltas within which four generations of the same family lived but they were becoming increasingly rare. Brothers and sisters often live side by side, having inherited the same plot of land and divided it, or sold off plots to one another. All this creates the impression of dynasties or familial groupings in particular territories.[3] In VGR brothers often work together as well, having learnt the same skills from their father, such as fishing, building or carpentry. This general proximity leads to a vast interrelated network, with people able to recognise relatives traceable through their great-great-grandparents. Often in conversation, people would immediately place another person as a relative and it seemed that they favoured relatives over non-kinsmen, however distant. A fisherman joked to a lazy youth to go and help his cousin, who happened to be hauling in a boat at the time, insinuating that he should do so as a close relative. Such examples help to confirm the depth of integration and potential reliance there is between kinsmen – an examination of family crews shows their kin-based organisation (see Macleod, 1993).

Cousins are commonly recognised to the third level, for example *primo tercero* being a male cousin related through the great-great-grandparents. There is no distinction made as to whether the cousin is related through the mother or father or whether s/he is a cross or parallel cousin. Many people were able to point out their third cousins with ease. Partly because of the closeness of the community and its isolation, the history and genealogy of many families are interrelated, allowing the people to accumulate a vast knowledge about their kin: a feature of small island communities. This proximity is shown in the genealogical plans of families (Figures 1 and 2), as well as on the map of the houses in Vueltas (Map 3).

Affinal relations are important in VGR and many people are able to use these relationships to improve their lives. Thus, someone's *cuñado* (brother-in-law) may help in finding a job or in building a house. It is usually one set of parents-in-law that provides the couple's first home together. The two sets of parents linked by the marriage of their offspring refer to one another as *compadres*. For example, a woman said that her parents were occasionally helped by the parents of her husband when it came to digging up potatoes: her husband's parents also brought along maize corn to be ground by her own mother for *gofio* and gave fish in return. The relationship can, therefore, be a close and supportive one. The spouses of a set of sisters or brothers also have a descriptive term, *concuño*, and, in some cases, they form a close relationship with each other: one girl recounted how she would chat with the wife of her brother-in-law, joking about their respective husbands, who of course were brothers. The network of kin may be profitably extended through marriage and this inter-familial relationship shows there are often potential socioeconomic advantages for members of the couple's families. The woman mentioned in this example was provided with a home to live in with her new husband by her parents, whilst her husband's parents helped out with provisions and were able to use their political connections to help her gain a job and give her legal advice.

Marriage between first cousins was, at one time, common, especially in the upper part of VGR at Casa de la Seda, and people say that it was also the norm in Tenerife some years ago. However, it was believed that the practice led to problems with offspring as one landlady pointed out: 'because of *mismo sangre* [the same blood] sometimes people were born *bobo* [simple]'. There were at least three contemporary examples of first cousin marriage in VGR in 1991. This example of an outdated marital custom, a suggestion of a type of endogamy, is really more of a reflection on the isolation of the community, again, characteristic of island communities where isolation leads to fewer choices for potential spouses. It is also a means of retaining wealth and established relationships in a kinship group and its demise shows how, in recent times, opportunities have opened up for local people. In the past the best chances for meeting prospective spouses were the fiestas whereas, nowadays, young people have much more freedom to mix with the opposite sex in other circumstances and meet people from other communities. Tourism has also introduced a new potential for meeting people and developing serious relationships and marriages are increasingly common between locals and foreigners who first arrived as tourists (Figures 1 and 2). We can see this development in

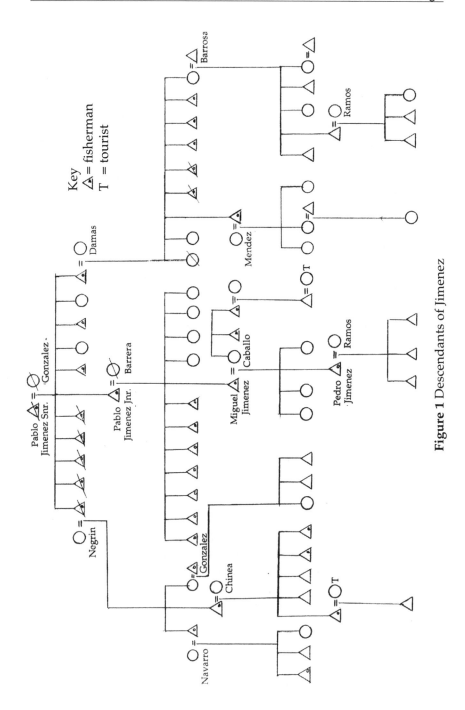

Figure 1 Descendants of Jimenez

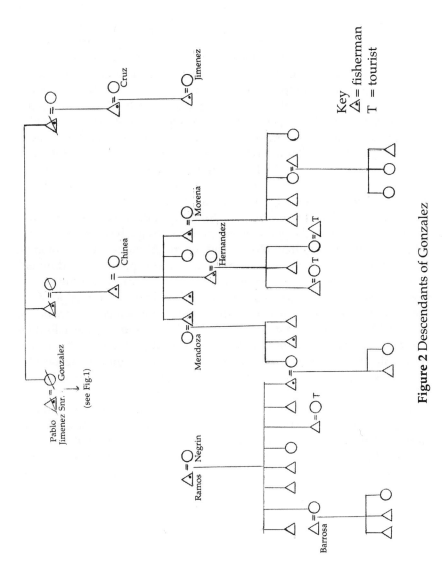

Figure 2 Descendants of Gonzalez

the outlines of the different families examined in the next section, all of which have a history going back to the original settlers of Vueltas.

The family as an enduring economic unit is important in Vueltas and kinship forms the organising principle governing many business operations such as shops and restaurants as well as the fishing crew (cf. Aceves, 1971: 131). This is a result of the historical development of livelihoods whereby the family would be the basic economic unit, living a subsistence lifestyle with children helping parents to wrest a living from the land or the sea. With fishermen, entire crews are instinctively drawn from the immediate family. This organisational principle also applies to other trades such as carpenters and builders as well as to service outlets, and it continues today with family-run businesses being the norm. However, with the growth in educational opportunities and the increase in available jobs in VGR, a greater mobility of labour has developed and more children now move away from their parents to find work.

In Vueltas the families tend to perpetuate the Catholic beliefs of the elder generation, although the younger generation does not have such a deeply religious attitude as their elders and religious piety varies amongst families. The two areas of economics and belief, pointing to different aspects of family life, serve to indicate the family's importance and fundamental centrality to the social life of La Gomera. In his examination of the family in Spain Lisón-Tolosana outlines the numerous characteristics of this kinship grouping. He states that the family is 'the locus of socialisation and development of the personality, law, sexual prohibitions, transition rites, obligations and laws, the moral and symbolic signifiers etc; besides being an economic unity and a focus of love and tension' (Lisón-Tolosana, 1980: 101).

These facets of the family are subject to variance between different examples and over time but, as a core grouping, it retains a central place in the lives of the people in Vueltas. All the more important then is the fact that foreign tourists are playing an increasingly large part in the lives and composition of families in Vueltas. The examples of three families, recorded in 1991, that have been settled in Vueltas since its beginnings illustrate some of these points.

Specific family groups

Jimenez

According to the 1991 electoral role, there were 19 adults in Vueltas whose first (paternal) surname is Jimenez and at least eight that have it as their second (maternal) surname. They are all descendants of the original fisherman, Pablo Jimenez, who arrived in VGR in 1910 and built one of the first houses in Vueltas for his family (see Figure 1). The grandchildren of the original Jimenez are now themselves grandparents: of those in Vueltas four men are fishermen, two having officially retired, although one still fishes regularly. One granddaughter is married to a former builder, who would have become a fisherman but was not physically suited to it. All these relations own tourist apartments, either built onto their homes or standing in separate buildings: Miguel and his cousin Pablo were amongst the first local people to build apartments and own up to 16 each.

The great-grandchildren of the original Jimenez, themselves aged between 20 and 40 in 1991, have pursued a variety of different professions. Of the seven sons of the fishermen, four are full- or part-time fishermen, a fifth was but now operates a restaurant in the village with his French wife whom he met whilst she was on holiday in Vueltas. Two others are involved in building and carpentry. The three sons of the granddaughter who married a builder all followed in their father's footsteps as builders. The daughters have remained housewives: one helps to run a bakery, and some work in the apartments cleaning and maintaining them. Of the most recent generation, the great-great-grandchildren, there was at least one who wanted to become a fisherman and started to fish with his father in the late 1990s giving the Jimenez family five generations of fishermen in Vueltas. Members of the Jimenez family themselves were aware that their ancestors were amongst the first of the settlers in Vueltas but this did not seem to affect their relationships with other inhabitants. Many fishermen would have arrived around the same time during the 1920s and most would have known the area due to the seasonal fishing in the Gomeran waters.

Gonzalez

The wife of Pablo Jimenez (mentioned earlier) arrived in Vueltas and settled in the 1900s. She was the daughter of a fisherman whose paternal surname was Gonzalez and met and married Pablo in Santiago del Teide, Tenerife: she joined him later in VGR. Eventually her brothers joined her in Vueltas. There are now 16 adults in Vueltas whose first surname is Gonzalez and seven who have it as their second (see Figure 2). All of the five male grandchildren of the first arrivals began their working lives as fishermen, four continued and two have retired. The fifth left for Venezuela aged around 26 with his wife and returned after 17 years having worked in a shop: on their return they opened up a general store, and are still running it together with additional outlets. This family also has apartments that they rent out: three more of the original grandchildren also rent out apartments.

The great-grandchildren of the Gonzalez brothers have followed a variety of career paths: one lives in Germany with a woman whom he met when she was a tourist in VGR, he works with computers. His brother is studying information technology at university and their sister studied law and tourism at university and now works in the family shop with her husband, an Italian whom she met whilst he was holidaying in Tenerife. Their cousin worked as a disc jockey in the local discotheque; his brother works as a painter; and their sister is a housewife also helping to clean a set of apartments. Another cousin is a cleaner for a set of apartments and one is a waiter in a hotel in Tenerife. None of them currently works as a fisherman, although one did work for a while on the large fishing boats. In 1991 some of this generation had children aged between 1 and 17 years, the eldest hoped to study business administration. All of the great-grand-children were brought up in adjoining houses in Vueltas.

Morales

One of the few non-fishing families to have settled in Vueltas before the 1940s is that of Domingo Morales (81 years old in 1991), and his wife. Domingo was brought up in the north of the island and met his wife in VGR in 1939. They built the house in which they still live. Domingo was a builder and his two sons, aged in their late fifties, are also builders, one having attended college to learn about construction. In 1991 the sons still worked in the construction industry, at one time having a business that employed some local men and built most of the apartments in Vueltas. Of Domingo's 11 grandchildren living in Vueltas, one of the teenage boys was already helping in the construction work with his father. Another was doing military service and the other five were students. Of the girls, one was a student of business at the university, another was at school, whilst the remaining three helped run apartments and worked in restaurants. By 1996, one of the girls was living with an Austrian boyfriend who worked for a tour company.

This brief examination of these three family groups has shown the tendency of men born before 1960 to follow the profession of their father, a determining feature of livelihood. This generation now forms the parental generation. They watch their children growing up, able to take advantage of the educational opportunities and, even more so in VGR, the work opportunities afforded by the tourism industry. The most striking feature of this change is the ability of women to find work in this way. The genealogical diagrams (Figures 1 and 2) showing whether the men are professional fishermen indicates that men have begun to find work in new professions outside fishing within the most recent generation. They also indicate that local men have married foreign women who visited the island as tourists. Moreover, this description of the families has shown that women are also beginning to establish serious emotional relationships with tourists. These changes emphasise the difference in opportunities and the expansion of choice available for the younger adult generation in comparison to that of their parents in earlier times.

La casa

The family is a central feature of socal life in Vueltas, and it is within the home that it is united and ultimately defined. *La casa* (the home/house) is the word that describes the physical building; but it also has another significance and implies the close parental unit, usually the nuclear family or, very occasionally, the extended family; it therefore possesses an emotional content. The two concepts of immediate family group and house are united in the term '*La casa*'.[4] In Vueltas, *la casa* was certainly the private concern of the inhabitants, although in general it was open to the many relatives and close friends that cared to visit: however, entertaining friends in the home was not the usual practice. *La casa* was also, at one time, the provider of the basic economic group in society but with the increasing division of labour and diverse employment within households this is diminishing.

One of the most profound facets of life in the *casa*, however, remains the division of activities based on gender. It is a noticeable feature in Vueltas that men and adolescent boys spend little time in the home whereas the mothers and daughters remain almost confined within its walls.[5] The women were not so free in their movements and they resented their lives confined to the home. The *casa* is dominated by the female presence, although in Vueltas it is generally agreed that the man is the ultimate authority. People publicly acknowledge that the men are the heads of the households in Vueltas; and yet there is a refrain that delivers the message:

La casa donde la mujer no es la jefa, no es una casa
(The house where the wife is not the boss, is not a home.)

The significance of being the boss is certainly a disputable notion and the real power of the man in the home deserves to be analysed further but this is outside the scope of this book. We are not here concerned to discover the ultimate reality of control within the *casa*, as clearly such a thing would differ within families and is never straightforward, with certain areas being the domain of either spouse. However, this is an area whereby acceptance of stereotypical roles is not enough and, with a little analysis, becomes exposed to many uncertainties.

As mentioned, women in Vueltas were expected to stay at home, whilst men were free to go out alone and enjoy the evening entertainment. This norm has been challenged recently by some of the North European women that have settled with local men in the village. Conflicts have arisen when a woman, an ex-tourist who is used to her freedom of movement, finds that she is expected to stay at home by her partner. Some insist on their right to go out at night and mix with friends. In this way tourism has led to funda-mental social attitudes being challenged within that most private refuge, the *casa*. This not only becomes a private and personal issue but develops into a public one because it tests the local assumptions of female behaviour, demonstrating that there are other possible roles for women in Vueltas, thereby offering a new opportunity for local women by example. In this way, choices for women, which may have remained at the imaginary or theoretical stage, now become real possibilities. Again, the foreign settler, refusing to act the prescribed role of domesticated housewife bound by the walls of her home, becomes a potential agent for change.

One of the activities which takes place within the *casa* and is regarded as the duty of the women of the household is the preparation of meals. This is an opportunity for the family to gather together, serving a ritualistic purpose as well as an alimentary one. In one household eight adult children would join their parents for the midday meal despite most having their own homes. The people of Vueltas tend to have four meals a day. These meals are *desayuno* (breakfast, coffee with milk) 8.00–9.00 a.m.; *almuerzo* (a big lunch, the main meal) between 1.00–3.00 p.m.; *merienda* (a light tea, coffee and a roll at 5.00 p.m; and *cena* (supper, soup, *gofio* (roasted maize flour), bread and cheese) between 8.00–10.00 p.m. The main meal of the day is *almuerzo* and the type of dishes served vary; however, some are made more often than others, depending on the availability of the ingredi-ents. Food consumed includes *potaje*, a soup which may contain beans, chickpeas, peas, pork, chicken, potatoes, poached egg, carrots and cabbage: this is particularly popular, and one soup may be reconstituted over many days. Other popular staples include *gofio*, fish, meat, bread, pasta and vege-tables. One landlady's brother was a fisherman who brought her fish regularly which consequently formed the main meal on most days. She often obtained potatoes from a close relative and occasionally fruit – usually given as a dessert with the main meal: bananas, mangoes, *higos pico* (cactus fruit), *higos leche* (fresh figs), oranges and pears. This indicates the importance of local produce for basic nutritional needs.

All the family gathers for the midday meal, which is followed by a resting period, the *siesta*. It is very unusual for non-relatives to join in with meals, just as it is rare for non-relatives to be invited into the home for a social event. Meeting others and socialising takes place in the bars and the open spaces such as the plaza or the port promenade: the *casa* is reserved for the family. It is usually the women who cook for the household and they also work on other household chores including washing up and cleaning the house. Many young women complained that the men in VGR do not help in the house; and when depicting the life of a married woman in VGR, local women would say, 'Staying in the house, looking after the children and not going out at night.' In contrast to the women's association with, and limitation to the home, the men are associated with their work outside the home.

Potential marriage partners

Te casastes, te apartaste [You marry, you will be apart].

People agreed that a couple normally go out together for about one year and then marry. A man will think seriously about a marriage partner after he has completed his military service and when he has a secure job. They also agreed that men usually marry at around 26 years and women around 22 years of age. Women explained that they married someone because of love (the romantic notion being intended); however, they did think that a man should have a job and preferably that a house should be available. Often, the first house or home was provided by one of the couple's parents, usually in the form of a small apartment near the parental home. There were no rules regarding which side of the family provides the home, although in Vueltas it was often the wife's side. The fact that many of the older generation now own additional apartments, built during the tourist boom, has changed the situation and makes it easier for young couples to live in them reasonably independent of their parents. Young couples usually prefer to be independent but not isolated: some say that when they married they experienced a sense of alienation from their families and friends. The women especially felt that their social lives were curtailed.

Mesa-Moreno stated that the marriages between the offspring of fishermen were subject to certain conventions, essentially requiring a fisherman to marry into a wealthier fishing family than his own: 'The family of the boyfriend must be of inferior status to that of the girlfriend'. This prescription has the following advantages: 'She not only offers a factory for sons and a seller of fish but offers also a house in which to live and a boat in which to fish' (Mesa-Moreno, 1982: 106). The father-in-law was expected to take his son-in-law fishing and the daughter was expected to look after her ageing parents. It seems that 'superior status' is defined by Mesa-Moreno in this context as wealth. However, questioning the young daughters and sons of fishermen in Vueltas did not unearth any desires to marry into particular families but uncovered a strong belief in freedom of choice and romantic love. One couple, both children of successful fishermen, that had married in 1986, disprove this theory, as they live in the paternal parents' property and the son fishes alone in his father's boat, even though his father-in-law operates a successful boat with two crew-members. The people of Vueltas scorned the idea of a contemporary hierarchy among fishing families, although the desire of women to find a man with a secure future was apparent. Perhaps Mesa-Moreno's contentions about marriage were applicable for earlier generations but they are not now, in practice or in ideology.

Nevertheless, the conventions indicated by Mesa-Moreno stress economic survival and its intimate relationship with the marital unit, a continuing relationship. Again, the home was the basic economic unit and survival for a fisherman often depended on his marital contract: the father-in-law providing a boat and the wife providing a home (with her parents) and acting as a vendor for the fish. The move away from this since the 1980s reflects the fundamental changes being experienced by people in Vueltas, affecting phenomena as seemingly diverse as economic and emotional decisions. Young men and women have far more opportunities to meet potential spouses than their parents did because of modern developments. One of these opportunities is present in the form of tourists and there have been numerous relationships between local men and foreign women. In contrast, very few local women have serious relationships with male tourists. As has been indicated in the discussion and in the genealogical diagrams (Figures 1 and 2), partnerships and marriages to tourists are becoming relatively common and most of the families examined in 1991 had, at least, one such marriage amongst their kin.

Belief and Values

This section concentrates on the spoken belief and actual activity of the indigenous people as observed and recorded during fieldwork. It is intended to highlight some important aspects of their communal lives as well as to give an insight into certain common beliefs that affect the society and their everyday lives. The focus is on the words and actions of people who are not connected in a professional way with religion or other belief systems.

Religious behaviour

The official religion of the Canary Islands is Roman Catholicism and in Vueltas this is indeed the popular religion, with everyone asked admitting to a belief in the Christian God. Many of the local homes have stickers on their front door proclaiming that they are Catholics and do not want anyone to change them: this is aimed at the proseletysing Jehovah's Witnesses who occasionally travel through the village. One of the bars in the port also sports such a sticker. In Vueltas, a mass is held in the chapel

Nuestra Senora Carmen at least once a month. The attendance is approximately 90% female, representing all ages, although most of those women are aged over 50 years: this ratio seems to be representative of the trend throughout VGR that changes only at funerals when the mass is attended almost entirely by men. On fiesta days, during the Christmas mass and the Easter masses, attendance is far higher than for the rest of the year, with standing room only in the larger churches in VGR: up to 300 people may attend at one time. Another popular occasion is the confirmation of school-children aged about 10 years: relatives and friends attend to see the youngsters in their special dress go through the elaborate ceremony confirming them as Roman Catholics.

When asked about the Christian doctrine, two young women, both university students and members of the local church choir, replied that they believed the Christian doctrine to be true. They became vague, however, when trying to describe God. When questioned about the tendency of men to avoid masses, they answered: 'Men don't trust the priest so they don't go to mass. But they do believe in God.' Some other local women admitted that they themselves did not trust the priest and, therefore, they avoided confession and mass. One said: 'Some of the people that go to church are sinners, they only go to church to be seen. Even though I don't go to church or confess I don't believe that I'm a sinner and I consider myself a Catholic.' When asked why they didn't go to mass some of the fishermen responded with: 'It's too much trouble to go: it means preparation, changing clothes and all that sort of thing. But we are Catholics, we believe in God.' Their words found real concrete support as they proudly recalled their donations towards the construction of the chapel: some had helped to build it with their bare hands.

A woman in Vueltas, the wife of a fisherman, came across an abandoned statue of St Mark when she was clearing a church in a village in the north of the island. She restored it, made a permanent shrine for it near the beach and established a procession with her family and friends on the relevant Saint's day. They carry it from the church to the shrine, having taken it to the church three days beforehand. This ritual began in the 1930s and the family still maintained the tradition in the 1990s, attracting quite a crowd. It is an example of grass-roots support for the religion and the ability of the local people to participate directly in and manipulate events. As a social community the villagers associate themselves strongly with their parish church: there is a structural centrality and a clear physical boundary defined and recognised during the processions (cf. Boissevain, 1991).

If a couple wish to get married the priest must be told of their desire to do so at least three months before the ceremony is intended to be held. One ceremony took place in the church at Calera at 7.00 p.m. It involved the priest reading the modernised version of the vows and getting the husband and wife to agree to them. The bride and groom dress in contemporary Spanish wedding style, the man in a suit and the woman in a bridal gown, and are normally attended by bridesmaids. Silver coins, usually 12, are then passed from the priest to the husband and then to the wife and back to the priest. A recently married bride questioned about the meaning of this replied: 'I think they symbolise prosperity in life together.' They are also said to represent the couple sharing their worldly goods. The coins are borrowed from a member of the family. Before the wedding, the husband may go out for some drinks with his male friends on a stag night, which often ends with the best man getting thrown into the water at the port. The wife also has her night out with girlfriends, the hen night, usually going for a meal and a drink. Many people agreed that couples often only courted together for a year before they get married and that there is a lot of pressure placed upon young people regarding their relationships with possible partners

Another major ritual that is always observed by Gomeran society is the funeral ceremony. Due to legal requirements, the deceased's body should be buried within 48 hours; this means that long preparations for the ceremony are not possible and that people discover the fact immediately before the service. The body will be watched over by close family members and female relatives and friends before the funeral, with comfort being given to the bereaved. During the funeral itself, women traditionally remain at the home of the bereaved and the tendency is for all the men of the family and male friends to attend. There is, therefore, a dropping of tools as people leave their tasks and travel, maybe for 3 hours, to the funeral location. It is not unusual for huge crowds, hundreds of men dressed in their Sunday best, to be inside the church and waiting outside to pay their respects. People tend to arrive a few hours before the service, gathering together and talking. At the end of the service (a virtual all-male affair) the coffin followed by the mourners is taken to the cemetery.

In VGR there is a stacking system for the bodies, the rock being too hard to allow graves to be dug. The coffins are slotted into a row of cell-like shelves and appropriate religious inscriptions are left to adorn the facing glass. After the funeral a widow will usually adopt the 'luto' mourning style of clothing, whilst males may wear a black button or other insignia for a period of time. The close relatives are expected to forgo public events of joyous celebration such as fiestas for up to a year, hence marking their respect and mourning for the deceased.

Supernatural powers
Many people attribute certain things that happen to them to the power of '*mal d'ojo*' (the evil eye). The possessor of the evil eye may not even be

aware of it or conscious of using it: the power might be invoked by the possessor through deliberate malicious intention, such as envy, or it might be innocently introduced simply by looking at someone or something. The evil eye is closely associated with envy. If a person possesses something that may enhance their status, others might be envious and the evil eye encouraged; hence, the protection of babies and the sensitivity about attractive characteristics. Anthropologists have drawn attention to the element of social control inherent in the context of evil eye accusations: the desire to keep people on an equal footing, to punish those who are exceptionally fortunate or challenge the status quo.[6]

One girl related how her hair began to fall out on her return to La Gomera following a period abroad with her parents. She attributed this to the evil eye, most likely invoked by another jealous girl who envied her beautiful hair or her good fortune in travelling abroad and wished to hurt her by damaging her looks. To cure this problem, she contacted two people whom she believed could cure her. These people were well known as *curanderos* (curers): they are also referred to as *brujas* (witches), the distinction depending on the individual concerned and their abilities, with witches being able to create harmful events. The *curanderos* are able to extract evil through a type of praying and chanting, utilising elements of Christian ritual, known as *santiguar* during which time they cough up the evil bile.[7] Often the *curandero* needs a personal item belonging to the 'possessed' individual, such as hair, fingernail or clothing, to allow the process to operate effectively. It is believed that babies who continually cry may be affected by the evil eye and one woman recalled how she phoned up a *curandero* and simply told her the name of the child, this being sufficient to allow the *santiguar* to be effective. There are numerous manifestations due to the evil eye, including sickness in animals, the inability of cheese to form properly and spots or hard areas forming on human skin. Many people claim to have the ability to cure certain things.[8]

It is said that people with the power of the evil eye can wilt plants by looking at them. A woman is believed to have cracked a pot on top of another woman's head by staring at it and some people are thought capable of causing physical pain in others. An impressive story concerns some German tourists in the 1980s climbing a ravine near Vuletas that was dangerous: it was used to pasture goats. They had been repeatedly warned not to climb in the area because it was perilous for themselves and for others who would have to rescue them and, furthermore, it was private land. Nevertheless, the tourists persisted on the climb. As he was halfway up the steep climb, one of the tourists experienced an excruciating pain in his knees: a pain that he had never experienced before. He buckled in agony and looked up the slope to see a large Gomeran woman at the top standing still, hands on hips, staring at him. He wondered why she was there and presumed that she must be the wife of the goat-herder. The woman walked off and he remained stationary. Unable to move because of the pain, his companions decided to go back to the village and enlist help. After his rescue and subsequent return to Germany, he asked doctors to examine his knees: they could not find anything wrong with them. He returned to La Gomera and told his story to foreign settlers who informed him that the woman was a well-known witch: he did not try to climb the ravine again.

On La Gomera, belief in the evil eye and witchcraft is widespread amongst men and women, young and old. People often wear a special cross to protect themselves from the power of the evil eye and most young children and babies have protective jewelry of some kind. The more malicious witches are said to make images of people and stick pins into them or damage them in other ways, thus inflicting problems on the real person. They may bury photographs of their victims, whose fading images are matched in real life by the destruction of the individuals and their relationship: a marriage can be destroyed in such a way. It is said that if a disfigured figurine of a victim is thrown into the sea the damage inflicted can never be healed by a *curandero*.

People are understandably very secretive about witchcraft and often a person will hide their activities from the rest of the family. There was one man in the village, said to be a witch who could read people's minds by looking into their eyes: he was widely feared and eye contact with him was avoided by many of the local people. One woman pointed to her neighbour who she believed was a witch (she reported this fact in a very hushed and scared manner, indicating genuine fear). This witch had spent many years working and living in Venezuela where a number of the witchcraft practices are said to have originated. The curanderos, in contrast, are well known and some are highly sought after for their curative ability, often for problems due to simple straightforward physical causes.

This short examination of belief shows a part of the people's lives that is prevalent but very difficult to reduce to confident statements of certainty. Each individual has his/her own personal opinion and relationship with religion and the supernatural and may not be able to articulate it, or even desire to do so. In addition, such relationships will change according to circumstances and over time – they are contextually influenced. It is an area of people's lives that is clearly manifest in physical activity and mental communication but which is not easily quantified and, like other things dealt with here, such beliefs have been subject to major changes during the 20th century. The younger generation is exhibiting different attitudes and behaviour from their parents, influenced as they are by formal education, mass media and encounters with tourists from different cultural backgrounds.

Envy, competition and criticism

Many local people described their fellow villagers as being envious or jealous and it was common for people to say that the Spanish as a whole were an envious people. They used this to explain the constant criticism to which people are subjected by others behind their backs and to explain the proliferation of material goods, cars, apartments, televisions and so on. Neighbourly competition – 'Keeping up with the Jones', as it is known in Britain – is a powerful factor in the lives of the villagers. One woman described with pride how well her children had done at school: 'One of my sons has been to college for many years to gain a professional qualification, none of them are drunkards or take drugs'. Because of this, she felt that other women were envious of her, some wishing her ill will: she could see that there were two sides to success. Another woman told of how her friends and other villagers were jealous because she had been to the European continent to visit a German friend. She had returned and described the villagers' reactions by saying: 'They were impressed but very envious of my experience'.

This social awareness of envy is, of course, not specific to La Gomera and other writers on European countries have commented on it including Kenny (1961: 85), Broegger (1990: 107) and Cole (1991). Envy can be a powerful motivating factor for action within a community. With envy comes competition and many local people felt that the sudden explosion of tourist apartment construction was due to envy and competitive feeling between families. It was suggested that once the villagers knew that the apartments were a safe investment, having seen the intrepid vanguard succeed, they quickly jumped onto the bandwagon. This shows how the local people were agents of change, using the tourist market to satisfy their interests that were motivated by locally held values of success. One young man aged 22 believed that before the tourism had expanded in VGR in the late 1980s, everyone was friendly, 'todo amigos ' [all friends]; however, he was sure that in 1996 this was not so, as there was too much competition, with everyone building apartments and buying luxury goods. This might be explained as his being overly sentimental about the past and that latent feelings of jealousy and competition had simply manifested themselves in a more tangible way. But the important thing is that he believed the loss of a friendly community to be a fact and others agreed. It is said that the tourist market has led to blatant competition and a preoccupation with money.

Envy and competition, powerful factors in the community, are all inter-related emotional and physical manifestations of mental experiences.

Another important and connected part of social life in Vueltas is criticism, which is one of the most powerful social forces in VGR. The phrase '*se critica*' (they criticise) was continually used to describe the group behaviour of others, almost always women; people would say that any group of women talking together would be criticising somebody else. One man, when describing former times, said: 'In the evenings or spare time the men would play cards or dominoes, whilst the women would gather together and criticise'.

Criticism acts as a strong form of informal social control. It also allows people to sound each other out on their opinions and the opinions of others, consequently establishing a general level of understanding and group cohesion, both shaping and redefining certain roles which men and women can play (cf. Aceves, 1971: 125; Zinovieff, 1987: 12). In Vueltas, it seemed that the inhabitants knew most of their neighbours' business and their knowledge about each other's tourist apartments was extensive. Often a neighbour would be talking about another person's apartment (usually an extension to the main home) and describe every detail down to the shower unit and its condition, passing comments on the cleanliness and cost of the apartments. This indeed was a very common topic as the apartments formed a market in which most of them competed directly, giving a good reason for envy, pride or insecurity.

The apartments proved to be an extremely sensitive area, with the local people regarding them as extensions of their own homes. Indeed, their recent development and the natural hospitality of the people would have led families into initially feeling that they were letting their rooms out to friends and many retain strong ties of friendship with regular customers, exchanging correspondence. However, with the passing of time and the arrival of an increasing number of tourists, attitudes and the reception have cooled.

A grave criticism of a home in Vueltas is to suggest that it is dirty and this was occasionally levelled at a set of apartments, thereby tarnishing the family that owned them. Goddard (1987) has revealed the link between cleanliness and sexuality in Naples, whereby a dirty home is associated with sexual misbehaviour and similar connotations would be inferred in the slander of another woman's domestic neglect. Such harsh words punish the victim and show how her neighbours feel themselves to be insulted as the whole community becomes tarnished. In Vueltas the apparent negativeness of criticism often serves a positive purpose: to warn against trouble, to share values, to cement relationships and to expose weaknesses. Moreover, it creates a boundary within which a community may be defined. Criticism helps to establish the parameters of certain roles whether gender related, parental or public; and the development of tourism in the community has offered abundant opportunities for the exercise of critical opinion.

Respect and shame

So far it has been argued that although there are clear ideas on gender divisions and their relative qualities in the public domain, these ideas become very vague and abstract when approached from the personal level: the public performance is not always an accurate representation of the private opinion. In this way, the phenomenon of tourism has led to great changes in opportunities and serious challenges to public behaviour and private belief. The vulnerability of local attitudes has been highlighted by the arrival of tourists, as witnessed by the sexual and personal freedom of German women challenging long-held gender stereotypes: this theme is continued by examining social values which are current within the community.

In many works on the Mediterranean region, the subject of honour and shame has played a large part, particularly in Pitt-Rivers (1954, 1963), Campbell (1964), Peristiany (1965a) and Peristiany and Pitt-Rivers (1992). The word *honor* (honour) was not used much amongst the people in VGR; however, the word *respeto* (respect) was certainly a common part of conversation. The phrase *faltar respeto* (to lack respect) was often employed: locals would say that tourists lacked respect for them or their property, treating the place like a playground. If someone acted in such a way that could be construed as insulting towards another person, it was said that they lacked respect towards that person. This type of situation may easily arise in the bar, an environment where high spirits and social relaxation combine to allow for jokes, insults and freedom of speech. For example, when the barman considered that a foreigner had been too provocative, he said: 'You have a lot of cheek, you lack respect'. Actions such as the payment for drinks, the order of a type of drink, the playing of games and the consumption of alcohol (too little or too much) can all lead to potential challenges to masculinity and recriminations concerning respect. On one occasion, a barman filled a fisherman's glass of wine to the brim, causing it to spill, and the fisherman accused him of lacking respect. This shows that there is a generally accepted level of interpersonal behaviour, a social norm where manners are mutually recognised and those breaking such norms are seen to be doing so deliberately.

People who knew their job and those who were formally educated gained respect from others because of their knowledge and experience. However, the mere wearing of a uniform did not confer respect, especially when the wearer was considered unworthy of his office. The officials appointed by the local council were often criticised by local people for not knowing their job or for acting self-importantly because they wore a uniform. The actor may be perceived as playing his public role but not deserving the status accorded to it: those in authority do not acquire it through donning a uniform, whereas the experienced fisherman in his role as teacher commands respect because he has earned it. We can see how 'respect' can fit into the broad concept of honour and, in their introduction to a book examining honour and grace, Pitt-Rivers and Peristiany define honor as '[a] conceptual field within which people find the means to express their self-esteem or their esteem for others' (Peristiany & Pitt-Rivers, 1992: 4). In fact, Cole, in her study of a Portuguese fishing community, goes as far as to say of honour that '[i]n Portuguese, honor probably best translates as respeito, or respect' (Cole, 1991: 77).

Honour is a broad concept and one that will have an influence on many lives.[9] However, while the concept is fine for articulating academic enquiries, it is difficult to capture in day-to-day ethnographic observation because of its paradoxical intangibility. Free (1991) examined the use of the term 'honour' in Mediterranean anthropology and draws attention to weaknesses in the academic analysis of this term. In the field, elements of behaviour and sentimental opinion, which may be perceived as components of honour, can be grasped by the fieldworker, which is one reason to concentrate on real people saying real things. The word honour was rarely used in Vueltas, and Herzfeld (1987) reports the same experience in his fieldwork in Greece; whereas, in Vueltas the words *respeto* and *vergüenza* (shame) were very common. It is also notable that certain families had acquired nicknames, pertaining to dishonourable acts including theft or serious violence – *roberos* (robbers) – and persistent drunkenness – *borrachos* (drunkards). Similar characterisations were used to describe successive generations of the same families (as was noted by Pitt-Rivers [1954] and Galván-Tudela [1980]).

The people of Vueltas use the word *vergüenza* often. It may be applied to both men and women and was often utilised in a humorous context. It was also used to infer embarrassment: '*Que vergüenza!*' ('What shame!' or 'How embarrassing!') might be said by one girl to another in reference to a situation. However, the concept has a more profound meaning in relation to women which lies in the context that anthropologists have highlighted: the sense of innate sexual shame. Women are expected to behave in a shy and constrained manner in their private and especially public behaviour. They are not to be brazen in a sexual sense and if they contravene these norms they are said to have no shame and labelled as *putas* (whores).

Rivière has pointed out the gender specificity of shame: 'As already mentioned, shameless behaviour, as defined by Pitt-Rivers for Andalusía, is that which is inappropriate to one's sex. This implies that a shameless person is taking on the attributes of the opposite sex' (Rivière, 1967: 580). Here, the emphasis on inappropriate role behaviour is important and, in VGR, the occasional sexual forthrightfulness of German women tourists, together with their relative independence, leads to instant problems of definition for local people: there is an unacceptable role reversal. In the same manner, a German girl told of how a German male friend, who accompanied her and her two girlfriends, was mocked by two Gomeran boys who had taken them all out for a drink: he was ridiculed as being effeminate because his association with the girls did not involve a sexual motive.

The behaviour of local women is under constant scrutiny: the older ones criticise the younger women's fashion, such as their short skirts and bikinis, saying that they have no shame. With this type of attitude, it is easy to see how the local people misinterpreted the behaviour of the female German tourists (with their penchant for sunbathing naked) believing them to be shameless and labelling them whores. One German woman said that she genuinely could not understand why the local people felt so strongly about nakedness. This is an example of the huge gap between the two sets of cultural perceptions.[10] We can see the relationship between respect and shame in the context of social control, with people showing admiration for those who know their place, are aware of the social status of others and perform their role according to commonly understood criteria. An extreme lack of respect, resulting in shame is, therefore, seen in those who seriously transgress appropriate roles, especially those based on gender.[11]

Local Attitudes and Global Ideas

It is not wise to say that the apparent influences of tourism are solely due to the visitors or to the industry without considering the impact of other globalising factors. Nevertheless, there are some outstanding examples of the direct influence of tourism and one of these is the use of the German language in the areas where German tourism predominates. Many notices are in German, postcards have German subtitles, menus are given with German translations and, of course, some people have learnt to speak German. The local people are encouraged to learn foreign words and broaden their lexical horizons for business and social advantage, as is the case with shop assistants.

The continual mixing of local youngsters with tourists also leads to an exchange of ideas, opinions, fashions, musical tastes and dancing techniques among other things. One woman mentioned how the Germans had introduced a completely new type of cuisine with the emphasis on health, such as vegetarian meals and different types of fruit and vegetables previously unknown to the local people: a new attitude towards eating, bodily well-being and the ethics of vegetarianism had arrived. With the tourists staying in private apartments and often being looked after by younger members of the family, the opportunities to exchange and communicate are manifold. Both parties, hosts and house-guests, want positive interaction: thus, hosts will often be instructive and protective towards their house-guests, befriending them in the street or bars and house-guests usually reciprocate with respectful attention, being pleased to make a local friend. This type of relationship is not usually found amongst mass (package) tourists who stay in large apartment complexes or hotels, where the local people operate solely in their professional roles as workers, roles that are too formal, constrained and impersonal for relaxed interaction with tourists (cf. Robinson, 1999: 10).

One German woman befriended the daughter of an apartment owner who was of a similar age, in her early twenties. They would visit the bars together and exchange ideas about fashion in which they were both interested. The local girl was able to visit her new friend in Germany and she considered bringing some German clothes back to Vueltas to sell. The German tourist had introduced her to new ways of thinking, encouraging her to be an independent businesswoman. Similarly, a local boy who helps to clean his parents' apartment became friends with a German tourist interested in sport and rock music: the German then invited him over to Germany where he was able to find some part-time work as a builder. He has since returned and values his experience in Northern Europe hoping some day to return there to work. Another local young man went to live in Amsterdam with his Dutch girlfriend whom he had met in VGR when she stayed in his family's apartments: he lived there for two years and, in his own opinion, has consequently become much more open minded in his relationship with foreigners. These experiences of visiting foreign countries have given the younger generation a far broader sense of the possibilities that life offers than their parents' generation could imagine. Even so, most confessed that they preferred the life in La Gomera to Northern Europe because of the people's friendliness, despite the severe limitations of village life on the island.

Many of these friendships begin through tourists meeting their apartment owners and families, as this is a situation where each party normally wishes to please the other and an element of mutual trust is needed and usually forms. For example, one English girl met a Gomeran boy through his sister whom she had befriended in the shop where she worked. She described how this boy was 'different' and they were able to talk about many things, saying:

He was one of the few boys that spoke good English and we would sit outside at night, talking about the stars, about films and acting, about art. I felt something very special with him.

She returned to the island regularly and tried to persuade him to visit England where she worked in the media, saying that he might even get a chance to do some modelling. This example and the previous ones illustrate the depth and richness of some of the relationships that start from casual acquaintance, usually through room renting. In contrast to this interpersonal communication between local people and tourists typical of backpacking tourism is the insularity of the 'timid' package tourist or 'group tourist', whom Zinovieff (1990: 49) describes as having no desire to discover the undiscovered and sticking to the main routes and major sites. Such tourists are relatively insulated from direct contact with their hosts as individuals and, consequently, enter very few relationships other than those involving direct economic exchange.

Another influence of tourism on La Gomera related to cultural differences and diverse home environments is that of nature conservation. The tourists' appreciation of the beauty of the island, the unusual flora, the breathtaking ravines with their terraced slopes and the natural splendour and power of the coast has probably increased the local people's realisation of their fortunate island heritage. Garajonay National Park, which takes up some 10% of the island's surface in its center, has brought an awareness of ecological and conservation issues to the forefront of the inhabitants' concern. It was listed as part of the World Heritage and, as such, is protected by international environmental concerns and managed by the Institute for the Conservation of the Environment (ICONA).[12] This organisation is encouraging a return to harmonious agriculture within the Park's periphery. Crick (1989) advocates that tourism should have a symbolic relationship with the environment; and Smith (1989b) draws attention to the Eskimos promoting the environment as a tourist attraction. This attitude is apparent now on La Gomera where the National Park promoters, who imagine the benefits from tourism, aim to create a balance between financial rewards and conservation: promotional material emphasises the ecological importance of the island.[13]

The island's environmental heritage is increasingly regarded as valuable and worthy of protection: a path running up the valley in VGR and along the mountain was designated a protected nature trail in the mid-1990s. Not only do visitors gain satisfaction from walking around the island and witnessing its beauty, local people are also increasingly aware of its charm and they talk proudly of the forest and the valleys. Recent worldwide interest in conservation and ecology, together with environmentally sensitive visitors, have given the Gomeros a greater realisation of their natural heritage, as was apparent in the protest against the beach development.

A Visitors' Centre placed on the border of the National Park contains information, exhibitions and literature pertaining to the park and its ecology, other parks in Spain and the history of La Gomera. It contains a reconstructed model Gomeran house with agricultural implements and traditional artifacts, as well as studios where craft workers make traditional items out of clay, wood and bamboo. The exhibitions are informative but do not have the complex reconstruction of social activities that Urbanowicz (1989) found in Tonga or Stanton (1989) writes of in Polynesia. However, the entire exhibition of housing and lifestyle is a sanitised version of history, appealing to the sentimental romantic gaze of the tourist as well as the cultural heritage seeker. It is a carefully constructed version of an idealised reality and forms a repositioning of carefully maintained island identity.

However, not all the folk traditions are as sanitised as those represented in the Visitors' Centre. As earlier chapters have illustrated, there are many occasions when the people dance in traditional style to local music played on homemade instruments (*chacaras, tambors*), notably during the fiestas. These are celebratory events, enjoyed by the people without reference to foreign spectators. A full-scale commodification of culture has not taken place on the island, as was the case with the historical celebration in Fuentarrabia, Spain, reported by Greenwood (1989). Similarly, this is not an example of cultural involution, as was noticed amongst the Amerindians (Deitch, 1989) and the Balinese (Mckean, 1989). Rather, the practice of dancing the *Tajaraste* to the *baile de tambor* (dance of the drums) in La Gomera is a continuation of a tradition that has only recently begun to reach the attention of the outside world through the experience of tourism and the mass media. Yet as the fiestas become more well known, so they attract a larger contingent of tourists. By 2000, a new dancing group, that wears traditional constumes and performs a specially choreographed traditional dance at fiestas, had formed. The traditional arts are growing in popularity among the younger generation, as is an awareness of environmental issues, both bound up with notions of cultural heritage and identity: and it is these young people who will shape the cultural and environmental landscape of the island in the future.

Notes

1. Galván-Tudela (1980: 236–7) in the first ethnographic monograph of a Canary Island community (Taganana, an agricultural village on Tenerife) gives a descriptive list of kinship terms to be found in Tenerife and these correspond to those terms encountered in VGR. They are of Spanish (Castilian) derivation.

2. The popularity of matrifocality in Vueltas has been noted by Mesa-Moreno (1982) in his study of the fishermen and their social community. He suggests that it arises because it is generally believed that the daughter will look after her ageing parents, whereas the son and his wife are less likely to do so. This contrasts with the matrilineal situation, in which inheritance goes to the daughter, as can be found in the Portuguese fishing village studied by Broegger (1990), where he recorded matrilineality and matrifocality as the norm, with a powerful matriarchy dominating the domestic lives of the fishermen

3. This type of sibling grouping was found by Cohen (1982c), in his study of a Shetland fishing community.

4. Gilmore (1980) has expressed the importance of this unit in his book examining and emphasising social class divisions in Andalusia: 'The casa unites its members defensively against a hostile world'. He promotes the importance of the casa as the operating economic unit and stresses the privacy of the casa, with the kitchen and bedroom always being off-limits to outsiders.

5. The situation accords with that noticed by Gilmore who writes about the men of Andalusía, saying that: 'In fact, after marriage, most men spend all their free time in the bars, and go home only to eat and to sleep' (Gilmore, 1980: 201).

6. See Pitt-Rivers (1954), Cole (1991) and Broegger (1990): all draw attention to the evil eye and its association with envy.

7. An explicit scene involving a woman performing *santiguar* was shown in the film *Guarapo* (1988).

8. One man in a bar casually assured me that he could personally cure people of skin problems.

9. Lisón-Tolosana (1980: 164) says: 'Honour is the most perfect individual attribute that can be applied to a mature man'. He also states: 'One of the components of honour is shame. He who is honourable has shame' (p. 165). Galván-Tudela, when discussing the concept of honour in a village in Tenerife, writes that the local men would say of honour that 'Here, honour is carried by women as much as by men. Women dishonour a family if they get pregnant. Men if they rob, are homosexual, or drunks. Shame is inherited. He who has seen shame in his home has shame.' (Galván-Tudela, 1980: 246).

10. Goddard (1987: 90) has highlighted the segregation of gender roles relating to work and linked this to honour, suggesting that these are ways of signifying boundaries and group identity. In this manner it is clear how visual appearances and group self-perception unite.

11. I have concentrated on words that can be heard being used in the everyday activities of the people and which for them have reasonably straightforward meanings. Although I bring these experiences into the general discussion of honour, I am aware of the pitfalls of stereotyping and categorisation and deliberately seek to avoid drawing finite conclusions and labeling such concepts as 'Mediterranean'. I am in agreement with Herzfeld (1987: 12) when he states: 'The study of a constructed phenomenon such as 'the Mediterranean code of honour and shame' is a study of our own relationship to the cultures in question'. A similar point concerns the comparability of concepts and the creation of anthropological 'regions'. Thus, it seems that many aspects of 'Mediterranean' cultures are recognisable in other geographical regions such as the North Atlantic coastline (as I have shown with the Canary Islands and Portugal), Latin America and Northern Europe (cf. Pina-Cabral, 1989: 404). This problem of delimiting cultural areas, particularly the 'Mediterranean', has exercised the

minds of many anthropologists recently. Notably in Goddard *et al.* (1994) who in their introduction to a collection of essays conclude that 'Europe' is a more worthwhile cultural region of comparison than 'The Mediterranean' where links are highly problematic. Llobera (1986) had previously described 'Mediterranean Anthropology' as the domain of the Anglo-Saxon anthropologists and pointed to the non-ubiquity of certain traits used to unite the Mediterranean region.

12. Olwig (1985) has written about an island in the Caribbean that became a national park, thereby reducing the availability of land for agriculture and housing and, consequently, creating problems for local people through the rising price of land. Gomera has not yet suffered from this reduction in agricultural land as the park was previously forested.

13. See Bianchi (2000) on the politics and sociocultural relations of world heritage in relation to Garajonay National Park.

Chapter 8

The Ability of Tourism to Change Culture

This, the final chapter, concludes the central arguments of this monograph and highlights tourism as a unique and powerful phenomenon with a tremendous capacity for changing culture. Tourism is seen as having a strong influence on a culture, understood in the holistic sense, with impacts spreading throughout the culture. These influences are especially penetrating when working on a small community – that of an island. The longitudinal research method and the use of many different voices, opinions and sources in the text, together with sensitivity towards history, have helped to give a fully rounded picture of these influences and placed them in the context of globalisation. The major issues addressed in these final concluding thoughts are identity, globalisation and cultural change, followed by a summary of the most striking areas of influence as addressed in this research.

The Environment and Identity

People on La Gomera associate strongly with their environment: the fishermen with the sea and the coast, the farmers with their land. They have pride in the products of nature – the fish, the bananas, the goat's cheese – all these items embody the Gomeros' productive power and qualities as hardworking capable people. Furthermore, there is the general contrast, reinforced by tourism, between rural Gomeros and the urbanised city dwellers that visit their island. The land, its products and the people that work on the land and at sea may become powerful symbols for a way of life, as witnessed with the '*mago*', a figure representing rural qualities, comparable to the proud, individualistic shepherd of many European folk ideals (see Mckechnie, 1993). Guarapo, the ecological and cultural conservation group on La Gomera, utilised the cultural traditions and environmental aspects of the island to stir up emotions amongst the people, highlighting the natural beauty and uniqueness of the island together with its special cultural traditions including *silbo*. The group even named itself after the palm-juice drink *guarapo*. People associate part of their identity with the environment in which they live and work and also through the roles they perform in relation to that environment. The fishermen have a distinct lifestyle and a definite sense of identity recognised by themselves and other groups in the valley. Their relationship with the environment, in this case the sea, is undoubtedly powerful: they spend most of their time either at sea, preparing to go to sea or talking about experiences at sea. People identify with the environment but this is also contingent upon their cultural understanding of it.[1]

Cultural context is of crucial relevance to events in La Gomera, where we have seen a history of resource exploitation, dependent upon the different 'cultural imagination' of groups of people, from the pre-Hispanic pastoralists, via the European plantation owners, the subsistence fishermen, the fish-processing plant owners, to the tourism promoters.[2] All these people have utilised the natural environment for particular purposes, principally for food and survival – but with the advent of tourism the collective perception of the place has changed dramatically. No longer is land primarily something to be cultivated to produce food or the sea solely harvested for marine life: the land and sea have recently acquired predominantly aesthetic and commercial value in relation to the interests of tourists and developers. Certainly the natural resources are being exploited but in a radically different way. The tourist gaze is subordinating the agricultural gaze. But the tourist gaze is not homogeneous: it is composed of various types.

There has been a radically new way of looking at VGR over the past decade: it has turned from a farming and fishing centre into a tourist resort. Those aspects which advertised its agricultural credentials – small plots of land, terraced fields, banana plantations – are giving way to apartments or being abandoned. The port, still the haunt of active fishermen, is becoming overrun by pleasure boats and tourists, as are the beaches. But the qualities which first attracted tourists, the relative isolation, natural beauty, ruggedness of landscape, unspoilt beaches and friendly people, are gradually being eroded by tourism development and the fast pace of life. That awful cliché, 'tourism destroys itself' is becoming a real possibility. Casanova, the socialist politician, voiced this fear in 1991, making public the commonly felt anxiety that VGR could lose the 'alternative' tourists through overdevelopment. The issue has become political in an overt manner.

Tourism in VGR is very much about the natural environment and tourism, as an industry, has a very strong relationship with the environment. To a large extent, it depends on the natural environment as an attracting factor and it can directly harm or benefit it. Some writers believe that tourism can be an effective benefactor of the environment, especially in the sense of conserving endangered resources through either offering a viable alternative to extractive industries or as a means of financing projects for ecological preservation.[3] Yet tourism and the environment share one thing in common – they are very much at the mercy of political events and power struggles: 'Sustainable development is concerned not so much to be about natural resources of the physical environment as about issues of control, power, participation and self-determination' (Croll & Parkin, 1992: 9). In this light it may be seen as subject to 'political ecology'.[4] We should become aware of the relationship between political power and the natural environment, as witnessed with the changing politico-economic climate and its impact on the environment in VGR over the period examined here, something which has become quite blatant with recent events relating political activity, tourism and development projects.

Issues of control and power are also very much tied up with issues of identity. In the case of La Gomera, particular groups wish to see the island 'developed' (hence the POI). This infers that certain projects, such as the building of roads and an airport, are carried out with the financial support of the EU and the National Government. As La Gomera was the only Canary Island without an airport, it became a matter of pride in some quarters for the island to build one: the continual arrival of people from urban areas in Germany and Tenerife exacerbates the awareness that the island lacks certain amenities commonly found in urban centres. The ambitious Casa Cultural in VGR is an example of civic pride but it is seen by some as a waste of resources. The huge roads that carve up the valley are vulgar but nevertheless modern: no tourists questioned liked the new roads but they do allow the coaches and big lorries easy and safe access to all corners of the municipality and, as one local woman in favour of them pointed out, they are illuminated at night and generally safer. The infra-structure is prepared for even more construction and apartments are going up in the expectation of more visitors.

The beach development proposal may have been shelved because of popular feeling against it manifested by the potent and successful petition but it remains to be seen how long the drive towards 'developing' the resort can be restrained. During 1996, a huge new complex, the first self-contained hotel, was under construction in VGR. It overlooks the sea on the main beach and is regarded by everyone asked (apart from the mayor) as an eyesore. This hotel was being advertised in the 1996/7 Neckermann Holiday Brochure. By 2002 it was well established and fully booked. The valley has reached a critical stage whereby it can either reduce construction and concentrate on maintaining its natural qualities or choose to continue the development programme and change irrevocably, turning itself into a micro-version of beach resorts found on Tenerife or Gran Canaria, catering for the mass-market tourist with all the attendant problems. The valley's identity and, consequently, that of its inhabitants is wholly bound up with events taking place over the next few years.

A way of approaching these issues, which relate to change and social construction, is to focus on the individual agent in terms of identity. It is valuable to consider the individual as possessing a complex set of identities which form the overall picture: not a simple two-dimensional identity which can be described as 'ethnic' or 'professional' but one which is multiplex, changing and adaptive, one which can be perceived differently by observers according to different contexts. The whole process is one of rearrangement and change. Individuals are constantly revising their own pasts in terms of their memories, albeit moderately, and revising their identities as well – physiologically and conceptually over time and socially through action according to changing contexts.[5]

Where tourism occurs, people may experience a change in identity on both a personal and a public level as individuals and groups – fishermen become shopkeepers or tour-guides, young women seek financial independence and emotional liberation, pressure groups revitalise local identity. In the case of the globalisation experience, people may encounter a broader range of role models, opportunities, networks of associates, as well as undergoing a new self-perception. Equally, people may experiment with traditional roles, re-interpret events, re-invent themselves or gain confidence in their lifestyles and values: all in accordance with postmodernist descriptions of de-differentiation and challenges to the metanarrative. Such personal and group changes may lead to other socioeconomic and physical transformations. This allows us to see the individual reacting to a situation and influencing that situation, which in turn emphasises the relationship between human identity and the environment as we have witnessed in VGR. The relationship allows us to contest the tendency to alienate people theoretically from their natural surroundings in terms of interaction. Thus, we move away from Cartesian dualism towards a position that regards the subject–object relationship as a continuum, not a clear division, and challenges the dualistic notion 'culture versus nature'.[6]

Hence, with the increasing complexity of life within the valley as regards the influx of people, ideas, technology and opportunities comes a complex array of potentialities for the livelihoods, lifestyles and identities of the inhabitants, which the terms 'post-modernism' and 'globalisation' only partially describe. By focusing on individuals and their identities, private and social, as perceived by themselves and others, we get an insight into change and social processes from a variety of sources. This has long been a quality of anthropological findings but we must endeavour to marry these findings to models of social processes such as world-system theory and, thereby, give a human, individual richness to theories that describe general processes without including the observations of individual agents. An ethnographic monograph is able to include a rich variety of cultural commentaries and individual viewpoints – providing not only a microcosm of the whole but occasionally a radical challenge to preconceptions. There are patterns of continuity and major transformations that are apparent to observers and interpreted differently relative to their vantage point and this includes the ethnographer. It has been political power supported by economic and military strength that has, in the past, largely determined the fate of the material environment on La Gomera. Nevertheless, local people's opinions and identities have been strongly influenced but never wholly determined by those holding power. This scenario remains so today.

Tourism and the Globalisation of an Island

The notion of globalising La Gomera may imply that the islanders are passive subjects in the process: in some instances, this has been the case. The island has been invaded and colonised by outsiders and this began the globalisation process. A trading network was established by the Spanish conquerors involving the Canary Islands in a vast geographical web of exchange. This development has continued and accelerated over the last century with its industrial production and invention, leading to the present situation in which La Gomera finds itself part of a vast finanscape, technoscape, ideoscape, mediascape and a rapidly diversifying ethnoscape (after Appadurai, 1990).

Despite all the rapid changes brought about by modernisation and new technologies, the indigenous people are not simply passive recipients of an imposed transformation. Instead they have become more actively involved with the processes of globalisation, particularly tourism. The local people have shaped their community's development and become engaged within a global exchange network. They are now fully active in the process of globalisation, not only in terms of dealing with tourism but in their trading of other export goods, migration, work, education and exhibiting elements of their culture to an external audience. Suffice it to say, there are many agents involved in globalising La Gomera and their number are growing as opportunities to communicate and exchange increase.

But what are the results of this globalisation? Some scholars argue that globalisation leads to a homogenisation of culture – for example Giddens (1997: 64), who sees it in terms of 'growing economic and cultural interdependence'. Others see a continuation of heterogeneity, disputing cultural convergences.[7] For the example of La Gomera, itself part of the Western world but with a distinct history including colonisation, we can perceive the process of homogenisation as well as the development of greater heterogeneity occurring simultaneously: the processes occur on different sociocultural levels. The homogenisation proceeds at the level of consumption, in terms of globally marketed goods, for example food, drink, clothing, music and film. This is accelerated with the arrival of tourists bringing new ideas and products, often reflecting urbanised, metropolitan ideals, even if counter-cultural.

In contrast to the relatively superficial homogenisation of the economy and consumption patterns, heterogeneity is retained through a continuation of cultural elements such as the role of the family, language, public education, religion, traditions including music, art and crafts, fiestas and a shared history: i.e. those qualities which create a sense of distinctive communal identity. And this sense of identity is increased by the arrival of palpably different people from different cultural backgrounds. These cultural qualities, which may be termed 'ethnic markers', often become accentuated in comparison with different cultural groups. As a consequence of tourism, the Gomeros have become increasingly aware of their individuality and group identity. In this sense, cultural diversity is made plainer. On a global scale, the awareness of such diversity leads to the consciousness of a greater wealth of difference – hence heterogeneity. Further to this, increased communication of ideas and experiences through mass media leads to the realisation among groups, peoples and nations that it is possible to strive for sovereignty and cultural recognition. Recent events within the EU show how a geopolitical area, increasingly homogenised in administrative, executive and judicial terms, may actually be perceived as increasing in heterogeneity in terms of national, regional and cultural enclaves promoted through the actions of interest groups and separatist movements.

Thus, despite the proliferation of media and commodities, individual communities often retain their distinct qualities. People maintain their links with social groups through a shared history whether folk or formal, and with family and friends, all of which profoundly influence their social identity and, hence, their uniqueness. We have seen that, despite rapid changes involving interactions with foreigners, mass media, economic transformation and geopolitical transition, people in Vueltas retain a sense of uniqueness because of their shared experiences. Despite the EU's increasing involvement in their lives and the regular arrival of foreign nationals, they have not lost a sense of themselves as a distinct group. In fact, they have occasionally been made more aware of themselves as a group in contrast with others and their peripheral location has become clear with new regulations from urban North Europe impinging on their lives – unrealistic rules made by anonymous metropolitan bureaucrats.

Globalisation describes a process involving different cultural flows: it may explain certain events but it is not a keen analytical tool. This book has used a model from world-system theory that has helped us understand the great historical process of colonisation and exploitation of the island by Iberian powers. Using the idea of a core and periphery we envision the power relationship between the colonists and colonised. From this we saw the establishment of a bourgeoise and proletariat class mentality that has lasted until today: people on La Gomera still conceive of society as divided between bosses (*caciques*) and workers. The island was drawn into a global network of trade and politics that began with the Iberian exploitation of natural resources and people, a network which continues today with the dominance of Western Europe and trans-national corporations. Neverthe-less, this examination of La Gomera has shown how ethnographic research can expose the more subtle aspects of such processes and has drawn our attention to the crucial involvement of the indigenous population in the development of VGR, specifically Vueltas. We are able to see the people involved in the process: globalisation loses its anonymity and is revealed as the collective result of individual human activity. For a relatively brief period, the people of Vueltas, those primary workers involved in the tourism economy, have been active and potent agents in globalising La Gomera.

Tourism and Cultural Change

General overview

Tourism, in its many aspects, makes a fascinating subject of study. This research has encountered numerous facets of the phenomenon, from the representation of the island as a tourist destination, the type of tourists, their motivations and experiences, to the manifold influences that tourism has had on the people of Vueltas. By studying the tourists themselves, we are examining aspects of the society from which they derive, in this instance predominantly Germany. It reveals to us the desires of people who have lived most of their lives in a western industrialised society with a distinct history. MacCannell's (1976) original thesis that the tourist was leaving modern society to seek something authentic proves to be a useful idea and is certainly applicable to the motivation of a number of tourists encountered in this study. However, the concept of 'authentic' when deconstructed leaves us unconvinced of its relevance to all cases, especially when the desire to escape 'authentic' everyday life for 'non-ordinary' experience is considered. Furthermore, in this climate of post-modernistic self-consciousness and parody, the new 'post-tourist' (Urry, 1990) who is well aware of pseudo-authentic 'exotica' actually revels in the pastiche of modern and traditional culture. All this leads us to regard MacCannell's views as relevant to only a minority of tourists.

Graburn's (1989) use of the notion of 'non-ordinary' experiences (after Durkheim) supports the idea of tourism as a 'sacred journey' and is also only partially relevant in explaining the motivation of tourists. Many of them certainly seek the non-ordinary experience, not in the sacred, neo-religious sense, but often simply as an escape from their ordinary lives – and, most interestingly, a significant number were actually searching for some truth within their lives. By this, we mean they were looking for space in which to resolve problems, to sort out personal relationships or difficulties within their working lives. In this way they sought to discover their own deeper feelings: they were embarking on an interior psychological journey, free of the constraints experienced at home. Therefore, an emphasis is placed on the personal and psychological aspects of the individual tourist, in terms of desires and experiences. The alternative tourists who formed the majority of visitors to Vueltas were often mindful of the situation into which they had sent themselves, being open to the indigenous community and the problems of the area and being very communicative with local people. Some were aware of the island's reputation as a meeting place for single people and so the topic of personal relationships became a preoccupation. We should consider the experience of tourism as both a physical and mental journey and continue to bear in mind the complexity of human identity and emotional experience when attributing motivational factors.

Much of this book has been concerned with the impact of tourism on a community, specifically Vueltas, a fishing settlement. Earlier chapters have detailed the influences of tourism giving examples of economic, social and cultural changes resulting from the arrival of tourists since the 1980s. A predominant theme of this research has been that the type of tourist has a specific influence on the host community. Due to the propensity of 'alternative' tourists to communicate with the local population, the type of accommodation they use, the places where they shop and eat, their general disposition (well educated, interested in others, young and adventurous), they are more likely to mix with the local population than the so-called 'timid' agency tourists described by Graburn (1989). Their 'willingness to engage with the other' places them into Hannerz's category of 'cosmopolitans' (Hannerz, 1992: 252). This mixing will result in more sociocultural influence. Thus, it is argued that, in assessing the impact of tourism on a host community, we must seriously consider both the types of tourism and the types of impact we want to measure.

The model of 'touristic impact upon a culture' proposed by Smith is not subtle enough to account for the cultural impacts which different types of tourism have on a community. It emphasises economic impact by regarding the number of visitors to a place as the determining factor: 'However, as the number of tourists progressively increases, it appears expectations emerge and more facilities are required to handle them' (Smith, 1989c: 14). Similarly, Graburn believes that greater numbers mean a greater impact and he discusses the 'timid' tourists: 'These tourists are likely to have the greatest impact on the culture and environment of the host peoples both by virtue of their greater numbers and by their demands for extensions of their home environments for which they are willing to pay handsomely' (Graburn, 1989: 35). But these tourists do not mix with the local people and, therefore, are less likely to have a deep cultural influence on them than the 'alternatives' who, although smaller in number, do actually interact with the host community at a more personal level. Cultural change is related to (and may be determined by) interpersonal communication and increasing change results from increasing communication.[8] This could form the basic equation for a number of comparative analyses. Clearly the types of host community, their history and relationship to visitors will affect any outcome but this gives us a new approach with which to examine the issue of impact.

A further consideration that arises, especially when we think of the historical relationship between two countries, is that of imperialism. Writers such as Nash (1989) and Crick (1989, 1994) have considered this theme and Nash supports the concept of tourism as a form of imperialism. He uses a broad definition of imperialism which is not especially helpful: '[v]oluntary acceptance by a native people and voluntary participation in transactions that further expatriate interests are an essential part of this conception of imperialism' (Nash, 1989: 38). Such a relationship and the perception of it as imperialistic seem to be tied up with the historical experience of the host country and may be an obvious analogy to be drawn by the local inhabitants of particular countries (for example Sri Lanka or Kenya). One factor that indicates imperialism is the power relationship, in terms of who is controlling the tourism. Thus, the business of mass tourism, if ultimately owned and controlled by outside investors, may well be overtly imperialistic, whereas a small-scale situation in which indigenous people are the agents of change in control of their businesses and locale could not be justifiably described as imperialistic. The latter situation has been largely the experience of people in VGR, although it could change in the near future.

Vested interests are becoming increasingly dominated by foreign nationals with the gradual expansion of tourist agency hotels and package tourism and the investment by the EU in infrastructure expansion (roads and the airport). Even the local businesses are becoming foreign owned (albeit by settlers) and, consequently, predominant tastes are oriented towards the tourists (mostly German) and the expanding foreign-settler community. Thus, expatriate interests are furthered and a neocolonial situation may arise if the original local community find themselves employed solely within the service industry in menial jobs. This situation leads to the growth of a 'creolised' community as described by Hannerz (1992: 264) in his search for a suitable metaphor for 'globalised' communities, with the majority peripheral population experiencing the influx of people from the 'core' (urbanised metropolis). Such a situation could develop within the valley and there is now a great demand amongst the young people of Vueltas to learn the German language in order to relate directly to the tourists and benefit from job prospects as intermediaries in positions such as receptionists, tour guides and shop assistants.

Studying the influence of tourism allows the anthropologist to address major intellectual issues that preoccupy many social scientists (see Nash, 1996). Tourism can create an environment in which reality is distorted, falsified, recreated and mocked. Things become symbols, differences disappear, values are challenged and inverted. Urry has examined postmodernism and focused on its quality of de-differentiation, i.e. the way in which it dissolves boundaries between high and low culture and different cultural forms, '[s]uch as tourism, art, education, photography, television, music, sport, shopping and architecture.' (Urry, 1990: 83). Tourism, a phenomenon that was once regarded as an outstanding example of modernism (MacCannell, 1976), is now being touted as an exemplary post-modern experience. Maybe tourism has changed or perhaps those talking about it have.

VGR would seem to be a place where modernism continues to shadow decisions, a place where projects are funded by the EU, with its ideology of progress including equalising economic standards between regions. The 'development' of this region is very much underway, and 'modern' roads and facilities are being constructed everywhere including streetlights, pathways, roundabouts and telephone kiosks (electricity has only recently been made available to everyone). Yet there are signs that the clear boundaries between cultural forms and activities are dissolving: tourists now go fishing in 'real' fishing boats whilst real fishermen work in supermarkets; a German settler advertises his fishing expeditions and competes with ex-fishermen who offer dolphin safaris; locals sit down in a recently built restaurant eating 'local' dishes whilst watching themselves performing in a promotional video for VGR; barefoot ex-urbanite hippies pass ex-barefoot peasants driving Mercedes cars. These are a few of the ironies that a tourist site can produce, which ultimately lead to more profound value changes and illustrate the complexity of identities.

The specific influences of tourism and tourists

It is worthwhile to review the influences of tourism and tourists at this stage, giving a brief summary of their main impacts, i.e. those that are unique to the phenomenon we have been examining as opposed to the more general processes of globalisation.

The most outstanding result of tourism in VGR is its impact on the built environment. The entire area has been changed: apartments have been added onto private houses, apartment blocks have been built by local residents, apartment complexes have been built throughout the coastal zone and a large hotel built overlooking the beach. Shops have opened to service the visitors: the majority of outlets in Vueltas are geared towards the tourism market. Roads have been widened and built to enable easier access for coaches and lorries. Beyond the valley, tunnels have been blasted out of mountains to ease access and an airport has been built in the south of the island. At the port, recreation vessels compete for space with fishing boats, large tour boats moor alongside the *falua* fishing boats – the economic transformation impacting on maritime activities. Similarly, tourism has indirectly displaced labour from the fields or provided more attractive land-use opportunities and once-cultivated terraced fields lie dormant, often awaiting transformation into land for construction: such is the case of the banana plantations between Vueltas and Borbalan.

Tourism has brought money into the region, which, in turn, has led to the multiplier effect improving the turnover of direct and indirectly associated businesses such as apartments and furniture suppliers. This has led to an increase in employment, especially in the service sector, and especially for women in apartments and shops. The growth in opportunities for women has also impacted on their private lives. Opportunities provided by tourism have led to the option for young men, the sons of fishermen and agricultural workers, to avoid the professions of their fathers and work in the service sector. As a consequence, there has been a reduction in the number of men going into the traditional primary industries – and the newly acquired wealth has encouraged others to go to university. There has been a more equitable distribution of wealth in terms of gender and social class, with many ex-fishermen and ex-agricultural workers able to rent out apartments and build on previously inexpensive land. One example is the grandson of the first fisherman to settle Vueltas: he now owns 16 apartments.

An increase in demand for land and property from local people desiring to stay in the region because of its economic success and incomers from other parts of the island and the world (often ex-tourists) has led to price rises. Some residential properties have increased in price beyond the pocket of local people and there is a shortage of suitable accommodation for young families. The property market has transformed from being local and informal into a global and commercialised venture. Land usage is subsequently changing as construction outbids agriculture.

With the increasing flow of wealth and the competition for resources has come a new challenge for politicians. Tourism is very much on the political agenda – it appears in manifestos and is a cornerstone of policies and electoral speeches. Monies come in from governmental bodies and can be claimed by parties in power as a consequence of their actions. Construction programmes provide employment for residents and the demand for licenses to operate service outlets have given those in positions of influence direct power over specific people. There has been blatant conflict over resources due to policies directly associated with tourism – the beach development proposal – and a clear delineation in local political opinion has become apparent. Furthermore, a new type of resident, the foreign settler, has added a new dimension to politics at many levels. Some refuse to accept traditional ways, as with patronage and personal favours, and they have openly challenged local social structures of power. With the (theoretical) support of the EU they will be able to challenge time-honoured practices.

Partly as a result of these influences, the identity of people in VGR has been subject to numerous changes. One of the most important areas of transition is the opportunity for women to work for others and themselves: this has led to repercussions in their home lives as well as on their sense of confidence. Furthermore, women have seen foreign visitors behaving in a manner quite alien from their previous experience and they have occasionally been influenced by this in their own relationships with men, their clothing and attitudes to bodily display, independent socialising, forthrightness and general expectations. Similarly, local men have had their behaviour put into question by German women and men, with the platonic relationship between a man and a woman becoming more acceptable, supporting the concept of equality.

The transforming economic landscape has led to a reduction in the relative importance of fishing and the actual number of full-time fishermen. This means that the dominance of this mode of livelihood has declined and, with it, the broader culture which it produces. The differentiation between the fishing village and the agricultural village is declining and patterns of livelihood have become blurred and faded as the younger men move towards different working ways. The older men have identified strongly with their profession: it governed their lives and largely determined their associates and marriage partners. All this is disappearing. Fathers may have taught sons the skills of fishing but this does not make the sons fishermen. As one old fisherman pointed out, you need to constantly work at fishing to understand the ways of the sea and be able to know what to fish for, how to fish for it, where and when. In other words, only a full-time fishing fleet can maintain the knowledge and, hence, the attendant culture of fishing.

Communities were once associated with the dominant form of economy underpinning them. This quality is fast fading as tourism supplies the workforce with employment and displaces traditional industries. However, the introduction of foreign visitors and the arrival of foreign settlers have given the indigenous population a strong sense of local and national identity. What was once a pattern of identity firmly based on family, neighbourhood, municipality, island and nation in relation to context remains; however, these factors have less impact due to constant intercommunication and movement. A greater sense of island and archipelago identity is prevalent because of the continual contact with people from other islands, especially Tenerife, and other countries, especially Germany. Furthermore, occasional travel abroad has given Gomeros a powerful sense of difference and the uniqueness of their own community. This sense of difference and uniqueness enables the islanders to be more confident in promoting their own cultural identity in terms of heritage, including the dance, music, silbo, crafts and food. They are able to commodify these with a greater sense of their intrinsic worth. Equally, the people who have been born before the coming of tourism have had an experience of the island which is unknown to the younger generation who have grown up surrounded by tourists and the trappings of tourism. This leads to a division between the older and younger generations in their experience and understanding of their native home.

The influence of tourism has reached deep into the experience of individuals that inhabit VGR: their personal identity. And similarly, it has entered an important part of their social lives: the family. Local men are marrying or living with foreign women (ex-tourists) and this has meant the introduction of foreigners into the family environment: it was, however, very unusual for Gomeran women to marry foreign men (ex-tourists). As a consequence, the family group is introduced to new ways of behaving by the incoming parent: the local families have initiated serious connections with people (and their families and friends) from other cultures. These are profound changes with profound consequences for the people of VGR and future generations. There are now children growing up in VGR with friends at school who speak a different language and who have parents from a different country: for a small island community, these are new experiences.

These marriages are a result of tourism introducing new potential partners to the local community. Local men have taken advantage of foreign women who are more willing to enter casual sexual relationships. This also leads to increased competition as far as local women are concerned, with resulting resentments and changing attitudes. It is a subject that provides material for envy and criticism: others include the apartments, the relative success of businesses and kinsmen and general personal comportment. Tourism has introduced a wealth of opportunities to supply material for social discussion and critique – and it has given the younger generation an unrealistic view of how foreigners behave. Some may argue that juvenile delinquency (including drug-taking and robberies) has increased because of the opportunities available due to tourism as well as the bad example given by tourists. This is not so obvious in VGR – and is also hard to differentiate from more general trends in social behaviour. Nevertheless, the fishermen regularly complain of the youth's inability to work hard, get up early, stick at a job – and their inclination to visit the disco until the early hours of the morning.

New people and opportunities, with different ways of behaving, different 'ways of seeing', have challenged traditional values but the moral template of 'respect and shame' remains part of the outlook of villagers in the region. But this attitude is under strong pressure and being destabilised by the new 'role' opportunities and choices exhibited by foreign visitors, especially women. As a result, old notions equating women with sexual shame are becoming viewed as outdated as foreign women behave in ways that blatantly contravene local codes of conduct. They are able to justify their behaviour in the face of criticism – this goes deeper than mere 'demonstration effect' imitation. The tourists have introduced radically different ways of behaving and also new ideas that reach into the heart of the local community. As well as attitudes toward gender roles, sexual conduct, marriage, education and parenthood, they have encouraged specific ways of understanding the environment – nature conservation, aesthetic approaches – and a new style of clothing, music, food and cooking, all of which change the indigenous population's experience of culture.

These examples draw our attention to the broad and deep impacts that tourism has had on the people of VGR. It seems to have infiltrated most areas of the culture as well as changing the physical environment. Many of the influences are distinctively due to tourism alone and depart from the more general effects of globalisation. Because of the community's relatively peripheral situation on an island in the Canary Islands archipelago, many of these phenomena have been especially powerful: partly due to the small scale of the society, the pressure on resources, the increased potential for dependence, the fragile infrastructure, the limited financial and cultural capital and related issues. This leads us to consider the importance of these findings for other similar communities, whether on islands or simply isolated through different factors, and to contemplate the profound cultural changes that can occur through tourism.

Notes

1. In a paper entitled 'Anthropology, the Environment and Development' Croll and Parkin (1992: 3) draw attention to the close association between people and their environment:

   > [m]ost peoples do ascribe a sometimes capricious agency to their environment which they are obliged to interpret and negotiate . . . they commonly regard themselves as inseparably part of it: the forest is the people, in the same way that the ancestors are, in a sense, extensions of the living'. 'As concepts, the environment and development together presuppose an interest in the management of natural resources. Anthropology adds to this a concern with the ways in which peoples bring their cultural imagination to bear on the utility of such resources.

2. Robinson (2000: 381) draws attention to the cultural context of human relations with the environment – and the importance of tourism in relation to the sustainability debate: 'It is the fact that tourism allows importation and exportation of different cultural constructs which is significant in the light of sustainable development as a global and globalising concept.'

3. 'Tourism has been called the leisure industry, but it has the opportunity now to broaden its contribution to society and become a prime economic agent for the sustainable development of our natural environment and cultural heritage' (Murphy, 1994: 289). See also Hawkins (1994).

4. For a broad discussion of the concept 'political ecology', see '*Journal of Political Ecology: Case Studies in History and the Social Sciences* (Vol. 1, 1994), Bureau of Applied Research in Anthropolgy , University of Arizona.

5. I liken the complexity and variability of an individual's identity to Edelman's (1992) model of the brain, in which there are no fixed 'hard-wired' computer-like programs but instead an infinite series of processes, particularly relating to the memory, which are being constantly revised and updated, with pathways being created, strengthened and broke.

6. See Macleod (1993) for a discussion on the continuum between objectivity and subjectivity – this intellectual stance has been noted by Milton (1996: 11) as representing a 'fundamental shift' in contemporary social science theory. See Wrangham and Peterson (1996) for an argument for combining culture and nature as determining factors of behaviour.

7. Featherstone and Lash (1995:4) argue that the homogenisers are modernists and that the heterogenisers, including Clifford and Marcus (1986) are postmodernists.

8. The importance of communication in relation to social change is noted by Milton (1993: 8) in her examination of environmentalism and anthropology and she states: ' In recent years the work of theorists such as Habermas, Touraine and Giddens has given rise to 'an actionist model of culture' which sees it as the process whereby social practice both constitutes and transforms itself. The principal mechanism through which this process operates is communication.'

References

Abram, S. and Waldren, J. (1997) Introduction. In S. Abram, J. Waldren and D.V.L. Macleod (eds) *Tourists and Tourism: Identifying with People and Places*. Oxford: Berg.

Abram, S, Waldren, J. and Macleod, D.V.L. (1997) *Tourists and Tourism: Identifying with People and Places*. Oxford: Berg.

Abreu-Padión, A. (1986) Historia de las Canarias. In P. Hernandez-Hernandez (ed.) *Natura y Cultura de las Islas Canarias* (pp. 223–91). Tenerife: Litografia P.H. G. Romera S.A.

Aceves, J. (1971) *Social Change in a Spanish Village*. Cambridge, MA: Schenkman.

Acheson, J. (1981) The anthropology of fishing. *Annual Review of Anthropology* 10, 275–316.

Albers, P.C. (1983) Tourism and the changing photographic image of the Great Lakes Indians. In J. Jafari (ed.) *The Anthropology of Tourism* (Annals of Tourism Research 10) (pp. 123–48). Wisconsin, USA: University of Wisconsin-Stout.

Anderson, R. (1973) Resource management and spatial competition in Newfoundland fishing. An exploratory essay. In P.H. Fricke (ed.) *Seafarers and Community: Towards a Scoial Understanding of Seafaring* (pp. 44–6). London: Croom Helm.

Appadurai, A. (1990) Disjuncture and difference in the global cultural economy. In M. Featherstone (ed.) *Global Culture: Nationalism, Globalization and Modernity* (pp. 295–310). London: Sage.

Appadurai, A. (1995) The production of locality. In R. Fardon (ed.) *Counterworks*. London: Routledge.

Armas, A. (1990) Valle Gran Rey: Ocupación traditional, transformations y expectivas. Singularidades de un modelo de transformación social en el contexto histórico y geográphico gomeron. Unpublished Masters thesis, Tenerife University.

Bardolet, E. (2001) The path towards sustainability in the Balaeric Islands. In D. Ioannides, Y. Apostolopoulos and S. Sonmers (eds) *Mediterranean Islands and Sustainable Tourism Development: Practices, Management and Policies*. London: Continuum.

Barke, M. (1999) Tourism and culture in Spain: A case of minimal conflict. In M. Robinson and P. Boniface (eds) *Tourism and Cultural Conflict*. Oxford: CAB International.

Barrett, R.A. (1974) *Benabarre, The Modernisation of a Spanish Village*. New York: Holt, Rinehart and Winston.

Bestard, J. (1991) *What's in a Relative?* Oxford: Berg.

Bhaba, H.K. (1994) *The Location of Culture*. London: Routledge.

Bianchi, R.V. (2000) The political and socio-cultural relations of world heritage in Garajonay National Park, La Gomera. In M. Robinson, N. Evans, P. Long, R. Sharpley and J. Swarbrooke (eds) *Tourism and Heritage Relationships: Global, National and Local Perspectives*. Sunderland: Business Education.

Black, A. (1996) Negotiating the tourist gaze: The example of Malta. In J. Boissevain (ed.) *Coping with Tourists: European Reactions to Mass Tourism*. Oxford: Berg.

Boissevain, J. (1966) Patronage in Sicily. *MAN: Journal of the Royal Anthropological Institute* (new series) 1, 1–9.

Boissevain, J. (1974) *Friends of Friends: Networks, Manipulators and Coalitions*. Oxford: Blackwell.

Boissevain, J. (1978) Tourism and development in Malta. In *Tourism and Economic Change* (Studies in Third World Societies 6). Williamsburg, VA. College of William and Mary.

Boissevain, J. (1991) Ritual, play and identity: Changing patterns in celebration in Maltese Villages. *Journal of Mediterranean Studies* 1(1), 87–100.

Boissevain, J. (ed.) (1996a) *Coping with Tourists: European Reactions to Mass Tourism*. Oxford: Berg.

Boissevain, J. (1996b) But we live here! Perspectives on cultural tourism in Malta. In L. Briguglio, L, B.V. Archer, J. Jafari and G. Wall (eds) *Sustainable Tourism in Islands and Small States: Issues and Policies*. London: Pinter.

Boorstin, D. (1964) *The Image: A Guide to Pseudo-events in America*. New York: Harper.

Bote Gomez, V. and Thea Sinclair, M. (1996) Tourism demand and supply in Spain. In M. Barke, J. Towner and M. Newton (eds) *Tourism in Spain: Critical Issues*. Oxon: CAB International.

Bouquet, M. (1986) 'You cannot be a Brahmin in the English countryside': The partitioning of status, and its representations within the farm family in Devon. In A.P. Cohen (ed.) *Symbolising Boundaries: Identity and Diversity in British Cultures* (pp. 22–39). Manchester: Manchester University Press.

Bouquet, M. (1987) Bed, breakfast and an evening meal: Commensality in the nineteenth and twentieth century farm household in Hartland. In M. Bouquet and M. Winter (eds) *Who From Their Labours Rest? Conflict and Practice in Rural Tourism* (pp.93–104) Aldershot: Gower.

Bowman, G. (1989) Fucking tourists: Sexual relations and tourism in Jerusalem's old city. *Critique of Anthropology* 9(2), 77–94.

Bramwell, B. and Lane, B. (2000) Collaboration and partnerships in tourism planning. In B. Bramwell and B. Lane (eds) *Tourism Collaboration and Partnerships: Politics, Practice and Sustainability*. Clevedon: Channel View Publications.

Brandes, S.H. (1975) *Migration, Kinship, and Community: Tradition and Transition in a Spanish Village*. New York: Academic Press.

Brandes, S.H. (1992) Sex roles and anthropological research in rural Andalusia. In J. Pina-Cabral and J. Campbell (eds) *Europe Observed* (pp. 24–38). London: Macmillan.

Briguglio, L, Archer, B.V., Jafari, J. and Wall, G. (eds) (1996) *Sustainable Tourism in Islands and Small States: Issues and Policies*. London: Pinter.

Broegger J. (1990) *Pre-bureaucratic Europeans: A Study of a Portuguese Fishing Community*. Norway: Norwegian University Press.

Burriel, E.L. (1982) *Canarias: Población y Agricultura en una Sociadad Dependiente*. Barcelona: Oikos-tau S.A.

Burns, P. (2001) Brief encounters: Culture, tourism and the local-global nexus. In S. Wahab and C. Cooper (eds) *Tourism in the Age of Globalisation*. London: Routledge.

Butler, R.W. (1980) The concept of a tourist area cycle of evolution. *Canadian Geographer* 24, 5–12.

Butler, R. and Stiakaki, E. (2001) Tourism and sustainability in the Mediterrranean: Issues and implications from Hydra. In D. Ioannides, Y. Apostolopoulos and S. Sonmers (eds) *Mediterranean Islands and Sustainable Tourism Development: Practices, Management and Policies*. London: Continuum.

Byrne-Swain, M. (1989) Gender roles in indigenous tourism: Kuna Mola, Kuna Yala, and cultural survival. In V. Smith (ed.) *Hosts and Guests: The Anthropology of Tourism* (2nd edn) (pp. 83–104). Philadelphia: University of Pennsylvania Press.

Byron, R. (1986) *Sea Change: A Shetland Society 1970–79*. St Johns: Memorial University of Newfoundland.

Campbell, J. (1964) *Honour, Family, and Patronage*. Oxford: Clarendon Press.

Chapman, M. (1986) A social anthropological study of a Breton village with Celtic comparisons. Unpublished DPhil thesis, Oxford University.

Cheater, A.P. (1995) Globalisation and the new technologies of knowing: Anthropological calculus or chaos? In M. Strathern (ed.) *Shifting Contexts: Transformations in Anthropological Knowledge*. London: Routledge.

Christian, W.A. (1972) *Person and God in a Spanish Valley*. New York: Seminar Press.

Clifford, J. (1986) Partial truths. In J. Clifford and G. Marcus (eds) *Writing Culture: The Poetics and Politics of Ethnography* (pp. 1–26). Berkeley, CA: University of California Press.

Clifford, J. and Marcus, G. (eds) (1986) *Writing Culture: The Poetics and Politics of Ethnography*. Berkeley: University of California Press.

Cohen, A.P.(ed.) (1982a) *Belonging: Identity and Social Organisation in British Rural Cultures*. Manchester: Manchester University Press.

Cohen, A.P. (1982b) Belonging: The experience of culture. In A.P. Cohen (ed.) *Belonging: Identity and Social Organisation in British Rural Cultures* (pp. 1–17). Manchester: Manchester University Press.

Cohen, A.P. (1982c) A sense of time, a sense of place: The meaning of close association in Whalsay, Shetland. In A.P. Cohen (ed.) *Belonging: Identity and Social Organisation in British Rural Cultures* (pp. 21–49). Manchester: Manchester University Press.

Cohen, E. (1972) Towards a sociology of international tourism. *Social Research* 39(1), 64–82.

Cohen, E. (1979a) The impact of tourism on the hill tribes of Northern Thailand. *Internationales Asienforum* 10, 5–38.

Cohen, E. (1979b) A phenomenology of tourist types. *Sociology* 13, 179–201.

Cohen, E. (1987) 'Alternative tourism' – a critique. *Tourism Recreation Research* XII(2). Lucknow: Centre for Tourism Research.

Cole, S. (1991) *Women of the Praia: Works and Lives in a Portuguese Coastal Community*. Princeton, NJ: Princeton University Press.

Concepción, J. (1989) *The Guanches Survivors and their Descendants*. Tenerife: Concepción.

Conlin, M. and Baum, T. (eds) (1995) *Island Tourism: Management Principles and Practice*. Chichester: John Wiley and Sons.

Cooper, C., Gilbert, D., Fletcher, J. and Wanhill, S. (1999) *Tourism: Principles and Practice*. Harlow: Pearson Education.

Crick, M. (1989) Representations of international tourism in the social sciences: Sun, sex, sights, savings, and servility. *Annual Review of Anthropology* 18, 307–44.

Crick, M. (1994) *Resplendent Sites, Discordant Voices: Sri Lankans and International Tourism.* Switzerland: Harwood.

Croll, E. and Parkin, D. (1992) Anthropology, the environment and development. In E. Croll and D. Parkin (eds) *Bush Base: Forest Farm. Culture, Environment and Development.* London: Routledge.

Cronin, C. (1970) *The Sting of Change: Sicilians in Sicily and Australia.* Chicago: University of Chicago Press.

Dalton, G. (1971) Introduction. In G. Dalton (ed.) *Economic Development and Social Change.* New York: National History Press.

Dann, G. (1981) Tourist motivation: An appraisal. *Annals of Tourism Research* 8, 187–219.

Dann, G. (1996) The people of the tourist brochures. In T. Selwyn (ed.) *The Tourist Image: Myths and Myth Making in Tourism.* Chichester: John Wiley and Sons.

Davis, A. (1991) Insidious rationalities: The institutionalisation of small boat fishing and the rise of the rapacious fisher. *Maritime Anthropological Studies* (MAST) 4(1), 1–12 . University of Amsterdam.

Deitch, L.I. (1989) The impact of tourism on the arts and crafts of the Indians of the Southwestern United States. In V. Smith (ed.) *Hosts and Guests: The Anthropology of Tourism* (2nd edn) (pp. 223–36). Philadelphia: University of Pennsylvania Press.

De Kadt, E. (ed.) (1979) *Tourism: Passport to Development? Perspectives on the Social Effects of Tourism in Developing Countries.* Oxford: Oxford University Press.

De Kadt, E. (1990) Making the alternative sustainable: Lessons from development for tourism. Discussion Paper, Sussex University Institute for Development Studies.

Denevan, W.M. (ed.) (1989) *Hispanic Lands and Peoples: Selected Writings of James J. Parsons.* Boulder, CO: Westview Press.

Douglass, W.A (1976) Serving girls and sheepherders: Emigration and continuity in a Spanish Basque village. In J. Aceves and W. Douglass (eds) *The Changing Faces of Rural Spain* (pp. 45–62). Cambridge, MA: Schenkman.

Duysens, B. (1989) Turismo, ocio, y cultura juvenil: El caso del turismo de mochila en la Gomera. In *ERES (Antropología)* 1(2), 115–26. Tenerife: Museo Arquelógico y Etnográfico.

Edelman, G. (1992) *Bright Light, Brilliant Fire. On the Matter of the Mind.* London: Penguin.

Editorial Event (2001) *La Gomera.* Leon: Editorial Event.

Eisenstadt, S.N. and Ranger, I. (1980) Patron-client relations as a model of structuring social exchange. *Comparative Studies in Society and History* 22, 42–77.

Ekholm-Friedman, K. and Friedman, J. (1995) Global complexity and the simplicity of everyday life. In D. Miller (ed.). *Worlds Apart: Modernity through the Prism of the Local.* London: Routledge.

Faulkner, B., Moscardo, G. and Laws, E. (eds) (2000) *Tourism in the 21st Century: Lessons from Experience.* London: Continuum.

Featherstone, M. (1990a) Global culture: An introduction. In M. Featherstone (ed.) *Global Culture: Nationalism, Globalization and Modernity.* London: Sage.

Featherstone, M. (ed.) (1990b) *Global Culture: Nationalism, Globalization and Modernity.* London: Sage.

Featherstone, M. and Lash, S. (1995) Globalization, modernity and the spatialization of social theory: An introduction. In M. Featherstone, S. Lash and R. Robertson (eds) *Global Modernities*. London: Sage.

Fernandez-Armesto, F. (1982) *The Canary Islands After the Conquest: The Making of a Colonial Society in the Early 16th Century*. Oxford: Clarendon.

Free, A. (1991) Patronage, honour, community and time in the ethnography of Spain. Unpublished MLitt. thesis, Oxford University.

Friedl, E. (1962) *Vasilika. A Village in Modern Greece*. Orlando, FL: Holt, Rinehart and Winston.

Fsadni, C. and Selwyn, T. (eds) (1996) *Tourism, Culture and Regional Development in the Mediterranean*. Malta: University of Malta.

Galván-Tudela, A. (1980) *Taganana: Un Estudio Antropológico Social*. Tenerife: Aula de Cultura del Cabildo Insular.

Galván-Tudela, A. (1987) *Las Fiestas Populares Canarias*. Tenerife: Ediciones Canarias.

Garcia, C. (1969) *La Pesca en Canarias y el Banco Sahariano*. Tenerife: CEIC.

Geertz, C. (1973) *The Interpretation of Cultures*. New York: Basic Books.

Gellner, E. and Waterbury, D. (eds) (1977) *Patrons and Clients*. London: Gerald Duckworth.

Getz, D. (1995) Island competitiveness through festivals and special events: The case of Newfoundland. In M. Conlin and T. Baum (eds) *Island Tourism: Management Principles and Practice*. Chichester: John Wiley and Sons.

Giddens, C. (1997) *Sociology* (3rd edn). Cambridge: Polity Press.

Gilmore, D. (1980) *The People of the Plain: Class and Community in Lower Andalusia*. New York: Columbia University Press.

Gilmore, D. (1987) The shame of dishonour. In D. Gilmore (ed.) *Honour and Shame and the Unity of the Mediterranean* (American Anthropological Association Special Publication 22) (pp. 2–21). Washington: American Anthropological Association.

Goddard, V. (1987) Honour and shame: the control of women's sexuality and group identity in Naples. In P. Caplan (ed.) *The Cultural Construction of Sexuality* (pp. 166–92). London: Routledge.

Goddard, V, Llobera, J. and Shore, C. (1994) Introduction: The anthropology of Europe. In V. Goddard, J. Llobera and C. Shore (eds) *The Anthropology of Europe: Identities and Boundaries in Conflict*. Oxford: Berg.

Goffman, E. (1969) *The Presentation of Self in Everyday Life*. London: Penguin.

Graburn, N. (1989) Tourism: The sacred journey. In V. Smith (ed.) *Hosts and Guests: The Anthropology of Tourism* (2nd edn) (pp. 21–36). Philadelphia: University of Pennsylvania Press.

Greenwood, D.J. (1989) Culture by the pound: An anthropological perspective on tourism as cultural commoditisation. In V. Smith (ed.) *Hosts and Guests: The Anthropology of Tourism* (2nd edn) (pp. 171–86). Philadelphia: University of Pennsylvania Press.

Guarapo (1990) Associación Cultural y Ecologista Yr 1, no 1.

Hall, C.M. (1994) *Tourism and Politics: Policy, Power and Place*. Chichester: Wiley.

Hall, S. (1996) Introduction: Who needs identity? In S. Hall and P. du Gray (eds) *Questions of Cultural Identity*. London: Sage.

Hannertz, U. (1992) *Cultural Complexity: Studies in the Social Organization of Meaning*. New York: Columbia University Press.

Harrison, D. (2001) *Tourism and the Lesser Developed Countries: Issues and Case Studies*. New York: Cognizant.

Hawkins, D. (1994) Ecotourism: Opportunities for developing countries. In W. Theobald (ed.) *Global Tourism: The Next Decade*. Oxford: Butterworth-Heinemann.

Hermans, D. (1981) The encounter of agriculture and tourism: A Catalan case. *Annals of Tourism Research* 8, 462–79.

Hernandez-Hernandez, P. (1986) *Natura y Cultura de las Islas Canarias*. Tenerife: Litografia P.H. G. Romera S.A.

Herzfeld, M. (1987) *Anthropology Through the Looking Glass: Critical Ethnography in the Margins of Europe*. Cambridge: Cambridge University Press.

M. Hitchcock, King, V.T. and Parnwell, M.J.G. (eds) (1993) *Tourism in South-East Asia*. London: Routledge.

Ioannides, D. Apostolopoulos, Y and Sonmers, S. (eds) (2001) *Mediterranean Islands and Sustainable Tourism Development: Practices Management and Policies*. London: Continuum.

Jafari, J. (ed.) (1980) Tourism and development. anthropological perspectives. *Annals of Tourism Research* 3(1). Wisconsin, USA: University of Wisconsin-Stout.

Jordan, J.W. (1980) The summer people and the Natives: Some effects of tourism in a Vermont village. In J. Jafari (ed.) *Annals of Tourism Research* 3(1), 34–55. Wisconsin, USA: University of Wisconsin-Stout.

Kenna, M. (1976) The idiom of family. In J.G. Peristiany (ed.) *Mediterranean Family Structures* (pp. 347–62). Cambridge: Cambridge University Press.

Kenna, M. (1988) *Islanders, Migrants and Tourists: Changing Relationships on a Greek Island* (Report to the ESRC). London: British Library Document Supply Centre.

Kenny, M. (1961) *A Spanish Tapestry: Town and Country in Castile*. London: Cohen and West.

Kenny, M. (1968) Parallel power structures in Castille. The patron-client balance. In J.G. Peristiany (ed.) *Contributions to Mediterranean Sociology* (pp. 155–62). The Hague: Morton.

King, B. (1997) *Creating Island Resorts*. London: Routledge.

Kinnaird, V., Kothari, U. and Hall, D. (1994) Tourism: Gender perspectives. In V. Kinnaird and D. Hall (eds) *Tourism: A Gender Analysis*. Chichester: John Wiley and Sons.

Kohn, T. (1988) Seasonality and identity in a changing Hebridean community. Unpublished DPhil thesis, University of Oxford.

Kottak, C. (1966) The structure of equality in a Brazilian fishing community. PhD thesis, Columbia University, New York.

Lanfant, M. (1995) International tourism, internationalization and the challenge to identity. In M. Lanfant, J.B. Allcock and E.M. Bruner (eds) *International Tourism: Identity and Change*. London: Sage.

Lanfant, M., Allcock, J.B. and Bruner, E.M. (eds) (1995) *International Tourism: Identity and Change*. London: Sage.

Lee, R.L. (1978) Who owns Boardwalk: The structure of control in the tourist industry of Yucatan. In *Tourism and Economic Change* (Studies in Third World Societies No. 6), (pp. 19–36). Williamsbug, VA: College of William and Mary.

Lett, J. (1983) Ludic and liminoid aspects of charter yacht tourism in the Caribbean. In J. Jafari (ed.) *The Anthropology of Tourism* (Annals of Tourism Research 10(1)), (pp. 35–57). Wisconsin, USA: University of Wisconsin-Stout.

Lienhardt, G. (1979/1964) *Social Anthropology*. Oxford: Oxford University Press

Linton, R. (1936) *The Study of Man*. New York: Appleton-Century.

Lisón-Tolosana, C. (1980) *Invitación a la Antropología Cultural de España*. Madrid: Akal/Bolsillo.

Llobera, J. (1986) Fieldwork in South Western Europe. *Critique of Anthropology* VI(2): 25–33.

Loizos, P. (1992) Unpublished paper on Greek masculinity given at All Souls College, University of Oxford.

Long, V and Wall, G. (1995) Small-scale tourism development in Bali. In M. Conlin and T. Baum (eds) *Island Tourism: Management Principles and Practice*. Chichester: John Wiley and Sons.

Loukissas, P. (1978) Tourism and environment in conflict: The case of the Greek Island of Myconos. In *Tourism and Economic Change* (Studies in Third World Societies 6) (pp. 105–32). Williamsburg, VA: College of William and Mary.

MacCannell, D. (1976) *The Tourist: A New Theory of the Leisure Class*. London: Macmillan.

Macdonald, S. (1993) Identity complexes in Western Europe: Social anthropological perspectives. In S. Macdonald (ed.) *Inside European Identities: Ethnography in Western Europe* (pp. 219–36). Oxford: Berg.

Macleod, D.V.L. (1993) Change in a Canary Island fishing settlement with reference to the influence of tourism. Unpublished DPhil thesis, Oxford University.

Macleod, D.V.L. (1997) Alternative tourists on a Canary Island. In S. Abram, J. Waldren and D.V.L. Macleod (eds) *Tourists and Tourism: Identifying with People and Places*. Oxford: Berg.

Macleod, D.V.L. (1998) Alternative tourists: A comparative analysis of meaning and impact. In W. Theobald (ed.) *Global Tourism: The Next Decade*. Oxford: Butterworth-Heinemann.

Macleod, D.V.L. (1999) Tourism and the globalization of a Canary Island. *Journal of the Royal Anthropological Institute* 5(3), 443–56.

Macleod, D.V.L. (2002) Disappearing culture? Globalisation and a Canary Island fishing community. *History and Anthropology* 13(1), 53–67.

Marcus, G.E and Fischer, M.M.J. (1986) *Anthropology as Cultural Critique: An Experimental Moment in the Human Sciences*. Chicago: University of Chicago Press.

Martinez, D. (1988) The Ama: Tradition and change in a Japanese diving village. Unpublished DPhil thesis, University of Oxford.

McCrone, D., Morris, A. and Kiely, R. (1995) *Scotland the Brand: The Making of Scottish Heritage*. London: Polygon.

McDonald, M. (1993) The construction of difference: An anthropological approach to stereotypes. In S. Macdonald (ed.) *Inside European Identities: Ethnography in Western Europe*. Oxford: Berg.

McIntosh, R.W., Goeldner, C.R. and Ritchie, J.R.B. (1995) *Tourism: Principles, Practices and Philosophies*. New York: John Wiley and Sons.

Mckay, L. (1987) Tourism and changing attitudes to land in Negril, Jamaica. In J. Besson and J. Momsen (eds) *Land and Development in the Caribbean* (pp. 132–51). London: Macmillan Caribbean

McKean, P. (1976) Tourism, cultural change and cultural conservation in Bali. In D. Banks (ed.) *Changing Identities in Modern Southeast Asia* (pp. 237–47). The Hague: Moulton.

McKean, P. (1989) Towards a theoretical analysis of tourism, economic dualism, and cultural involution in Bali. In V. Smith (ed.) *Hosts and Guests: The Anthropology of Tourism* (2nd edn) (pp. 119–38). Philadelphia: University of Pennsylvania Press.

Mckechnie, R. (1993) Becoming Celtic in Corsica. In S. Macdonald (ed.) *Inside European Identities: Ethnography in Western Europe* (pp. 219–36). Oxford: Berg.

McNutt, P. and Oreja-Rodriguez, J.R. (1996) Economic strategies for sustainable tourism in islands: The case of Tenerife. In L. Briguglio, B.V. Archer, J. Jafari and G. Wall (eds) *Sustainable Tourism in Islands and Small States: Issues and Policies.* London: Pinter.

Mesa-Moreno, C. (1982) Antropologica Social de las Communidades Pesqueras en Valle Gran Rey. In C. Mesa-Moreno, J. Pascual-Fernandez and A.J. Perez-Soza (eds) *La Pesca en Canarias* (pp. 73–115). Tenerife: CCPC.

Milton, K. (1993) Introduction: Environmentalism and anthropology. In K. Milton (ed.) *Environmentalism: The View From Anthropology* (ASA Monologue 32). London: Routledge.

Milton K. (1996) *Environmentalism and Cultural Theory: Exploring the Role of Anthropology in Environmental Discourse.* London: Routledge.

Moeran, B. (1983) The language of Japanese tourism. In J. Jafari (ed.) *The Anthropology of Tourism* (Annals of Tourism Research 10(1)) (pp. 93–108). Wisconsin, USA: University of Wisconsin-Stout.

Moore, K. (1976) Modernisation in a Canary Island village. In J. Aceves and W. Douglass (eds) *The Changing Faces of Rural Spain* (pp. 17–28). Cambridge, MA: Schenkman.

Ministerio de Obras Publicas y Urbanismo (1988) *Ecoplan Para La Isla de La Gomera.* Madrid: Ministerio de Obras Publicas y Urbanismo.

Mora, M. (1988) *Inside La Gomera.* Tenerife: Editorial Globo.

Murphy, P. (1994) Tourism and sustainable development. In W. Theobald (ed.) *Global Tourism: The Next Decade.* Oxford: Butterworth-Heinemann.

Nash, D. (1989) Tourism as a form of imperialism. In V. Smith (ed.) *Hosts and Guests: The Anthropology of Tourism* (2nd edn), (pp. 37–54). Philadelphia: University of Pennsylvania Press.

Nash, D. (1996) *Anthropology of Tourism.* Oxford: Pergamon.

Olwig, K.F. (1985) *Cultural Adaptation and Resistance on St John: Three Centuries of Afro-Caribbean Life.* Orlanda, FL: University of Florida.

Ortner, S. (1989) *High Religion: A Cultural and Political History of Sherpa Buddhism.* Princeton, NJ: Princeton University Press.

Owen, R. and Dynes, M. (1989) *The Times Guide to 1992.* London: Times Books.

Palsson, G. (1991) *Coastal Economies, Cultural Accounts: Human Ecology and Icelandic Discourse.* Manchester: Manchester University Press.

Parman, S. (1990) *Scottish Crofters: A Historical Ethnography of a Celtic Village.* Orlando, FL: Holt Rinehart and Winston.

Pascual-Fernandez, J. (1982) San Miguel de Tajao o la historia de la familia de Domingo el Palomo. In C. Mesa-Moreno, J. Pascual-Fernandez and A.J.Perez-Soza (eds) *La Pesca en Canarias* (pp. 10–72). Tenerife: CCPC.

Pearce, D.G. (2001) Islands and coastal tourism: Demand and supply perspectives from Samoa, Sarawak and New Zealand. *Tourism* 49(3), 255–66.

Pearce, P.L. and Moscardo, G.M. (1986) The concept of authenticity in tourists experiences. *Australian and New Zealand Journal of Sociology* 22(1), 121–32.

Peristiany, J.G. (1965a) *Honour and Shame: The Values of Mediterranean Society.* London: Weidenfeld and Nicholson.

Peristiany, J.G. (1965b) Introduction. In J.G. Peristiany (ed.) *Honour and Shame: The Values of Mediterranean Society* (pp. 9–18). London: Weidenfeld and Nicholson.

Peristiany, J.G. (ed.) (1976) *Mediterranean Family Structures.* Cambridge: Cambridge University Press.

Peristiany, J.G. and J. Pitt-Rivers, J. (eds) (1992) *Honour and Grace in Anthropology.* Cambridge: Cambridge University Press.

Pina-Cabral, J. (1989) The Mediterranean as a category of regional comparison: A critical view. *Current Anthropology* (June), 399–405.

Pina-Cabral, J. and Campbell, J. (eds) (1992) *Europe Observed.* London: Macmillan.

Pi-Sunyer, O. (1977a) States of technological change in a Catalan fishing community. In M.E. Smith (ed.) *Those Who Live from the Sea: A Study in Maritime Anthropology* (pp. 41–57). New York: West.

Pi-Sunyer, O. (1977b) Through native eyes: Tourists and tourism in a Catalan maritime community. In V. Smith (ed.) *Hosts and Guests: The Anthropology of Tourism.* Philadelphia: University of Pennsylvania Press.

Pi-Sunyer, O. (1989) Changing perceptions of tourism and tourists in a Catalan resort town. In V. Smith (ed.) *Hosts and Guests: The Anthropology of Tourism* (2nd edn), (pp. 187–220). Philadelphia: University of Pennsylvania Press

Pitt-Rivers, J. (1954) *The People of The Sierra.* London: Weidenfeld and Nicolson.

Pitt-Rivers, J. (ed.) (1963/1977) *Mediterranean Countrymen: Essays in the Social Anthropology of the Mediterranean.* Westport, CT: Greenwood Press.

Puijk, R. (1996) Dealing with fish and tourism: A case study from Northern Norway. In J. Boissevain (ed.) *Coping with Tourists: European Reactions to Mass Tourism.* Oxford: Berg.

Rivière, P. (1967) The honour of Sanchez. In *MAN* Journal of the Royal Anthropological Society 2(4), 569–83.

Robertson, R. (1990) Mapping the global condition: Globalization as the central concept. In M. Featherstone (ed.) *Global Culture: Nationalism, Globalization and Modernity.* London: Sage.

Robinson, M. (1999) Cultural conflict in tourism: Inevitability and inequality. In M. Robinson and P. Boniface (eds) *Tourism and Cultural Conflict.* Oxon: CABI.

Robinson, M. (2000) Collaboration and cultural consent: Refocusing sustainable tourism. In B. Bramwell and B. Lane (eds) *Tourism Collaboration and Partnerships: Politics, Practice and Sustainability.* Clevedon: Channel View Publications.

Rodriguez-Martin (1988) *La Emigraciòn Clandestina de la provincia de Santa Cruz de Tenerife a Venezuela en los años cuarenta y cinquenta.* Tenerife: S.A. Romeo ACT.

Romero-Maura, J. (1977) Caciquismo as a political system. In E. Gellner and D. Waterbury (eds) *Patrons and Clients* (pp. 53–62). London: Gerald Duckworth.

Roseberry, W. (1989) Peasants and the world. In S. Plattner (ed.) *Economic Anthropology.* Stanford: Stanford University Press.

Rozenberg, R. (1995) International tourism and utopia: The Balaeric Islands. In M. Lanfant, J.B. Allcock and E.M. Bruner (eds) *International Tourism: Identity and Change.* London: Sage.

Sant Cassia, P. (1991) Authors in search of a character: Personhood, agency and identity in the Mediterranean. *Journal of Mediterranean Studies: History, Culture and Society in the Mediterranean World* 1(1), 1–17.

Sawyer, J.E. (1971) Social structure and economic progress. In G. Dalton (ed.) *Economic Development and Social Change* (pp. 401–12). National History Press.

Scott, J. (2001) Gender and sustainability in Mediterranean island tourism. In D. Ioannides, Y. Apostolopoulos and S. Sonmers (eds) *Mediterranean Islands and Sustainable Tourism Development: Practices, Management and Policies.* London: Continuum.

Selannieni, T. (2001) Trapped by the image: The implication of cultural tourism in the insular Mediterranean. In D. Ioannides, Y. Apostolopoulos and S. Sonmers (eds) *Mediterranean Islands and Sustainable Tourism Development: Practices, Management and Policies*. London: Continuum.

Selwyn, T. (ed.) (1996a) *The Tourist Image: Myths and Myth Making in Tourism*. Chichester: John Wiley and Sons.

Selwyn, T. (1996b) Tourism, culture and cultural conflict: A case study from Mallorca. In C. Fsadni and T. Selwyn (eds) *Tourism, Culture and Regional Development in the Mediterranean*. Malta: University of Malta.

Selwyn, T. (2001) Tourism, development and society in the insular Mediterranean. In D. Ioannides, Y. Apostolopoulos and S. Sonmers (eds) *Mediterranean Islands and Sustainable Tourism Development: Practices, Management and Policies*. London: Continuum.

Shannon, T. (1989) *An Introduction to the World-System Perspective*. Boulder, CO: Westview Press.

Sharpley, R. (2001) Sustainability and the political economy of tourism in Cyprus. *Tourism* 49(3), 241–54.

Sinclair, M.T. and Bote-Gomez, V. (1996) Tourism, the Spanish economy and the balance of payments. In M. Barke, J. Towner and M. Newton (eds) *Tourism in Spain: Critical Issues*. Oxon: CAB International.

Smith, M.E. (ed.) (1977) *Those Who Live from the Sea: A Study in Maritime Anthropology*. New York: West.

Smith, V. (ed.) (1977) *Hosts and Guests: The Anthropology of Tourism*. Philadelphia: University of Pennsylvania Press.

Smith, V. (ed.) (1989a) *Hosts and Guests: The Anthropology of Tourism* (2nd edn). Philadelphia: University of Pennsylvania Press.

Smith, V. (1989b) Eskimo tourism: Micro models and marginal men. In V. Smith (ed.) *Hosts and Guests: The Anthropology of Tourism* (2nd edn), (pp. 55–82). Philadelphia: University of Pennsylvania Press.

Smith, V. (1989c) Introduction. In V. Smith (ed.) *Hosts and Guests: The Anthropology of Tourism* (2nd edn) (pp. 1–20). Philadelphia: University of Pennsylvania Press.

Stanton, M.E. (1989) The Polynesian cultural centre: A multi-ethnic model of seven Pacific cultures. In V. Smith (ed.) *Hosts and Guests: The Anthropology of Tourism* (2nd edn) (pp. 1247–64). Philadelphia: University of Pennsylvania Press.

Strathern, M. (ed.) (1995) *Shifting Contexts: Transformations in Anthropological Knowledge*. London: Routledge.

Theobald, W. (ed.) (1994) *Global Tourism: The Next Decade*. Oxford: Butterworth-Heinemann.

Theobald, W. (ed.) (1998) *Global Tourism* (2nd edn). Oxford: Butterworth-Heinemann.

Thompson, J. and Heelas, P. (1986) *The Way of the Heart: The Rajneesh Movement*. Northamptonshire: Aquarian Press.

Todorov, T. (1984) *The Conquest of America*. New York: Harper and Row.

Trujillo, R. (1978) *El Silbo Gomero: análysis lingüístico*. Tenerife: Editorial Islas Canarias.

Turner, L. and Ash, J. (1975) *The Golden Hordes: International Tourism and the Pleasure Periphery*. London: Constable.

Tylor, E.B. (1871) *Primitive Culture: Researches into the Development of Mythology, Philosophy, Religion, Art and Custom*. London: John Murray.

Urbanowicz, C.F. (1989) Tourism in Tonga revisited: Continued troubled times? In V. Smith (ed.) *Hosts and Guests: The Anthropology of Tourism* (2nd edn), (pp. 105–18). Philadelphia: University of Pennsylvania Press.

Urry, J. (1990) *The Tourist Gaze. Leisure and Travel in Contemporary Societies.* London: Sage.

Wagner, U. (1986) Going north and getting attached: The case of the Gambians. *Ethnos* 51(3–4), 199–222.

Wagner, U. (1977) Out of time and place: Mass tourism and charter trips. *Ethnos* 42(1–2), 173–90.

Wahab, S. and Cooper, C. (2001) Tourism, globalisation and the competitive advantage of nations. In S. Wahab and C. Cooper (eds) *Tourism in the Age of Globalisation.* London: Routledge.

Waldren, J. (1989) Insiders and outsiders in a Mallorquin village community. Unpublished DPhil thesis, University of Oxford.

Waldren, J. (1996) *Insiders and Outsiders: Paradise and Reality in Mallorca.* Oxford: Berghahn Books.

Wallerstein, I. (1974) *The Modern World-System.* New York: Academic Press.

Walton, J. (1993) Tourism and economic development in ASEAN. In M. Hitchcock, V.T. King and M.J.G. Parnwell (eds) *Tourism in South-East Asia.* London: Routledge.

Wang, N. (1999) Rethinking authenticity in tourism experience. *Annals of Tourism Research* 26(2), 349–70.

Waters, M. (1995) *Globalization.* London: Routledge.

Wilson, D. (1993) Time and tides in the anthropology of tourism In M. Hitchcock, V.T. King and M.J.G. Parnwell (eds) *Tourism in South-East Asia* (pp. 32–47). London: Routledge.

Wolf, E. (1966) Kinship, friendship and patron-client relationships in complex societies. In M. Banton (ed.) *The Anthropology of Complex Societies* (ASA Monograph 4) (pp. 1–20). London: Tavistock.

Wolf, E. (1982) *Europe and the People Without History.* Berkeley, CA: University of California Press.

Wrangham, P and Peterson, D. (1996) *Demonic Males: Apes and the Origins of Human Violence.* New York: Houghton Mifflin.

Zinovieff, S. (1987) Inside out and outside in. Gossip, hospitality and the Greek character. *Cambridge Anthropology* 12(3), 1–15.

Zinovieff, S. (1990) Dealing in identities: Insiders and outsiders in a Greek town. Unpublished PhD thesis, Cambridge University.

Index

Abreu-Padion, A. 41
accommodation, on La Gomera 24
– in Vueltas 38
acculturation 8
Acheson, James 118, 168
advocacy, of tourism for development 8
agency, as deliberate action 9
agriculture 27
– activity 36
– crops 44
airport, La Gomera 215
Albers, P.C. 96n
Anderson, R. 123
anthropology 11
– and ideas about 'the journey' 12
Appadurai, Arjun 217
authenticity 11, 12, 78-79, 88
– deconstruction of 219

bananas, as export crops 44
– and plantation work 113
– packing station 114
Bardolet, E. 15
Barke, M. 135
belonging, and identity 175,
– *hijo del pueblo* 175
Boissevain, Jeremy 64n
Boorstin, D. on authenticity 78
Bouquet, M. 125
Bramwell, B. and B. Lane 54n
Brandes, Stanley 172
Britain, British couple as settlers 178
brochures, and stereotypification 87
Broegger, Jan 120, 130
bubble, as home lifestyle and environment
    13, 68
business, in Vueltas 38, 105-115 *passim*
– attitudes towards 128, 129
– competition 129
Burns, Peter 21n
Butler, R. and E. Stiakaki 15
Butler, Richard 94
Byrne-Swain, M. 132n
Byron, Reginald 138, 168

caciques 45, 46, 59
– local council 95, 146, 148
– politicians 142
Campbell, John 187
Canary Islands 24
capital, socio-cultural capital advantage 63,
    94, 126
carrying capacity, of islands 16
Cartesian dualism 216
casa, la, house design in Vueltas 39-41
– the home 195-197
Chapman, Malcolm 168
Cheater, Angela 6
Christian, William 185n
class, bourgeoisie 63
– conflict over resources 153, 219
Clifford, James 65n
Cohen, Anthony 185n, 186n
Cohen, Erik, on tourist types 68, 69
Cole, Sally, on respect 206
Columbus, Christopher 18
– and history 42
– as signifier 87
– celebrations of 43
commodification, of culture 16, 210
– of history 87
Common Fisheries Policy 137
Communication and change 209, 210
competition, and envy 203
Concepción, 44
Conlin and Baum 14
conservation, Guarapo group 213
– of nature 209
– tourism and resources 215
Cooper *et al.*
– on motivation 78
– on TALC 94
cosmopolitans 220
Crafts, ancient traditions 158
Crick, Malcolm 108, 133n, 209
criticism, as social control 204, 226
Croll, Elizabeth, and David Parkin 215
Cuba, migration to 59
culture, as commodity 16, 210

– and stereotypification 85
– anthropological definitions 20n
– change, homogeneity and heterogeneity 217, 218
– cosmopolitan 91, 93
– cultural perceptions of nudity 207
– cultural change and mode of livelihood 224
– cultural context and environment 214
– cultural involution 210
– disappearance of 125
– folkloristic 181
– local concepts of 176
– official vision of 181
– youth 180

Dalton, G. 154n
Dann, Graham 77
Davis, A. 133n
De Kadt, Emmanuel 99, 108, 132n, 135, 154n
Demonstration Effect 16, 226
development 8
– beach development proposal and protest 148, 215
– development stage in cycle 94
– EU, FEDER funds 137
– of La Gomera 137
– of the port 35
– personal views 62
– sustainable development 215
– tourism development and environment 214
Duysens, Bart 83, 95n

ecology 11
– and La Gomera 26
– destruction of 149, 150
– marine ecology 123
– protest group 153
economy, of islands 15
– EU funding 137
– globalised 120
– influence of tourism 223
– influence of tourism 99-101
– *la casa* as economic unit 195
– La Gomera history 101, 102
– multiplier effect 100, 101
ecotourism 27
ecotourists 69
employment, 103-105
– impact of tourism 223
– settlers 126
– women 110
English, tourists 86, 175

– as settlers 179
entrepreneurs, foreign ideas 62
– tours 127
ethnic markers 217
ethnography 19
– qualities of an ethnographic monograph 217
European Commission (EC) 32, 102, 103
– and fishing regulations 120
European Union (EU) 7, 11, 14, 17
– and marine conservation 123
– funds 43, 137, 218
– impact on Vueltas 136-138
– law 131
– Single European Market 117, 136
evil eye 200, 201
– belief in 202
– power of 201
exploitation 45
– of fishermen 119, 219
– of workers 58, 93, 94, 115
export items 18

fishermen, number in Vueltas 54
– EU restriction on 138
– lifestyle 163-168
– recreational 122
– social identity 163
fishing, settlement 19
– as a business 115-124 *passim*
– changes due to tourism 225
– early history of 45
– history in Vueltas 52,53
– methods of 54
– personal history 56
– processing industry 46
– the activity of 163-165
folklore, arts and crafts 156-158
Foucault, Michel, on the gaze 12
Franco 50
Free, Tony, on honour 206
funeral ceremony 200

Galván-Tudela, Alberto 211n
gaze, the tourist gaze 10, 11, 80, and land use 214
Gellner, E. and D. Waterbury 145
gender, roles and change 62, 81
– and work 124
– fishermen 165
– masculinity 167
– shame 206
genealogies, kinship diagrams 190, 191
German, attitudes towards Germans 61-63

– German women 81
  and behaviour 207
– influences on culture 92
– mixing with locals 176
– settlers and business 126
– stereotypes 86
– use of German language 207
Geertz, Clifford 20n
Getz, Don 16
Giddens, Anthony 217
Gilmore, David 184n, 211n
globalisation 4-8, 10,14,19,52
– and identity 216
– and local agency 217, 219
– homogeneity versus heterogeneity 217, 218
– relation to tourism 217-219
Goddard, Victoria 124
– on sexuality and cleanliness 204
Goffman, E. 21n, 184n
Gomero, Gomeran women 82, 83
– as an identity 161-163 *passim*
– Gomeran men 81
– self-image 89
Graburn, Nelson 12, 13
– on impact of tourism 220, 221
– on timid tourists 72, 93
Guanche 18
– and cave dwelling 160
– and identity 156
– and livelihoods 159
– culture of 41, 42
– descendants of 44
– local notions of 55

Hall, C. Michael 135
Hall, Stuart 155
Hannertz, Ulf, on creolization 222
Harrison, David 21n
heritage, pre-Hispanic 160
– cultural 210
– natural 209
– promotion of 225
Hernandez-Hernandez, P. 45, 64n
Herzfeld, Michael, on honour 206, 211n
hippies 71, 77, 91
history, as interpretation and construction
  of experience 17, 18
– of La Gomera 41
– of the Canary Islands 41
– of Valle Gran Rey 44-47 *passim*
– of Vueltas 52-54 *passim*
honour 170, 206
host–guest encounters 208
hotel, Valle Gran Rey 215

ICONA 26, 67, 209
identity 11
– 'hijo del puelblo' 175
– and environment 153, 213
– and media 156
– and power 215
– and religion 181
– and social change 215
– as a concept 155
– as a theme 20
– Guanche 157
– historic influences on 156
– homogeneity and heterogeneity 217, 218
– influence of tourism 224
– local divisions 162, 163
– multinational roots 173
– multiplex personal 215
– social mask 'facha' 180
– the Gomero 161-163 *passim*
imperialism 13, 14, 93
– Nash's definition 221
Ioannides *et al* 15
islands, and tourism 14
– and economy 16
– and insularity 15

jealousy 203

Kenna, Margaret 184n
Kenny, M. 146
King, Brian 16
kinship, family group 192-195 *passim*
– and belief 192
– and economics 192
– diagrams 190, 191
– influence of tourism 225
– networks and importance 189
– terms 189
– the family in Vueltas 187

Lanfant, M. 155, 156
Lett, James 80
Liminoid, and ludic 80-81
Lison-Tolosana, Carmelo 192, 211n

MacCannell, Dean 11
– on authenticity 78, 219
mago 45, 46
– and identity 163
– qualities of 213
Marcus, G.E. and M.M.J. Fischer 22n
marriage 189, 197, 198
– ceremony 199, 200
– influence of tourism on 225

Martinez, Dolores 132n
McIntosh, R.W. *et al.*, on motivation 78
McKay 130
media, and stereotypes 86
– and identity 180
– television 93
– the influence of mass media 207, 208
Mediterraneanists, and kinship 187
– anthropology 206
Mesa-Moreno, Ciro 119, 168
– on marriage 197
Milton, Kay 228n
miseria, la 58
Modern World System Theory 5-7, 10
– and change 217, 219
– core and periphery 222
– development of 44
– Roseberry, W. 21n
modernisation 10
modernism 222
modes of livelihood 30
– changing attitudes towards 124
– tourism's influence on 224
Moeran, Brian 95n
Moore, Kenneth 86
motivation, of tourists 77, 78, 80
multiplier effect 101, 106, 108, 223
Murphy, P. 227n

Nash, Dennison 8, 9, 13
– on imperialism 93, 221
– on stereotypes 85
National Park Garajonay 209, 210

Olwig, Karen Fog 104-105
Ortner, Sherry 184n
Owen, R. and M. Dynes 137

Palsson, Gisli 123
patronage 144
– and foreign settlers 146
– examples of 144-146
Peristiany, J.G. 187
Pi-Sunyer, Oriol 86
– on fishermen 120
Pitt-Rivers, J. and J.G. Peristiany, on honour 206
plantations, crops 29
– exportation 43
– work on 109, 113
POI 103
– and the protest 137
political ecology iv, 11, 153
political economy, of islands 15

politics, Canary Islands system 138
– beach development protest 148
– elections 139, 144
– influence '*manga*' 143
– influence of tourism 224
– mayor and powers 139
– patronage 144
– personalities 141
– political graffiti 143, 144
– political parties 64n, 139
postmodernism 17
– and culture 222
– and identity 216
– and the post-tourist 220
proletariat 45, 63, 94, 115
property, in Vueltas 31
– and tourism 224
– attitudes towards 127
– inheritance 131
– prices of 130

respect 168, 179, 226
– and concept of honour 205
– and gender role play 207
– and self-control 171
– in social setting 205
Rivière, Peter, on shame 206
Robertson, Roland 5
Robinson, Mike 135, 185n, 227n
Rocca, Tony 87
role, concept of 9
– as a tourist 79
– challenge to roles 90
– criticism and control 204
– gender 83, 84
– gender and respect 207
– gender roles in the home 195
– Goffman, E. 21n
– influence of tourists 171
– local gender role construction 171
– masculinity in the bar 168 – 170
– new roles 226
– role as a professional
Roman Catholicism 198
– belief in God 199
– mass 199
Romantic Movement 23
Romero-Maura, J. 64n
Roseberry, W. 21n

sacred journey 12
– on personal quest 88
– on self-discovery 81
Sant-Cassia, Paul 184n

Scott, J. 154n
self-discovery 81, 88
– tourism as a personal journey 220
Selwyn, Tom, mono-cropping on islands 15
sexual relations 60
– influence of tourists 171, 226
– liberation and encounters 83
– sexuality and dress 82
shame, and nudity 81
– and respect 205-207
– in public 170
– sexual shame 206
verguenza 206
Shannon, T. 5
Sharpley, Richard, on islands and resources 15
Silbo 156, 157
Smith, Valene 6, 10
– impact of tourism 13
– tourist impact model 221
– tourist types 39
– typology 68, 108, 209
Spain, as colonising power 18, 19, 23, 42, 43
– and the EC 102
stereotypes, cultural 85, 86
– and gender 173
– personal 88
strangers, as foreigners 174
– identity 177
– influence of foreign settlers 225
sustainability, on islands 15
sustainable development 215

Tenerife, volume of tourism to 23
– as opposed to La Gomera 162
– local attitudes towards 89
tourism, impact of 13
– alternative, mass charter and backpacking 13
– and envy 203
– and housing 41
– and marriage partners 189, 194, 197, 198
– and nature conservation 209
– and party politics 152
– and wealth 132
– as a physical and mental journey 220
– as historical watershed 183

– as provider of new social roles 183
– growth in Spain 23
– growth in VGR 66,67
– historical growth 51
– influence on economy 223
– influence on landscape 32
– influence on politics 224
– influence on property 224
– local views on 57-62 *passim*
– mass tourism 221
– on La Gomera 24
– package tourism 222
– specific influences on Valle Gran Rey 223-227 *passim*
Tourist Area Life Cycle 94
tourists, descriptions of 6
– alternative 69, 80, 93, 220
– backpackers 67, 71, 93
– British 73
– influencing religious ideas 182
– influencing social identity 182
– local views of 60-62
– package 77
– specific economic impacts of types 104
– timid tourists 221
– types and impacts 220-221
– types in Vueltas 39
– typologies 68
– *veranistas* 67, 74-76, 88, 89
tours, dolphin-watching 122, 124
transnational groups 14

UNESCO, Natural Heritage Park 26
Urry, John 12, 222

Venezuela, migration to 59

Wahab, S. and C. Cooper, 5
Waldren, Jacqueline 185n
Walton, J. 100
Wang, Ning 79
witches 201
– *curanderos* 201
– *santiguar* 201
Wolf, Eric 7

Zonovieff, Sofka 95n, 96n, 184n, 185n, 209